REUTERS
SPORTS
IN THE 21ST CENTURY

REUTERS
SPORTS
IN THE 21ST CENTURY

NEW EDITION

with 766 color illustrations

Thames & Hudson

PAGES 2–3 Mexican Laura Sánchez dives during the women's three metre springboard final at the XIV Pan American Games in Santo Domingo. Sánchez finished in fourth place. 8 August 2003, Jorge Silva.

Reuters project director Jassim Ahmad
Reuters picture editors Hamish Crooks, Catherine Benson

License pictures from Reuters and Action Images for professional use at reuters.com/pictures and actionimages.com

First published in 2007 in hardcover in the United States of America by Thames & Hudson Inc., 500 Fifth Avenue, New York, New York 10110

thamesandhudsonusa.com

New edition 2009

Library of Congress Catalog Card Number 2008908253

ISBN 978-0-500-28808-5

Printed and bound in China by C&C Offset Printing Co. Ltd

CONTENTS

6 **Sport in the 21st Century**
Introduction by John Mehaffey

20 **Sporting Glory**
Courage / Talent / Drama / Triumph

148 **Heroes and Zeroes**
Champions / Celebrities / Fallen Idols

230 **The Spirit of Sport**
Dreams / Passion / Offbeat and Global Sports

328 **Off the Field**
Media / Marketing / Behind the Scenes

356 **World Timeline of Sport**

377 Additional Photo Credits

378 Acknowledgments

380 Index

Sport in the 21st Century

Introduction by John Mehaffey

Steam rises off the head of soccer player Mikael Silvestre of Manchester United.
6 January 2002. Michael Regan

Sport in the 21st Century

On a crisp 2008 October day, the New Orleans Saints defeated the San Diego Chargers in the second regular season National Football League match to be played at Wembley stadium in north London, the traditional home of English soccer. A third match at Wembley is scheduled between the New England Patriots and Tampa Bay Buccaneers in 2009. Earlier in the month the U.S. National Basketball Association staged an exhibition game in London's O2 centre. At a media conference before the match between the New Jersey Nets and the Miami Heat, commissioner David Stern outlined ambitious plans to expand the game in China.

Australia and New Zealand preceded their November 2008 rugby union tours of Europe with a Bledisloe Cup clash staged in Hong Kong's steamy heat, the first outside home territory. Belying its name, the

executive Richard Scudamore called for a 39th regular-season game for the 20-team league. Scudamore proposed staging 10 fixtures in five different cities across the world in the middle of a two-week break in the domestic soccer season every January.

'We cannot stand still,' Scudamore said. 'We are sitting in a privileged position but we are also in a vulnerable position. Sport is globalizing whether we like it or not.'

The most audacious merger between show business and sport took place at an unprecedented auction on 20 February in Mumbai. Eight Indian city-based franchises bid a total $20 million for players from around the world to play in the new Indian Premier League Twenty20 cricket competition, a frenetic three-hour version of a

Force India's Formula One team drivers Adrian Sutil (second left) of Germany, Giancarlo Fisichella (right) of Italy and compatriot Vitantonio Liuzzi (left) pose with team chairman Vijay Mallya during the launch of their new F1 team in Mumbai. 10 January 2008, Punit Paranjpe.

Argentina's soccer legend Diego Maradona (centre) visits al-Sadd club in Doha. Maradona and Brazil's Pelé headlined the guest list for the official unveiling of the world's biggest covered sports dome, the ASPIRE Academy of Sports Excellence, in Qatar. 18 November 2005, Fadi Al-Assaad.

2009 European golf tour started in Shanghai and will climax in Dubai.

'A hundred years ago your community was your local town and village,' remarked Mark Waller, a senior National Football League vice-president. 'Two thousand of you wandered down to the stadium or the church or whatever, and that was your focal point. Then it became your county or your country, and now it is a global community. There are no boundaries now. Brands, entertainment and sports properties operate at a global level, and our job is to make sure that we cater to these people.'

Sport's authorities have become acutely aware of the need to promote their brands in the 21st-century global village. The English Premier League, the most lucrative and popular soccer competition in the world, is a notable example. Early in 2008, Premier League chief

game that stretches to five days in traditional test matches.

Indian captain Mahendra Singh Dhoni attracted the highest bid, emerging richer by $1.5 million before a ball had been bowled in a competition designed specifically to appeal to the country's huge television audiences who devour soap operas and Bollywood films. Bollywood star Preity Zinta is a part-owner of the Mohali franchise.

Cricket's world governing body had little option other than to accept a competition it did not organize and does not control.

'Transformation is something that has affected the entire globe in all areas; politics, cricket, whatever. The world is a changed place. We have to learn to adapt,' said International Cricket Council chief executive Haroon Lorgat.

Television and money reshape sport

One of the most powerful forces reshaping sport has been television. Match play, the most exciting form of golf and the basis of the biennial Ryder Cup team event between the United States and Europe, pits one player against another over 18 holes, and was used in two of the four tournaments when Bobby Jones won the grand slam in 1930. But because a match ends as soon as one player has taken an unassailable lead, bringing a premature halt to television coverage, it was abandoned in standard tournaments in favour of stroke play, in which the lowest aggregate score over four completed rounds of 18 holes wins.

Tennis had an opposite problem. Under rules in force until the early 1970s, players had to win every set by a two-game margin, culminating

'There are no boundaries now. Brands, entertainment and sports properties operate at a global level.'

in the 112-game, two-day epic between Pancho Gonzales and Charlie Pasarell at the 1969 Wimbledon championships. To prevent matches from stretching to eternity, the tiebreak was introduced at the 1970 U.S. Open, employed when a set is tied 6–6. Similarly, soccer devised the penalty shootout. A cruel but undeniably dramatic device, the shootout concludes matches unresolved after extra time that would otherwise present the logistical headache of staging a replay.

Television money underwrites modern sports. The U.S. network NBC paid $3.5 billion for broadcast rights to stage five summer and winter Olympics from Sydney 2000 through to Beijing 2008. Television and marketing revenues will bring $3.2 billion to the world governing soccer body FIFA for the 2010 World Cup in South Africa.

English football was transformed by the creation of the Premier League in 1992, when Rupert Murdoch's BSkyB television company signed an exclusive deal to broadcast matches, worth around 300 million pounds. Although the two traditional European powerhouses, the Primera Liga in Spain and Serie A in Italy, continue to attract outstanding players, it is English clubs that have become the magnet for talented and ambitious youngsters throughout the world.

Added to the influx of television revenues has been the arrival of the super-rich, headed by Russian oil billionaire Roman Abramovich, who bought Chelsea in 2003 in a cash deal worth nearly 60 million pounds. Five years later, representatives of the Al Nahyan dynasty, which has ruled Abu Dhabi since the 18th century, purchased Manchester City, historically the poor relations of cross-town rivals Manchester United. At the start of the 2008–9 season, nine Premier League clubs were under foreign ownership.

McLaren's Formula One driver Lewis Hamilton of Britain and Ferrari's Felipe Massa (left) of Brazil wave to the crowd before the Brazilian Grand Prix in São Paulo. F1 is a prime example of a global modern sport, its protagonists commanding the salary and attention of their counterparts in the music and film industries. 2 November 2008, Paulo Whitaker.

In Chelsea's case money did buy success, with consecutive titles in 2005 and 2006, although Manchester United, a true global brand with the biggest overseas fan base of any club, trumped them in 2008 by winning the Premier League title and beating the west London side in the Champions League final in a penalty shootout. Long-suffering fans of the New York Yankees, who shell out around $200 million a year to their players, might well compare these achievements with those of their team, who have not won the baseball World Series since 2000 despite the enormous payroll.

Motor racing may be the supreme fusion of television, technology and sport, whether in Formula One or in stock cars on the American NASCAR circuit. The daredevil days of the old Grand Prix Circuit, when drivers were the earthbound equivalents of wartime fighter pilots or the early supersonic test aviators, are long gone. But so too are the frightening casualty rates. Instead of building cars to go as fast as possible, designers now balance speed with safety. In 2008, the sport's authorities also successfully experimented with a night-time race through the streets of Singapore.

An explosion in the sports/leisure business, with sports gear doubling as casual wear for a generation increasingly focused upon the goal of physical fitness, has also generated enormous revenues and directly benefited the world's outstanding athletes. Spanish tennis player Rafael Nadal, who took over from Roger Federer as world number one in 2008, could have strolled off a beach with his piratical

A view of the media area during the men's preliminary Pool A volleyball match between the U.S. and China at the Beijing 2008 Olympic Games. 16 August 2008, Stefano Rellandini.

bandana holding his unruly hair in check, baggy shorts and minimalist tops revealing impressive biceps.

Much of this money comes from shoe companies, which have been associated with athletics since Adolf and Rudolf Dassler, sons of a German cobbler, began making spiked shoes for track athletes in the 1920s. After a family split, Adolf set up adidas, which supplied the footwear for Jesse Owens at the Berlin Olympics in 1936, and also for Muhammad Ali and Joe Frazier when they fought for the world heavyweight title in 1971. In the following year adidas was named as official supplier for the Munich Olympics.

Twenty years later, the American company Nike (named after the Greek goddess of victory) was pre-eminent, sponsoring Michael Jordan and Tiger Woods among others. Both companies were still locked in a

fierce rivalry at the 2008 Olympics, with adidas sponsoring the Chinese National Olympic Committee while Nike had signed up 22 of the Chinese teams.

Against the odds

Sustained excellence makes Tiger Woods the pre-eminent athlete in the first decade of the 21st century and television exposure ensures he is one of the most widely recognized men in the world.

According to a table published in the *Economist* weekly news magazine, Woods is also sport's biggest earner, with annual earnings of $127.9 million. Another golfer, Phil Mickelson, is a distant second with $62.4 million, followed by English footballer David Beckham who earns $48.2 million.

Woods's singular achievement since he won the U.S. Masters by 12 strokes in 1997 has been to bring glamour to the game while succeeding Chicago Bulls basketball phenomenon Michael Jordan as the best-known sportsman in the world. After doffing his cap to the gallery and flashing a smile only slightly less dazzling than the sun, it is all business for Woods, who concentrates the resources of an acute intellect, a gym-honed body and a relentless will on mastering the course and vanquishing his rivals. Body speed allied to strength gives him length from the tee. His touch is uncanny, his putting sure and fearless, and he had the humility to twice take time out to reshape a swing already coveted by his rivals. Woods is also an incredible competitor, as he showed in 2008 when he won the U.S. Open virtually on one leg after a potentially crippling injury to his left knee. A birdie at the last hole took Woods into a playoff with Rocco Mediate, won on the first extra hole to give him his 14th major, only four behind Jack Nicklaus's record. Anterior cruciate surgery on his knee then brought a premature end to Woods's season and his unending quest for perfection was put on hold while he underwent a painstaking recuperation programme.

His income, image and high profile exploited to the full by the advertising industry have made Woods a perfect representative of corporate America. But he has not forgotten his early battles against bigotry in a middle-class neighbourhood in Cypress, California. 'I was always treated as an outsider,' he said. 'We were the first and only black family for many years and we had many problems. I've been denied many things because of the colour of my skin.'

Coincidentally, a similar struggle had been taking place in Los Angeles, where another black American, Richard Williams, coached his daughters Venus and Serena on public tennis courts, accompanied at times by the sound of gunfire as rival gangs took pot shots at each other. Against the odds, both women went on to dominate tennis with their power and aggression. When fully fit and focused the Williams sisters still remain the women to beat.

Formula One's youngest ever champion Lewis Hamilton, who went from sixth to fifth on the final lap of the last Grand Prix of the 2008 season to win the title by a point, is also the sport's first and only black driver. Hundreds of racist hate messages were posted on a Spanish website before the season-ending race in São Paulo. His success in a glamorous sport patronised by the international jet set has shattered barriers every bit as intimidating as those dismantled by Woods a decade earlier.

Although claims are often made for its superior moral values,

> **Although claims are often made for its superior moral values, in reality sport more often reflects than influences society.**

in reality sport more often reflects than influences society. However, in the field of race relations, it has undoubtedly helped to change the world for the better. At the 1936 Berlin Olympics Jesse Owens, the grandson of slaves, exposed the malign Nazi ideology of Aryan white supremacy by winning four gold medals. Then came the fierce black baseball genius Jackie Robinson, who helped to break down his sport's unspoken racial barriers while playing for the Brooklyn Dodgers in the 1940s and 1950s. During the turbulent 1960s Ali, stripped of his world heavyweight boxing titles for three years for refusing to serve in the Vietnam War, became a hero on the unsettled American campuses with his articulate denunciations of racism.

An international sporting boycott played a role in the crumbling of the apartheid regime in South Africa, where rugby union, chosen sport of the Afrikaner, is a passion. In an inspired gesture of reconciliation, South African President Nelson Mandela, imprisoned for 27 years for

his militant opposition to apartheid, wore a replica Springbok jersey before their 1995 rugby World Cup final against the New Zealand All Blacks. South Africa's formerly all-white national team won in extra time against the tournament favourites.

Zinedine Zidane, the son of an Algerian warehouseman born in the Mediterranean port city of Marseille, acquired his soccer skills on dusty public pitches. He needed no special grants or schools of excellence to become the supreme player of his generation, scoring from two headers in France's 3–0 victory over Brazil in the 1998 World Cup final at the Stade de France in Paris.

In 2006 Zidane emerged from international retirement to recapture the magical essence of his youth and take France to the World Cup

Tennis champions Venus Williams (left) and Serena Williams (centre) and *Vogue* Editor-in-Chief Anna Wintour attend the Zac Posen Spring 2009 collection at New York Fashion Week. 11 September 2008, Joshua Lott.

final against Italy in Berlin. After converting an audacious penalty via the crossbar, Zidane looked set to join Brazil's Pelé as the greatest player to display his skills on the global stage. Instead, after a header which would surely have decided the match was tipped over the bar, Zidane was shown a red card for head-butting Italian defender Marco Materazzi in the chest. A career apparently set to reach its climax on soccer's greatest stage will always have an asterisk attached.

Zidane's impact beyond the confines of the playing field was problematic. Some white Frenchmen condemned him and his team mates as foreign mercenaries; others praised him as a role model for Muslim immigrants. As with Robinson and Ali, the more enlightened response seems the likeliest legacy.

Nationalism and internationalism

The reshaping of political forces since the fall of the Berlin Wall means nationalism is no longer the force it was in the post-World War Two Olympics, when the United States and the Soviet Union viewed the medals table as an extended arena of the Cold War. Yet it is still a powerful presence at the summer and winter Games. The 2008 Games in Beijing, the third Asian city to host the world's greatest sports festival, proved no exception.

After Beijing was awarded the Games seven years earlier in Moscow, the hosts launched Operation 119, the number of gold medals available in individual sports with high medals counts, such as swimming, canoeing and kayaking. China won only four gold medals in those sports at the 2004 Athens Olympics but its campaign proved such a success that it easily topped the medals table in Beijing with 51 golds. The old Cold War adversaries, the United States and Russia, were second and third with 36 and 23 respectively, while Britain, hosts of the 2012 Games, came in fourth with 19.

International and regional competitions still exert a powerful nationalistic pull, but the old thrill of seeing new and exciting athletes from exotic locales for the first time has all but disappeared now that the best perform in all seasons throughout the world. Soccer has a huge pool of exponents from around the globe playing for clubs in lucrative European leagues. Many are from impoverished African nations, notably George Weah, the 1995 world player of the year who, after a distinguished career with AC Milan, Chelsea, Monaco, Paris Saint-Germain and Olympique Marseille, stood unsuccessfully in 2005 for the presidency of his native Liberia.

In tennis Russian women have flourished, their game honed by relentless practice from an early age, often at American academies. Anna Kournikova, their most notable export, was paradoxically the least successful, playing in only four Women's Tennis Association (WTA) finals and failing to win one. But, in another sign of the times, her exceptional good looks earned her millions in endorsements.

Africans, primarily Kenyans and Ethiopians, chase each other on the world's running tracks, both outdoor and indoor, on roads and across country. The outstanding long-distance exponent at the moment is the light-footed Ethiopian Kenenisa Bekele, who has proved uniquely adept on any surface and won the 5,000–10,000 double in Beijing. Bekele's older compatriot Haile Gebrselassie successfully graduated from the track, where he won successive Olympic 10,000 metres titles, to the road to become the first person to clock a sub-two-hour-four-minute marathon, in Berlin in September 2008.

One interesting side-effect of today's freedom of movement has been the steady trickle of African runners emigrating to the Gulf States and changing their nationality in exchange for riches they could not hope to earn representing their native countries. The prime example is world steeplechase record holder Saif Saaeed Shaheen, who competed for his native Kenya under his original name of Stephen Cherono, and is now paid substantially more to run for his adopted country Qatar.

In a parallel case, Switzerland, a country without a coastline, twice won the America's Cup, the world's oldest yachting trophy, with a team of renegade New Zealanders.

Some sports have slipped from the limelight in one part of the world only to be enthusiastically embraced in another. Boxing, once an American preserve, is now dominated in the lower weight divisions by Asians and Latin Americans, and among the heavyweights by fighters from former Eastern Bloc countries. Promoter Don King, always quick to spot an opportunity, believes China will be the new powerhouse. 'China has 1.7 billion people, so content is King,' he punned.

Olympic renaissance

The new millennium opened in a spirit of wary optimism as the global economy rebounded following the threat of an Asian meltdown two years earlier which foreshadowed the even more frightening global economic turmoil to come a decade later. It was celebrated with New World exuberance at the 2000 Olympics in Sydney, the city which had been unexpectedly awarded the Games ahead of Beijing. A sun-burnt continent grasped the opportunity to parade the attractions of one of the world's most vibrant harbour cities in a country that pursues sports and the outdoor life with unrestrained vigour.

During the 1950s, Australia came to dominate most of the sports either invented or codified during an astonishing burst of energy in Victorian England. They still punched well above their weight at the start of the 21st century, particularly in swimming, where 17-year-old Ian Thorpe won three golds and two silvers in Sydney, and in cricket, where their national team is consistently the best international side in any sport in the world.

OPPOSITE ABOVE Yang Wei of China performs on the rings during the men's team artistic gymnastics final at the Beijing 2008 Olympic Games. Yang, who won gold in the individual all-around and team final, finished second. But China easily topped the medals table in Beijing with 51 golds. 12 August 2008, Dylan Martinez.

OPPOSITE BELOW World champion Saif Saaeed Shaheen of Qatar competes in the men's 3,000 metres steeplechase at the Zurich Golden League meeting in Switzerland. Formerly known as Stephen Cherono in his native Kenya, Shaheen is the most high-profile track and field athlete to change nationality for economic reasons. 19 August 2005, Pascal Lauener.

In a public relations masterstroke, aboriginal Australian Cathy Freeman lit the Olympic flame as a symbol of reconciliation between the once shamefully downtrodden indigenous people and European settlers. Freeman went on to win the 400 metres gold on an unforgettable night at the Olympic stadium.

Sydney was a perfect tonic for the International Olympic Committee (IOC) following a corruption scandal over the vote to award the 2002 winter Olympics to Salt Lake City. With sponsors threatening to defect in droves after revelations that several members of the unelected body had taken bribes or inducements before the vote, it was no exaggeration to suggest that the future of the Games was threatened.

she would go one better. Jones planned to win the same four titles as Owens and Lewis and also run in the 4x400 relay. In a heartening testament to the progress of women in sports over the course of the previous century, it was Jones who seized the headlines and dominated the magazine covers in the run-up to Sydney.

Women were excluded from the first modern Games in Athens in 1896 but took part four years later in Paris, where British tennis player Charlotte Cooper became the first woman to win an Olympic gold medal. Prejudice, though, still permeated the upper echelons of sports administration. At the 1928 Amsterdam Games several competitors collapsed at the finish of the women's 800 metres. Subsequently, women's races over 200 metres were banned from the Games for

Australian runner Cathy Freeman speeds to a first place finish in the semi-final of the women's 400 metres at the Olympic Games in Sydney. She went on to claim gold in the final. 23 September 2000, Gary Hershorn.

Yelena Isinbayeva of Russia competes during the women's pole vault final of the athletics competition in the National Stadium during the Beijing 2008 Olympic Games. 18 August 2008, Mike Blake.

'The vultures of the sport/leisure industry were waiting in the wings for any sign of weakness that they might exploit, with the potential to entice willing international federations to create a new multi-sports commercial venture,' wrote Olympic historian David Miller in *Athens to Athens*, the official history of the modern Games.

The 1984 Los Angeles Games had been the first to openly embrace commercialism and make a profit. They featured Carl Lewis, who announced he would emulate Owens and win gold medals in the 100, 200 and 4x100 metres relay plus the long jump. Lewis succeeded without, to his frustration, ever gaining the adoration and praise he craved from the American public.

In the year before the Sydney Games, Marion Jones announced

32 years and IOC president Count Henri de Baillet-Latour spoke for the reactionaries when he said that, as in ancient Olympia, women should not take part in the Games at all.

The Belgian aristocrat's views were already out of touch with the times when he voiced them and by 2000 women were taking part in all track and field disciplines, with the exception of the 3,000 metres steeplechase, which was finally introduced at the 2005 Helsinki world championships.

In Sydney, Jones completed the first part of her ambitious programme with sweeping victories in the 100 and 200 metres. But she faltered in the long jump, finishing third behind a superior technician in German Heike Drechsler. Another bronze in the

4x100 metres relay meant Jones could not equal Owens and Lewis, although she went on to a third gold with an astonishing run in the third leg of the 4x400 relay.

Fifteen months later, the global mood had darkened dramatically. The first winter Olympic Games of the new century, staged in Salt Lake City in February 2002, was also the first major sporting event since the attacks on New York and Washington on September 11, 2001. In the fraught weeks after 9/11, there had been serious doubts in the sporting community that the Games and the subsequent soccer World Cup in Japan and South Korea would go ahead at all. Both did, but at an enormous cost, with organizers in Salt Lake spending an unprecedented $310 million on security.

Marion Jones of the U.S. crosses the finish line in the 100 metres during the Golden Gala IAAF meeting at Rome's Olympic Stadium. 14 July 2006, Max Rossi.

September 11 was never far from the hearts and minds of the thousands of spectators who poured into the Utah state capital, where they mingled with hundreds of under-cover security agents. A tattered U.S. flag, rescued from the rubble of the World Trade Center, was carried into the stadium during the opening ceremony and later that year fluttered over the U.S. Open tennis tournament.

Against this emotional backdrop, Janica Kostelić, a 20-year-old Croatian who began her skiing career while her native Yugoslavia disintegrated in bloody discord, claimed three gold medals and a silver. Despite suffering 11 operations on her battered knees and the removal of her thyroid gland she was still around four years later in Turin where she won the combined and took a silver medal in the Super G.

The drugs nightmare

Scientists have transformed sport legitimately through nutrition and fitness, remarkable surgical techniques to speed up rehabilitation and healing, and improved materials and equipment. One notable example of the latter is the pole vault, which graduated through bamboo, steel and aluminium before it was transported into another dimension by the introduction of fibreglass, which acts essentially as a catapult and has underpinned the dramatic evolution of the women's pole vault in the past decade. American Stacy Dragila won the first Olympic women's title at the Sydney Games. She has been succeeded by Russian Yelena Isinbayeva, an outstanding athlete who has set world records in consecutive Olympics and is the first woman to vault over five metres.

Performance-enhancing drugs are without doubt the most serious issue facing sport today.

But scientists have also been at work in the sinister underworld of performance-enhancing drugs, without doubt the most serious issue facing sport today, as the establishment of the World Anti-Doping Agency (WADA) in 1999 under the forthright former IOC vice-president Dick Pound, testifies. The drugs nightmare has haunted the Olympics since Canadian Ben Johnson tested positive after winning the 100 metres final in world-record time in 1988. It descended on sunny Sydney during the Games when it was revealed that Jones's husband CJ Hunter, the world shot put champion, had tested positive four times for huge amounts of the anabolic steroid nandrolone during the previous year. The hulking American had pulled out of the Games, citing injury, but was still present in Sydney and wept openly at a packed news conference while Jones stood stony-faced by her man.

Anabolic steroids, drugs that mimic the effects of the male sex hormone testosterone, produce rapid muscle growth, a corresponding increase in strength and stamina, and sometimes dramatic mood changes. They emerged during the 1930s, when German scientists fed them to the Nazi storm troopers. During the 1950s they were administered to Eastern Bloc schoolchildren in a bid to build a master race of Olympic athletes. In the following decade they became part of the Californian bodybuilding cult. Steroid use in sport has been most marked in speed and strength events such as sprinting and, in particular, weightlifting, a sport always popular at the Olympics but plagued by periodic drugs busts.

A Canadian government inquiry in the year after Johnson's fall from grace had already revealed in shocking detail the extent of drug abuse in athletics, much of it supplied under oath by the sprinter's coach Charlie Francis. Francis admitted that he had turned to performance-enhancing drugs for his athletes after the 1976 Montreal Olympics. The medals table in Montreal had been dominated by athletes from the Soviet Union and East Germany, where state-controlled doping was rife, as confirmed in documents released since the fall of the Berlin Wall.

Sitting unnoticed among Hunter's entourage at the Sydney news conference was a former jazz musician who had played bass with the pianist Herbie Hancock and who was now enjoying a lucrative career as a nutritionist. Victor Conte ran the BALCO laboratory in California, and Hunter and Jones, as well as baseball slugger Barry Bonds, were listed among his clients.

Three years later, everybody in the world of sport knew the name of Victor Conte, following a drugs scandal that was to end, in disgrace, the careers of Jones, Tim Montgomery, the father of her child, and her coach Trevor Graham. The furore erupted after Graham anonymously sent a syringe containing a previously unknown drug to the U.S. Anti-Doping Agency (USADA). Scientists at the Los Angeles Olympic Analytical Laboratory under leading anti-doping campaigner Don Catlin identified and devised a test for the new drug, dubbed tetrahydrogestrinone, or THG, which had been designed specifically to fool the testers.

As a result, federal agents raided the BALCO laboratory and a number of athletes, including Bonds, were subpoenaed to give grand jury testimony. Bonds had bulked up dramatically and become baseball's premier slugger, extending Hank Aaron's previous career home record of 755 to 762 in 2007. He was committed to stand trial in 2009 after pleading not guilty in a federal court to charges that he had lied about past steroid use.

By the 2002 outdoor season, Jones had separated from Hunter and found a new partner in Montgomery. In September of that year,

Montgomery became the first man to run faster than Johnson, whose Seoul mark of 9.79 seconds had not been recognized as a world record but had also never been bettered. In the following year the pair attracted controversy when they were coached briefly by Francis, who had been banned for life from coaching Canadian athletes. Jones took the rest of the year off to have Montgomery's child and in her absence Kelli White won the 100–200 double at the Paris world championships. Two years later both Montgomery and White had been banned after USADA produced sufficient evidence – the so-called non-analytical positives based on circumstantial evidence rather than positive test results – to prove they had taken a frightening variety of banned substances, including THG, supplied by BALCO. Retesting of samples showed European 100 metres champion Dwain Chambers had taken a similar cocktail of drugs and the Briton was banned for two years.

The northern hemisphere summer of 2006 proved a triumph for the drugs testers and a disaster for devotees of speed and endurance. Justin Gatlin, who shared the world record of 9.77 seconds with Jamaican Asafa Powell, had won the 2004 Athens Olympic gold medal followed by the 100–200 sprint double at the Helsinki world championships. But just as the world was salivating at the prospect of a sprint rivalry to match that between Lewis and Johnson a generation earlier, Gatlin tested positive for excessive amounts of testosterone. Within days Gatlin's fellow American Floyd Landis, winner of the world's most celebrated cycling endurance race, the Tour de France, had also tested positive for testosterone. Gatlin had escaped a ban early in his career after a positive test for an amphetamine, arguing that he was taking the stimulant for a medical complaint. This time he was banned for four years. Landis was suspended for two years.

For those struggling to retain their belief in athletics, the core sport of the summer Olympics, even worse was to follow. After years

OPPOSITE ABOVE Justin Gatlin of the U.S. celebrates after setting a 100 metres world record at the Qatar Super Grand Prix in Doha, with a time of 9.77 seconds. In July 2006 it was announced that Gatlin had tested positive for unusual amounts of the male hormone testosterone after a relay race in Kansas. 12 May 2006, Fadi Alassaad.

OPPOSITE BELOW Italian Marco Pantani (centre) rides among the pack during the sixth stage of the 83rd Giro d'Italia in 2000. One of the greatest climbers in the history of cycle racing, Pantani won both the Tour de France and the Giro d'Italia in 1998. But the following year he was disqualified from the Giro d'Italia after failing a random blood test. He was put on trial, accused of using the banned performance-enhancing drug erythropoietin (EPO). The trial collapsed but three years later Pantani was suspended for six months after a syringe containing insulin was found in his hotel room. He died of a cocaine overdose on 14 February 2004, leaving a note saying that years of police inquiries and judicial investigations had made him deeply depressed. 19 May 2000, Vincenzo Pinto.

of denial, Jones confessed to taking drugs, including THG, before the Sydney Games and spent the Beijing Olympic Games in jail after she was convicted of lying to federal prosecutors. Montgomery's life spiralled out of control and in 2008 he was jailed for five years for conspiring to possess heroin on top of a 46-month sentence for his role in a money-laundering scheme.

Conte later revealed that Chambers, who tried unsuccessfully in 2008 to get a British Olympic Association ban from the Beijing Games overturned, had been taking seven different drugs at the same time. Graham, who had also coached Gatlin, was banned from coaching and sentenced to a year's house arrest in 2008 for lying during the investigation into BALCO.

Seven-times Tour de France winner Lance Armstrong of the U.S. cycles down a mountain during the 204.5-km (127-mile) 17th stage of the Tour. 22 July 2004, Stefano Rellandini.

A tainted sport

The Tour de France was first devised in 1903 by Henri Desgrange with the express purpose of selling more copies of his newspaper *L'Auto*, and has since become a national institution. But because of the unique demands of this three-week race, which includes the mountain outreaches of the Pyrenees plus the French Alps, drug use has been endemic, and 2007 proved a particularly bad year. One of the oldest sponsors, Deutsche Telekom, ended its support of team T-Mobile in order 'to separate our brand from further exposure from doping in sport and cycling specifically'. T-Mobile had embraced a policy of zero tolerance, sacking German Patrik Sinkewitz and Italy's Lorenzo Bernucci following positive dope tests and dismissing Ukrainian rider Serhiy Honchar for breach of conduct.

The company's withdrawal came a month after the International Cycling Union and WADA announced the creation of the toughest anti-doping measures in sport, a plan to take blood samples from all professional riders to create medical profiles. The original profile is to be kept in a database and compared to the findings after a rider has undergone a dope test to see if there are any significant discrepancies indicating drug use, even if the athlete has not tested positive.

Also in 2007, former Tour de France winner Bjarne Riis admitted he had doped during his victorious ride in 1996, while fellow Dane Michael Rasmussen was sacked by his Rabobank team as he led that year's Tour for lying about his training programme. Kazakh Alexander Vinokourov was found guilty of blood doping during the race. He and his Astana

> Sponsors, crucial to modern sport, need their products to be associated with glowing health and clean-cut performers and not a sordid trail of used needles and empty vials.

team were expelled, and Vinokourov retired after he was suspended for a year. The Cofidis team pulled out of the Tour after Cristian Moreni tested positive for excessive testosterone, while Erik Zabel, who had won a record six green jerseys on the Tour, also admitted to doping.

In 2008, U.S. cyclist Lance Armstrong announced his return to the sport. The most successful rider in Tour history, Armstrong won seven successive Tours before he retired in 2005. He had previously returned to racing after recovering from testicular cancer which had spread to his lungs and brain. At one point he had been given less than a 40 percent chance of survival.

'There was one unforeseen benefit of cancer,' he wrote. 'It had completely reshaped my body. I now had a much sparer build. I was leaner in build and more balanced in spirit.'

Armstrong too has come under suspicion. But he denied any involvement in doping after the French sports newspaper *L'Equipe* devoted four pages in 2005 to a story that he had tested positive for the blood-boosting drug erythropoietin during his first win in 1999, the year before a test was introduced at the Sydney Olympics.

The continued popularity of the Tour de France suggests that spectators may not necessarily care what their heroes ingest. But the sponsors, crucial to modern sport, need their products to be associated with glowing health and clean-cut performers and not a sordid trail of used needles and empty vials.

A golden age

For all its problems, sport is enjoying a golden age. So too are sports fans. Through a wide array of dedicated channels, fans in any part

everyday life, there is usually only one winner. Sport inspires awe in the feats of American swimmer Michael Phelps, who won eight gold medals and broke seven world records in Beijing, and amazement at the sight of the laidback Jamaican Usain Bolt unwinding his elongated body out of the blocks to eradicate the previous world 100 and 200 metres records in the imposing Bird's Nest stadium.

For sheer drama, few spectacles could beat the 2008 Wimbledon men's final, where the concentrated fury of Nadal finally prevailed over the balletic grace of Federer as dusk fell over south London. Woods's battle against his failing knee, the course and his opponents in the U.S. Open reached epic proportions. Isinbayeva soaring through the air is both an athletic and an artistic marvel.

Michael Phelps and Garrett Weber-Gale celebrate after the U.S. won the men's 4x100 metres freestyle relay swimming final during the Beijing 2008 Olympic Games. 11 August 2008, David Gray.

Rafael Nadal of Spain (left) embraces Roger Federer of Switzerland after winning their men's final at the Wimbledon tennis championships in London. 6 July 2008, Toby Melville.

of the world can now watch a Tour de France stage climax in the Netherlands. Random flicks through the channels yield tennis from Monte Carlo, one-day cricket in the Caribbean, Primera Liga soccer from Barcelona, baseball in Chicago, a triathlon in Sydney Harbour. The fans can relive the experience through replays, the expanding sports sections of daily newspapers and a dizzying array of websites.

The cast for this collection of teams, individuals and competitions is young men and women with outstanding physical gifts, determination, pluck, and the good fortune to be in the right place at the right time.

Sport's special appeal is its unpredictability. Unlike the theatre, where Hamlet will always die at the end of the final act, the result may be uncertain until the final whistle. Unlike the messy compromises of

'The roads from all the dusty pitches of the world now converge on a satellite feed,' observed the American sportswriter Robert Lipsyte. 'Yet at the heart of it all is the true glory of sports, the individual daring to be better. How society can nurture the dream without cynically exploiting it may be the true sports challenge of the century.'

John Mehaffey

Sporting Glory
Courage / Talent / Drama / Triumph

Yuliya Nesterenko of Belarus runs to victory in the women's 100 metres
at the Athens Olympics. 21 August 2004. Shaun Best

JUMP!

ABOVE German striker Miroslav Klose turns a somersault after scoring against Ecuador in Berlin in the 2006 World Cup. Klose scored five goals from seven matches to win the Golden Shoe award as the tournament's top scorer. It was the lowest winning tally in a World Cup since 1962. He scored two goals against Costa Rica, two against Ecuador and a header in the quarter-final against Argentina, bringing his total tally in World Cups to 10. 20 June 2006. Shaun Best

RIGHT Chelsea fans applaud Frank Lampard as he celebrates with team mate Damien Duff after scoring a second goal in a Premier League match against Aston Villa at Stamford Bridge in London. Lampard, a powerful midfielder with a savage shot from long range, was a key member of Chelsea's 2005 and 2006 Premiership winning sides. He was runner-up in the 2005 European and world player of the year awards but had a disappointing 2006 World Cup, where he failed to reproduce his club form for England. 24 September 2005. Dylan Martinez

THE LINE-UP

LEFT Italy captain Fabio Cannavaro challenges for the ball Ghana's Richard Kingston (third left) and Michael Essien (second left) during their 2006 World Cup group match in Hanover. Awaiting the outcome are Ghana's Eric Addo (centre) and Samuel Osei Kuffour (second right), and Italy's Daniele De Rossi (third right) and Alberto Gilardino (far right). Italy won 2–0 with Andrea Pirlo scoring in the 40th minute and substitute Vincenzo Iaquinta sealing victory in the 83rd. Italy went on to win their fourth World Cup. 12 June 2006. Shaun Best

BELOW Argentine players (left to right) Ariel Ortega, Javier Zanetti, Gabriel Batistuta, Juan Verón and Diego Simeone protect themselves against a Jay Jay Okocha free kick in their 2002 World Cup group F match against Nigeria in Ibaraki, Japan. The Argentines, among the pre-tournament favourites, edged Nigeria 1–0 but then lost by a similar margin to England after a David Beckham penalty and were eliminated after a 1–1 draw with Sweden. 2 June 2002. Ruben Sprich

STRIKER

BELOW Italian striker Francesco Totti in action during the 2006 World Cup semi-final against Germany. This consistently entertaining match between the eventual champions and the hosts, which went 90 minutes without a goal, exploded in extra time. The Italians hit the woodwork twice but still seemed set for penalties, a German speciality, until Fabio Grosso beat keeper Jens Lehmann with a minute to go and then Alessandro Del Piero chipped into the net with the last kick of the game. 4 July 2006. Kieran Doherty

DEFENDER

OPPOSITE Tigres' goalkeeper Edgar Hernandez grimaces as he dives after the ball during a Mexican championship match against América at the Azteca stadium in Mexico City. The Tigres are one of the most popular teams in Mexico. 13 August 2006. Henry Romero

WILKINSON'S WORLD CUP WINNER

England flyhalf Jonny Wilkinson strikes the drop goal that broke Australian hearts and took the rugby World Cup to the northern hemisphere for the first time. Both Wilkinson and England had struggled for form during the 2003 tournament in Australia until the rain-drenched semi-final against France. The final in Sydney was tied 17–17 in the final minute of extra time when Wilkinson, a natural left-footer, let fly with his right boot. 22 November 2003. Kieran Doherty

RUGBY RAMPAGE

TOP New Zealand's All Blacks perform the haka before the rugby test against Italy in Rome. In 2006, the All Blacks upset rugby's authorities by including a throat-slitting gesture at the end of the haka. 13 November 2004. Tony Gentile

ABOVE Stephen Hoiles of the Waratahs receives a hand to his face from an Auckland Blues defender during a Super 14 rugby match at Aussie Stadium in Sydney. The Waratahs, who went on to reach the semi-finals, won 43–9. 24 March 2006. Will Burgess

TOP South African wing Bryan Habana soars through the air to score a try against Argentina in their 2007 Rugby World Cup semi-final at the Stade de France in Paris. Habana scored twice in the 37–13 victory to equal New Zealand wing Jonah Lomu's World Cup record eight tries at the 1999 tournament. 14 October 2007. Eddie Keogh

ABOVE Trevor Woodman of England is tackled by Keven Mealamu and Carl Hayman of New Zealand in the second test at Eden Park, Auckland. The All Blacks won 36–12 to complete a 2–0 series win against the world champions. 19 June 2004. Andrew Budd

FIELDS OF PLAY

LEFT New Orleans Saints fans cheer as their team takes the field to play the Atlanta Falcons in the first National Football League game at the Louisiana Superdome since Hurricane Katrina devastated the city. The Superdome, the largest fixed dome structure in the world, was used as an emergency shelter when the hurricane struck in August 2005. The Saints, who had spent the previous season on the road while the Superdome was restored, brought some much-needed relief to a crowd of around 70,000 with a 23–3 victory after a pre-game show by rock groups U2 and Green Day. 25 September 2006. Tami Chappell

BELOW A rainbow arcs over the pitch at an African Nations Cup qualifier in which Rwanda (in yellow) beat Liberia 3–2 in Monrovia. 8 October 2006. Christopher Herwig

GRIDIRON GREATS

OPPOSITE ABOVE LEFT New Orleans Saints running back Reggie Bush (25) breaks a tackle by Atlanta Falcons Darrell Shropshire (71) during the second quarter of their NFL game in New Orleans at the newly restored Louisiana Superdome, 13 months after Hurricane Katrina had ravaged the city. 25 September 2006. Sean Gardner

OPPOSITE ABOVE RIGHT Michigan defensive back Jashaad Gaines (29) keeps Notre Dame wide receiver David Grimes from making a catch during the first quarter of their college football game in South Bend, Indiana. 16 September 2006. John Gress

OPPOSITE BELOW LEFT New York Giants' David Tyree celebrates his touchdown against the New England Patriots during the fourth quarter in Super Bowl XLII in Glendale, Arizona. The Giants won 17–14 to prevent the Patriots from becoming the first side since the 1972 Miami Dolphins to go through the season unbeaten. 3 February 2008. Shaun Best

OPPOSITE BELOW CENTRE Indianapolis Colts quarterback Peyton Manning calls a play during the second quarter of the NFL's Super Bowl XLI against the Chicago Bears in Miami. The Colts won 29–17 to take their first NFL title since 1971, when they were based in Baltimore. 4 February 2007. Mike Blake

OPPOSITE BELOW RIGHT Pittsburgh Steelers running back Willie Parker dives into the endzone to score a touchdown on a 75-yard run against the Seattle Seahawks in the third quarter of the NFL's Super Bowl XL in Detroit. It was the longest touchdown run from scrimmage in title game history. 5 February 2006. Rebecca Cook

RIGHT Seattle Seahawks wide receiver D.J. Hackett fails to reach an incomplete pass in the endzone from quarterback Matt Hasselbeck as he is guarded by Pittsburgh Steelers cornerback Bryant McFadden in the first quarter of the NFL Super Bowl XL in Detroit. Pittsburgh won 21–10 for a record-equalling fifth title. 5 February 2006. Lucy Nicholson

DIAMOND HEROES

LEFT Curt Schilling of the Boston Red Sox pitches to New York Yankees batter Gary Sheffield during their game in Boston. The Red Sox won 10–1 to earn the American League wildcard playoff spot. 2 October 2005. Gary Hershorn

LEFT Boston Red Sox players celebrate after clinching their first World Series win since 1918 with victory over the St Louis Cardinals, in St Louis. 27 October 2004. Mike Blake

RIGHT Detroit Tigers' Craig Monroe breaks his bat as he grounds out in the third inning against the St Louis Cardinals during Game One in Major League Baseball's 2006 World Series in Detroit. The Cardinals won their first MLB title in 24 years with a Game Five victory. 21 October 2006. Rebecca Cook

RIGHT New York Yankees fans wave to shortstop Derek Jeter on the field during the final regular-season MLB game at Yankee Stadium in New York. The stadium, built in 1923, was being replaced by a new baseball park bearing the same name. 21 September 2008. Gary Hershorn

PLAYING TO THE CROWD

Andre Agassi stretches into his serve during the final match of his professional career against Benjamin Becker at the 2006 U.S. Open. Agassi, 36, who needed four injections during the week to relieve the pain in his aching back, lost in four sets to the 112th-ranked German qualifier in an emotional farewell to Flushing Meadow, New York. 'I don't take pride in my accomplishments,' the eight-times grand slam winner told the crowd. 'I take pride in the striving.' 3 September 2006. Mike Segar

EYE ON THE BALL

OPPOSITE Andy Roddick serves during his quarter-final against Russia's Nikolay Davydenko at the Australian Open in Melbourne. The American was leading 6–3 7–5 4–1 when Davydenko retired injured. Roddick lost in the last four to Lleyton Hewitt. 26 January 2005. David Gray

TOP Marat Safin lunges for a backhand as he helps Russia to win the Davis Cup men's team trophy for the first time with a 3–2 victory over France in the Paris final. 29 November 2002. Philippe Wojazer

ABOVE Novak Djoković serves to Sweden's Robin Soderling at the Rogers Cup tournament in Toronto. In January 2008 Djoković won the Australian Open to become the first player representing Serbia to win a grand slam title. 24 July 2008. Mark Blinch

TOP Britain's Andy Murray chases down a shot from Switzerland's Stanislas Wawrinka during his 6–1 6–3 6–3 fourth-round win over the 10th seed at the U.S. Open at Flushing Meadows in New York. Murray went on to defeat world number one Rafael Nadal in the semi-finals before losing to Roger Federer in the final. 1 September 2008. Jeff Zelevansky

ABOVE Australia's Lleyton Hewitt returns the ball to American Justin Gimelstob during his straight-sets win in the third round at the Wimbledon championships in London. Hewitt lost to eventual champion Roger Federer in the last four. 24 June 2005. Dylan Martinez

TOP OF THEIR GAME

OPPOSITE ABOVE LEFT Lindsay Davenport hits a forehand to Maria Sharapova of Russia during the WTA Tour Championships in Los Angeles. The American, who has won three grand slam titles, quit at the end of 2006 to have a baby. She returned to the WTA tour in the following year. 10 November 2005. Lucy Nicholson

OPPOSITE ABOVE CENTRE Justine Henin serves to Amélie Mauresmo of France during the Australian Open final in Melbourne before she was forced to retire with a stomach upset. The Belgian reached the final of all four grand slam events in 2006. 28 January 2006. Tim Wimborne

OPPOSITE ABOVE RIGHT Amélie Mauresmo returns the ball en route to beating Justine Henin in the round-robin stage of the WTA Championships in Madrid. Henin got her revenge two days later when she defeated Mauresmo in the final. 10 November 2006. Andrea Comas

OPPOSITE BELOW Belgium's Kim Clijsters stretches to return the ball to Lindsay Davenport during the fourth round at Wimbledon. Clijsters, who went on to win the U.S. Open the same year, announced plans to retire at the end of 2007. 27 June 2005. Dylan Martinez

THIS PAGE In 2004, at the age of 17, Maria Sharapova became the third youngest champion in Wimbledon's 120-year history and the first 13th seed to win the title. The Russian beat Serena Williams in the final. 24 June 2004. Tony O'Brien

SÖRENSTAM'S SWING

ABOVE Swede Annika Sörenstam tees off on the 13th hole during the second round of the 2004 LG Skins Game at La Quinta, California. Skins is a golf betting game with money placed on each hole. The winner of the hole takes the money; if it is halved the money is carried over to the next hole. A player winning a hole is said to have won a 'skin'. Fred Couples won this game for the fifth time, taking 11 skins and earning a total $640,000. 28 November 2004. Lucy Nicholson

RYDER CUP TRIUMPH

OPPOSITE Spectators watch as Darren Clarke plays a practice drive before the 2006 Ryder Cup at the K Club in Ireland. The Northern Irishman made himself available for the biennial team golf match against the United States as a wildcard selection for captain Ian Woosnam just three weeks after his wife Heather died following a long battle against cancer. 'Every single one of us has dedicated this to Heather and Darren,' said Woosnam after Europe triumphed for a third consecutive time. 19 September 2006. Kieran Doherty

BEACH SHOT

Fijian Vijay Singh is silhouetted against Carmel Bay as he hits his approach shot
on the ninth fairway at Pebble Beach golf links during the final round of 2004
of the AT&T National Pro-Am. The tournament was originally known as the
Bing Crosby Pro-Am after the American crooner and keen golf fan. Singh
went on to win the tournament with a four-round total of 272, 16 under par.
8 February 2004. Robert Galbraith

ON COURSE

BELOW Adam Scott of Australia hits from a bunker on the third day of practice for the 88th PGA Championship in Medinah, Illinois. Scott was tipped as a future world number one after winning the 2004 Players Championship aged 24. 16 August 2006. John Gress

BOTTOM Lee Westwood and Sergio Garcia check their shoes at the 34th Ryder Cup at the Belfry. Europe beat the U.S. in a contest that had been postponed for a year because of the September 11, 2001, attacks on the United States. 28 September 2002. Win McNamee

BELOW Ernie Els hits a shot on the sixth hole at the Singapore Open. The South African lost to Adam Scott in a three-hole playoff for the title after a tropical downpour had reduced the tournament to 54 holes. 7 September 2006. Vivek Prakash

BOTTOM Padraig Harrington pitches out of the rough during his final round at the Tour Players' Championship at Gut Kaden near Hamburg. Harrington won the British Open in 2007, retaining the title in 2008 before becoming the first European to win the PGA championship since 1930. 18 May 2003. Kai Pfaffenbach

BOWLED OVER

TOP Pakistan's Shoaib Akhtar bowls on the opening day of the second test against India in Lahore. India went on to win their maiden test series in Pakistan. Akhtar, the first bowler to be measured bowling at 160 kph (100 mph), is nicknamed the 'Rawalpindi Express.' 5 April 2004. Arko Datta

ABOVE Chris Gayle of the West Indies celebrates his century against South Africa during their ICC Champions Trophy semi-final in Jaipur. West Indies lost to Australia in the final. 2 November 2006. Arko Datta

TOP Australia wicketkeeper Adam Gilchrist dives for a catch during a World Cup pool match against England in Port Elizabeth, South Africa. Australia went on to beat India in the final. 2 March 2003. David Gray

ABOVE New Zealand's Andre Adams is bowled by Pakistan's Shoaib Akhtar for five in the fifth one-day game at the Westpac Stadium in Wellington. 17 January 2004. Anthony Phelps

BOUNDARY BOUND

Australia captain Ricky Ponting crashes the ball under a leaping Ian Bell at silly point while England wicketkeeper Geraint Jones watches intently on the third day of the fourth test of the 2005 Ashes series at Trent Bridge in Nottingham. England won an exciting match in a consistently enthralling series to go 2–1 up in the five-match series. They then drew at The Oval in London to win a series against their oldest rivals for the first time in 18 years. 27 August 2005. Darren Staples

ABOVE THE RIM

ABOVE Milwaukee Bucks forward Joe Smith (8) attempts a shot that fails with Philadelphia 76ers forward Chris Webber and centre Steven Hunter (45) providing a tight defence in the first quarter of NBA action at the Bradley Center in Milwaukee. 23 November 2005. Allen Fredrickson

ABOVE RIGHT Dallas Mavericks' Brandon Bass (right) shoots over Ben Wallace of the Chicago Bulls during the second half of their NBA game in Chicago. 3 December 2007. John Gress

OPPOSITE ABOVE LEFT Jason Kidd of the New Jersey Nets defends against Phoenix Suns guard Steve Nash in the third quarter of their NBA game in East Rutherford, New Jersey. 27 March 2006. The Nets won 110–72. Jeff Zelevansky

OPPOSITE ABOVE RIGHT Phoenix Suns forward Quentin Richardson watches the ball hang on the rim during first-half action against San Antonio Spurs in Game 4 of the 2005 NBA Western Conference Finals in San Antonio, Texas. 30 May 2005. Lucy Nicholson

OPPOSITE BELOW LEFT LeBron James of the U.S. goes for the basket during a Group B men's basketball game against Angola at the 2008 Beijing Olympics. The U.S. defeated Spain 118–107 in the final. 12 August 2008. Lucy Nicholson

OPPOSITE BELOW RIGHT Lebanon's Basseem Balaa (bottom left) goes for a rebound against Iran's Mohammad Nikkhah (bottom right) during the final game of the Asia basketball championship in Tokushima, western Japan. Iran won 74–69. 5 August 2007. Issei Kato

GRECO-ROMAN GRAPPLE

Egypt's Karam Ibrahim (right) grapples with Georgia's Ramaz Nozadze on his way
to a gold medal in the men's Greco-Roman 96 kgs competition at the 2004 Athens
Olympics. The flamboyant Ibrahim, a women's underwear manufacturer from
Alexandria, won Egypt's first Olympic gold medal since 1948. He then raised a
finger in triumph, kissed the mat and flipped his exultant coach to the floor before
performing a perfect somersault. 26 August 2004. Yves Herman

WRESTLEMANIA!

Canadian Chris Benoit grimaces at the referee as Chavo Guerrero pins him to the floor during a World Wrestling Entertainment show in Madrid. Professional wrestling, compared to its Olympic cousins Greco-Roman and freestyle, is pure spectacle with such rules as there are designed to be entirely secondary to entertainment. In June 2007 Benoit killed his wife and seven-year-old son before hanging himself. 6 December 2006. Susana Vera

HEAVY HITTERS

Referee Joe Cortez reacts as Bernard Hopkins (centre) of the U.S. hits Welshman
Joe Calzaghe during their light-heavyweight boxing fight at the Thomas and Mack
Arena in Las Vegas, Nevada. Calzaghe recovered from a first-round knockdown to
outpoint Hopkins in his first fight in the U.S. 19 April 2008. Marsh Starks

TOP Oscar de la Hoya, one of the best and most glamorous boxers at the turn of the 21st century, is instructed by trainer Floyd Mayweather Snr during his title fight with Shane Mosley. De la Hoya, the son of Mexican immigrants who was brought up in Los Angeles, won a gold medal at the 1992 Barcelona Olympics and after turning professional won world titles in six different divisions. He met his match in Mosley, who outpointed him twice over 12 rounds, winning their Las Vegas fight for the World Boxing Council and World Boxing Association super-welterweight titles. 13 September 2003. R. Marsh Starks

ABOVE Ricky Hatton (left) of England hits World Boxing Association welterweight champion Luis Collazo of the U.S. in the eleventh round in Boston. Hatton won on a unanimous decision. 13 May 2006. Brian Snyder

TOP Dariusz 'Tiger' Michalczewski of Poland takes a punch from Fabrice Tiozzo of France during their World Boxing Association light heavyweight fight in Hamburg. Tiozzo retained his title with a sixth-round technical knockout. 26 February 2005. Christian Charisius

ABOVE A bloodied John Simpson faces up to defending champion Derry Matthews in their World Boxing Union featherweight title fight in Liverpool, England. Local fighter Matthews was knocked down in the first round and also docked two points but still managed to outpoint the British champion. 10 March 2007. Carl Recine

HOLMES STRIKES GOLD

Years of disappointment and injury are forgotten as Britain's Kelly Holmes wins
the women's 800 metres final at the 2004 Athens Olympics. Holmes beat her
training partner Maria Mutola, who had dominated the event for a decade. She went
on to complete an 800–1,500 double, a feat which had previously been beyond any
Briton, including twice Olympic 1,500 metres champion Sebastian Coe who won
800 metres silver medals at the 1980 Moscow and 1984 Los Angeles Games.
23 August 2004. Gary Hershorn

KNOCKOUT AT LAST

World Boxing Organization junior welterweight champion Miguel Cotto rejoices after repulsing an unexpectedly torrid challenge from Colombian Ricardo Torres in Atlantic City, New Jersey. Cotto felled the challenger four times but each time Torres came back to rock the champion, including a right hand to the chin which had the Puerto Rican reeling. In the seventh round, Cotto finally prevailed, pounding Torres around the head and body and scoring a knockout with a left hook to the Colombian's face. 24 September 2005. Tim Shaffer

DOWN AND OUT

TOP U.S. sprinter Jon Drummond lies on the track in protest after he was disqualified in the second round of the 100 metres at the 2003 Paris world athletics championships. Competition was suspended for nearly an hour as officials tried to get Drummond to leave the track. The former U.S. champion, who alternately lay down, beat his chest and burst into tears, was finally persuaded to leave. He later withdrew from the 4x100 metres relay squad and said: 'I honestly believe I did not false start. My spirit is broken because it has always been my desire to provide entertainment for the fans.' 24 August 2003. Yannis Behrakis

ABOVE Portugal striker Hélder Postiga crouches on the pitch in dejection after his team lose 1–0 to France in a World Cup semi-final in Munich. 5 July 2006.
Alessandro Bianchi

TOP Jesus Hernandez of Spain sits injured after a crash during the 16th stage of the Tour of Spain cycling race between Almería and Calar Alto. 12 September 2006.
Victor Fraile

ABOVE Los Angeles Lakers' Derek Fisher lies on the floor after being knocked down during Game Two against the Minnesota Timberwolves in the Western Conference Finals in Minneapolis. 23 May 2004. John Gress

THE LIMITS OF ENDURANCE

A runner bites his arm in pain as he receives first aid after collapsing at the finish line in the 2005 Nairobi marathon. The race was won by Samson Barmao in two hours 12 minutes 15 seconds. The Nairobi marathon, first held in 2003, is part of a four-stage race including the Hong Kong, Mumbai and Singapore marathons. In 2006, London, New York City, Boston, Chicago and Berlin combined to form a marathon majors grand slam circuit with the overall men's and women's winners gathering half a million dollars each. Runners score points in each race they contest over a two-year period. 23 October 2005. Radu Sigheti

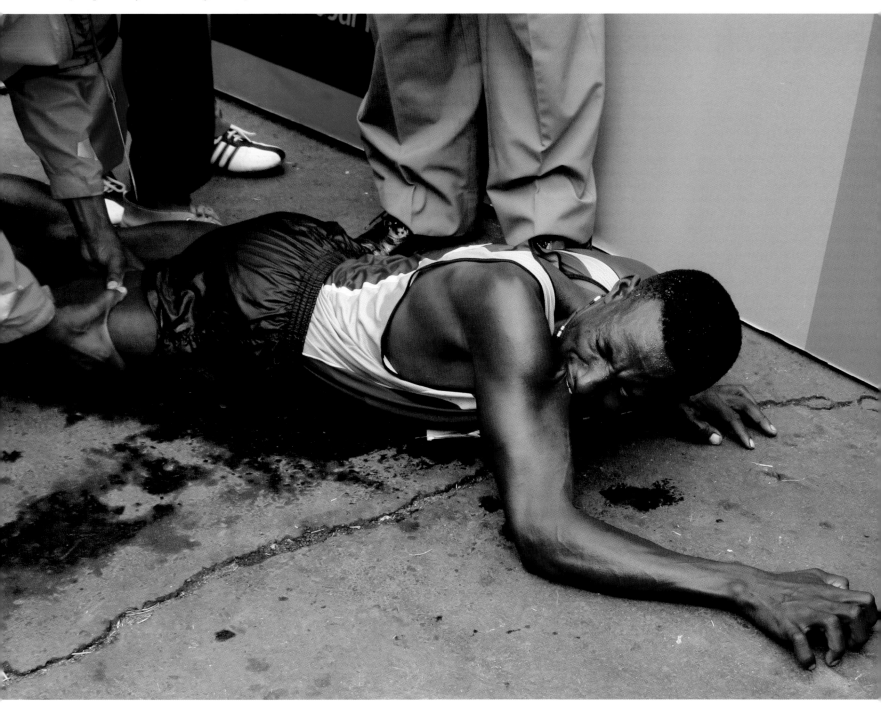

WAITING FOR THE OFF

TOP New Zealand's All Blacks gather before their rugby test against Italy in Rome. After a routine 59–10 defeat of Italy, the All Blacks had a record five-try 45–6 defeat of Six Nations champions France two weeks later. 13 November 2004. Alessandro Bianchi

ABOVE Riders are reflected in Francisco Mancebo's sunglasses before the start of the 16th stage of the 2004 Tour of Spain from Olivenza to Cáceres. The Tour of Spain is one of the world's big three cycling endurance races along with the Tour de France and the Giro d'Italia. 21 September 2004. Victor Fraile

TOP England sprinter Darren Campbell waits to start his men's 200 metres heat at the Commonwealth Games in Melbourne. He was later disqualified for running outside his lane. 22 March 2006. David Gray

ABOVE Athletes wait for the start of the 100 metres event of the men's decathlon at the European athletics championships in Gothenburg. 10 August 2006. Kai Pfaffenbach

OPPOSITE St Louis Cardinals pitcher Anthony Reyes listens to the playing of 'God Bless America' during Game One of Major League Baseball's World Series against the Detroit Tigers in Detroit. The Cardinals won the series 4–1. 21 October 2006. Brian Snyder

LIMBERING UP

OPPOSITE TOP LEFT A surfer stretches before the qualifying series of the Pantin Classic Pro World championships at Pantin Beach in Ferrol, northern Spain. 7 September 2006. Miguel Vidal

OPPOSITE TOP RIGHT Spain's coach Luis Aragonés encourages players during a training session in Cádiz before their friendly soccer match against Romania. 14 November 2006. Marcelo del Pozo

OPPOSITE CENTRE LEFT Scotland's Dougie Hall (centre) and fellow players practise scrummaging in training at Murrayfield Stadium in Edinburgh, Scotland, before the test against Romania. 6 November 2006. David Moir

OPPOSITE CENTRE RIGHT Sarah Drury of the United States stretches during a practice session for the FIVB women's volleyball world championships in Kobe, western Japan. 2 November 2006. Toru Hanai

OPPOSITE BELOW LEFT An athlete trains for the discus by throwing bicycle tyres in Nauru, the world's smallest republic. 13 September 2001. Mark Baker

OPPOSITE BELOW RIGHT Australian cricketers warm up at a training session at the WACA Ground in Perth, three days before the third Ashes test against England. 11 December 2006. David Gray

THIS PAGE ABOVE Canadian swimmer Morgan Knabe rests on the swimming pool deck next to team mate Scott Dickens during a morning training session at the Olympic aquatic centre ahead of the 2004 Athens Games. 11 August 2004. David Gray

THIS PAGE BELOW France's short track speed skating team begin free practice for the Short Track World Cup and Olympic qualifying competition in Bormio, northern Italy. 10 November 2005. Max Rossi

RETURN TO ATHENS

LEFT An athlete passes by a statue on the final lap of the men's marathon, the last event of the 2004 Olympic Games. Runners followed the approximate route covered by Spiridon Louis at the first modern Games in 1896. That in turn supposedly traced the course taken in 490 BC by Phidippides from the battlefield at Marathon to Athens, where he announced the Greek victory over Persia. The athletes finished in the Panathinaiko stadium, the ancient stadium that was fully rebuilt to stage the athletics in 1896. 29 August 2004. Damir Sagolj

BELOW Gianna Angelopoulos, president of the 2004 Athens Olympics organizing committee, holds a torch lit with the Olympic flame in the Panathinaiko stadium. The Olympic torch relay, carrying a flame lit by the rays of the sun at the site of Ancient Olympia, was introduced at the 1936 Berlin Olympics. The flame is borne by a series of relay runners to the host city where it is used to light the cauldron at the opening ceremony. 31 March 2004. Yannis Behrakis

LUNGE FOR THE LINE

World record holder Dayron Robles of Cuba crosses the finish line to win the men's
110 metres hurdles final in the National Stadium at the 2008 Beijing Olympics.
On the left is David Oliver of the U.S. who finished third and on the right another
American David Payne, who won the silver medal. 21 August 2008. Dylan Martinez

OUT BEFORE THE FIRST HURDLE

China's Liu Xiang limps disconsolately from the track after failing to start his 110 metres hurdles first-round heat at the 2008 Beijing Olympics. Liu, the first Chinese man to win an Olympic track title with his victory at the 2004 Athens Games in world-record equalling time, publicly apologized while his coach said he had been suffering from a right Achilles tendon injury. 18 August 2008. Gary Hershorn

MAKING A SPLASH

OPPOSITE Saif Saaeed Shaheen of Qatar splashes through the water barrier on his way to the gold medal ahead of Olympic champion Ezekiel Kemboi in the final of the 3,000 metres steeplechase at the 2005 Helsinki world championships. Shaheen, formerly known as Stephen Cherono in his native Kenya, is the highest profile track and field athlete to change nationality for economic reasons. He was granted Qatari citizenship in 2003 and nine days later set an Asian steeplechase record. He won Qatar's first world championships track and field medal in the same year when he finished first at the Paris world championships. Shaheen did not compete at the 2004 Athens Olympics after Kenya refused to agree for the International Olympic Committee's qualification rules to be waived. In his absence Kemboi led a Kenyan clean sweep. 9 August 2005. Kai Pfaffenbach

ABOVE Olga Kaniskina of Russia strides towards the finish line in the 20 kilometres walk final in the National Stadium during the 2008 Beijing Olympics. Kaniskina led from the start and battled through relentless rain to win in Olympic record time. 21 August 2008. Jerry Lampen

ATHLETE FROM HEAD TO TOE

ABOVE Bahrain's Ruqaya Al-Ghasara gives thanks after winning the 200 metres gold medal at the 2006 Asian Games in Doha. The 24-year-old wore a hijab, a scarf which covers the hair and neck, along with leggings and long sleeves. Only her face and hands were exposed. 'Wearing conservative clothes has encouraged me,' she said. 'Wearing a veil proves that Muslim women face no obstacles. This is a glory to all Muslim women.' 11 December 2006. Jerry Lampen

RIGHT South Africa's Dina Phakula risks injury as she runs barefoot in the women's 1,500 metres heats at the 2006 Melbourne Commonwealth Games. Ethiopia's Abebe Bikila is the most famous barefoot runner, winning the men's marathon at the 1960 Rome Olympics. He retained the title four years later in Tokyo wearing running shoes. South African Zola Budd, who was controversially granted British citizenship shortly before the 1984 Los Angeles Games, also ran barefoot. 20 March 2006. Andy Clark

CITIUS, ALTIUS, FORTIUS

TOP Czech Roman Šebrle competes in the long jump on his way to winning the decathlon gold at the 2004 Athens Olympics. In 2001, Šebrle became the first man to break 9,000 points in the 10-event competition. 23 August 2004. Ruben Sprich

ABOVE Jan Železny wins javelin bronze at the 2006 Gothenburg European championships in his last international appearance before he announced his retirement. The Czech won three Olympic and three world titles and set five world records. 9 August 2006. Kai Pfaffenbach

TOP Shot putter Reese Hoffa throws during the U.S. Olympic trials in Sacramento. Hoffa placed second to earn a spot on the team for the Athens Olympics, where he failed to make the cut for the final. 10 July 2004. Jason Reed

ABOVE Lithuania's Virgilijus Alekna throws the discus to win the gold medal at the European athletics championships in Gothenburg. It was the double world and Olympic champion's 18th win in as many competitions in a year. 12 August 2006. Kai Pfaffenbach

BELOW Dwight Phillips soars through the air during the men's long jump competition at the 2004 U.S. Olympic trials in Sacramento. Phillips completed a rare treble at the Athens Olympics the following month. The man dubbed Spiderman at the 2003 Paris world championships because of his distinctive blue-and-white body suit won the Olympic long jump gold comfortably with a leap of 8.59 metres after winning both the world indoor and outdoor titles. 11 July 2004.
Jason Reed

RAISING THE BAR

Yelena Isinbayeva of Russia soars to her 24th world record with a vault of
5.05 metres during the women's pole vault final at the 2008 Beijing Olympics.
Isinbayeva, who broke the mark of 5.04 she set in the previous month, has
specialized in breaking the world record by a centimetre at a time, earning
$100,000 each time. 18 August 2008. Kai Pfaffenbach

TOP Sweden's Olympic and world heptathlon champion Carolina Klüft (third from right), seen here in a 200 metres heat on the first day of her event, added a second European title on a day of high emotion in front of her home fans in Gothenburg. 7 August 2006. Phil Noble

ABOVE Russia's Tatyana Lebedeva, the Olympic long jump champion, switched to triple jump in Gothenburg to win a European gold medal. 9 August 2006. Kai Pfaffenbach

TOP Croatian Blanka Vlašić competes in the women's high jump final in the National Stadium at the 2008 Beijing Olympics. Vlašić finished second to Belgian Tia Hellebaut on a countback after both women had cleared 2.05 metres, ending an unbeaten streak of 34 victories. 23 August 2008. Jerry Lampen

ABOVE World record holder Tatyana Lysenko of Russia competes in the women's hammer throw at the European athletics championships in Gothenburg, where she won gold with a throw of 76.67 metres. 8 August 2006. Kai Pfaffenbach

HEADSTRONG

Japan's Hisashi Mizutori dismounts from the parallel bars at the 2005 world gymnastics championships in Melbourne. Mizutori finished second to team mate Hiroyuki Tomita, who became the first Japanese to win the all-around title since Shigeru Kasamatsu 31 years earlier. Japan is one of the traditional powerhouses of men's artistic gymnastics, winning every Olympic team title from 1960 through 1976. They won again at the 2004 Athens Games, with both Tomita and Mizutori on the team. 24 November 2005. Tim Wimborne

FEET FIRST

Venezuela's Keisa Monterola wins bronze in the women's pole vault at the 2006 Central American and Caribbean Games in Cartagena, Colombia. The women's pole vault was not introduced into major competition until 1997, when American Stacy Dragila won the world indoor title in Paris. Dragila was again successful when the first outdoor world competition was staged in Seville in 1999 and completed an historic treble with gold in the inaugural Olympic event at the 2000 Sydney Games. 25 July 2006. Daniel Munoz

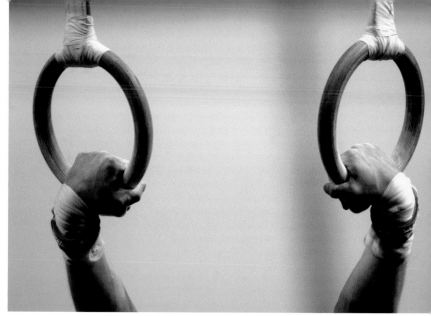

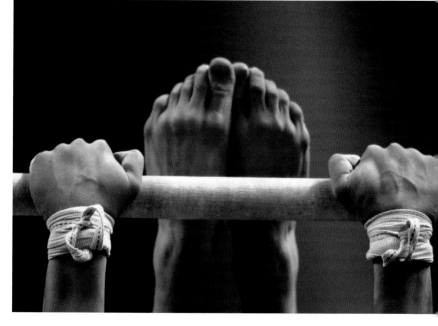

A FIRM GRIP

TOP Daniel Popescu of Romania goes through his horizontal bar routine during an artistic gymnastics test event for the Olympic Games in Athens. Popescu went on to win a team bronze at the Olympics. 18 March 2004. Yannis Behrakis

ABOVE Romanian Marius Urzică presents his pommel horse routine at the 25th European artistic gymnastics championships in the Greek town of Patras. Urzică won the gold medal in the floor competition. 28 April 2002. Yannis Behrakis

TOP Sasha Artemev of the U.S. performs on the rings at the Athens Olympic test event. His compatriot Paul Hamm won the Olympic all-round gold in Athens in controversial circumstances after a mix-up over the scoring. 18 March 2004. Yannis Behrakis

ABOVE Soultana Kosaxi of host nation Greece hangs from the uneven bars during the test event for the 2004 Olympics in the Athens indoor arena. The arena hosted trampoline and basketball as well as gymnastics at the Games. 17 March 2004. Yannis Behrakis

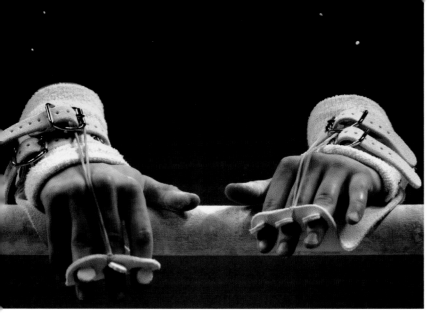

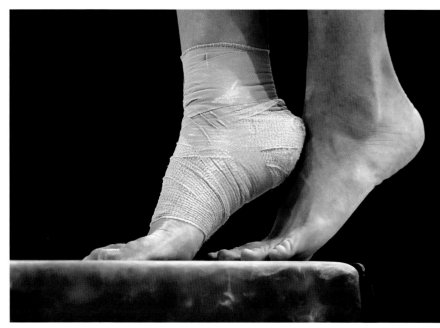

TOP Canadian Melanie Banville performs on the asymmetric bars during the test event in the Athens Olympic indoor arena. 18 March 2004. Yannis Behrakis

ABOVE An Argentine gymnast chalks her hands before starting her asymmetric bars routine in the team final at the 14th Pan American Games in Santo Domingo in the Dominican Republic. Argentina failed to win a medal in the event, with the U.S. taking gold. 2 August 2003. Jason Reed

TOP Argentina's Maria Sol Poliandri competes in the asymmetric bars final at the South American Games in Buenos Aires. Argentina topped the medals table at the Games with 107 golds. 13 November 2006. Enrique Marcarian

ABOVE A gymnast balances on the beam in practice for the world championships in Aarhus, Denmark. Surprise winner Irina Krasnianska gave Ukraine their first gold medal in 11 years after an ankle injury ruled out Chinese favourite Zhang Nan. 12 October 2006. Max Rossi

CHINESE GRACE

China's Pang Panpan competes in the women's floor final at the 2006 Shanghai
World Cup. Pang won the beam title at the event and three months later helped
China to win the women's world team title in Aarhus, Denmark. It was one of a
record eight world gold medals for China, boosting the team's hopes of outclassing
all comers at the 2008 Beijing Olympics. 16 July 2006. Aly Song

DUTCH STRENGTH

Dutchman Yuri van Gelder dismounts from the rings en route to winning the bronze medal at the 2006 world championships in Aarhus. Van Gelder went into the event as the defending champion but lost out to world championship debutant Chen Yibing of China. Van Gelder's sculpted biceps reveal the strength required to perform on this demanding apparatus. 20 October 2006. Max Rossi

PARALLEL PERSPECTIVE

OPPOSITE Romania's Dorin Razvan Selariu competes on the rings at the same time as Switzerland's Niki Böschenstein performs on the floor during the 2006 world gymnastics championships in Aarhus, Denmark. After a judging fiasco at the 2004 Olympic Games, when noisy protests from the crowd forced judges to increase Russian Alexei Nemov's mark in the horizontal bar, the old 10 scale was scrapped and a new, open-ended scoring system made its global debut in Aarhus, though it puzzled many fans. 14 October 2006. Max Rossi

BOUNCE BACK

ABOVE Olympic champion Yuri Nikitin from Ukraine (left) and bronze medallist Henrik Stehlik of Germany perform on the trampoline during a gymnastics exhibition at the 2004 Athens Olympics. The first Olympic men's trampoline champion was 30-year-old Russian Alexandre Moskalenko who decided to come out of retirement when the sport was introduced at the 2000 Sydney Olympics. The former world champion had to lose 24 kg (53 lb) to get back into shape but won easily. 24 August 2004. Kim Kyung-Hoon

TO THE WATER

Some of the 1,800 contestants at the start of the swimming leg of the 2004 Nice triathlon. Competitors swim 4 km (2.5 miles), cycle 120 km (74.5 miles) then finish with a 30-km (18.6-mile) running race. The triathlon originated in France with a report in the French newspaper *L'Auto* in 1920 describing a competition featuring a 3-km race, a 12-km bike ride and a swim across a channel. It was introduced at the 2000 Sydney Olympics where local fans claimed the first champion, Canadian Simon Whitfield, as their own on the grounds that he had an Australian father. 26 September 2004. Eric Gaillard

TO THE COURSE

Cross-country skiers at the start of the 2006 Engadin ski marathon in Maloja, Switzerland. About 12,000 competitors took part in the race over the Olympic marathon distance of 42.2 km (26.2 miles) between Maloja and S-chanf in the Engadin valley via the ski resort of St Moritz. The course includes 'Mattress Hill', a steep drop through a forest where organizers tie mattresses to tree trunks to protect skiers who crash. The annual race has been staged since 1969. 12 March 2006.

Sebastian Derungs

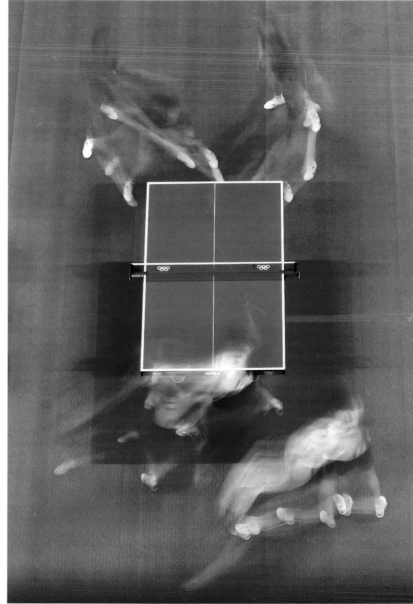

TURNING THE TABLES

ABOVE Paey Fern Tan of Singapore serves to U.S. doubles pair Whitney Ping and Jasna Reed during the second round of the 2004 Athens Olympics table tennis tournament. Doubles is the most exciting form of table tennis, a sport originally devised as an indoor, miniaturized version of lawn tennis. It is immensely popular in east Asia, particularly in China, where the game was instrumental in bringing a rapprochement with the United States. In 1971 a U.S. team in Japan for the world championships was invited by the Chinese team to visit the republic. They were the first Americans to visit Beijing for 22 years, clearing the way for President Nixon's historic visit in the following year. 15 August 2004. Mike Hutchings

ABOVE China's Qi Chen and Lin Ma (top) play Hong Kong's Lai Chak Ko and Ching Li to win the men's doubles table tennis gold medal at the Athens Olympics. China won three of the four table tennis titles in Athens. 21 August 2004. Kieran Doherty

SHUTTLECOCK SMASH

France's Hongyan Pi, the world number three and leading European badminton player, lines up a smash against Elena Nozdran of Ukraine during the second round of the 2005 world badminton championships in Anaheim, California. China has become the dominant force in world badminton. In 2006, Chinese players won four of the five golds at the Madrid world championships, the Thomas Cup men's team event for the sixth time and their fifth successive women's Uber Cup. 17 August 2005. Lucy Nicholson

HANDS UP FOR VOLLEYBALL

Cuba team members' hands pictured above the net during the women's volleyball quarter-final against Italy at the 2004 Athens Olympics. Volleyball, a combination of basketball skills and tennis scoring, was given full Olympic status at the 1964 Tokyo Games. Cuba have dominated the women's game but after winning the Olympic gold three times in a row they lost to China in the semi-finals in Athens, gaining some consolation by beating Brazil in the third-place playoff. 24 August 2004.

Jorge Silva

BELOW Brazilian Jacqueline Carvalho on the attack as Caroline Wensink (right) and Alice Blom of the Netherlands attempt to block during a first-round match at the 2006 world championships in Kobe, Japan. Brazil were hot favourites but were surprisingly beaten 3–2 in the final by Russia, who won their first title since 1990. The Brazilian men fared better the following month, overwhelming Poland 3–0 to retain their world title. 3 November 2006. Toru Hanai

TAKING THE PLUNGE

Peter Vanderkaay dives into the pool at the start of the men's 400 metres freestyle final at the 2006 U.S. swimming championships in Irvine, California. Vanderkaay was a member of the U.S. 4x200 metres relay team, with Michael Phelps, Ryan Lochte and Klete Keller, who upset the Australian quartet of Ian Thorpe, Grant Hackett, Michael Klim and Nicholas Springer at the 2004 Athens Olympics. He won a world gold medal in the relay the following year. 1 August 2006. Lucy Nicholson

CHAMPIONS OF THE POOL

ABOVE Cullen Jones competes in the men's 50 metres freestyle heats at the U.S. national championships in Irvine. A fortnight later, Jones helped the American 4x100 freestyle relay team to break the world record at the Pan Pacific championships in Victoria, Canada. They set a blistering time of three minutes 12.46 seconds, more than seven-tenths of a second faster than the previous record set by surprise gold medallists South Africa at the 2004 Olympics. 3 August 2006. Lucy Nicholson

TOP Laure Manaudou of France swims the butterfly leg of the women's 200 metres individual medley final on her way to winning one of four gold medals she collected at the European Aquatic Championships in Budapest. 3 August 2006. Laszlo Balogh

ABOVE Britain's Rebecca Adlington swims next to Camelia Potec (left) of Romania in the women's 800 metres freestyle final at the National Aquatics Centre during the 2008 Beijing Olympics. Adlington won the 400–800 double to become the first British woman since 1960 to win an Olympic swimming gold and the first Briton for 100 years to win two swimming titles at the same Games. 16 August 2008. Wolfgang Rattay

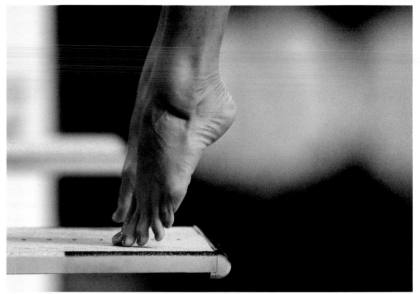

POWER AND GRACE

ABOVE Alexandre Despatie from Canada sprays water as he dives during a practice session before the preliminary competition in the three-metre springboard at the 17th Commonwealth Games in Manchester. At the age of 17, Despatie won two golds and a bronze at the Games. His haul over the following years included two world titles in 2005 and three more Commonwealth Games golds in 2006 in Melbourne, as well as an Olympic silver in Athens. 26 July 2002. David Gray

TOP The feet of South African diver Jenna Dreyer push away from the three-metre springboard during the Commonwealth Games in Melbourne. Dreyer placed 10th. 25 March 2006. Andy Clark

ABOVE Bermuda's Commonwealth Games team member Katura Horton-Perinchief floats to the surface during a diving practice session in Melbourne. 14 March 2006. Tim Wimborne

ABOVE Yulia Pakhalina of Russia holds her position as she dives on her way to winning the bronze medal in the three-metre springboard final at the Athens Olympic Games behind China's Guo Jinjing and Wu Minxia. Pakhalina also won silver in the synchronized event. 26 August 2004. Damir Sagolj

ABOVE Kwon Kyung-min and Cho Kwan-hoon of South Korea plunge into the water in the men's three-metre springboard synchronized event at the 14th Diving World Cup in the Athens Olympic Aquatic Centre. 18 February 2004. Yannis Behrakis

TREADING WATER

ABOVE Triathletes gather in the water before swimming in the 2006 Ironman Triathlon in Kailua-Kona, Hawaii. Introduced in 1978, the Hawaii Ironman event comprises a 4-km (2.4-mile) swim, a 180-km (112-mile) bike ride and a 42.2 km (26.2-mile) run. Today it is the world's premier triathlon with 1,500 athletes enlisted on the 25th anniversary in 2003. 21 October 2006. Hugh Gentry

FISHEYE VIEW

RIGHT Members of Spain's synchronized swimming team practise at the National Aquatics Centre, also known as the Water Cube, ahead of the 2008 Beijing Olympics. Originally known as water ballet, synchronized swimming began in Canada in the 1920s. It spread to the United States in the early 1930s, where a display at the 1934 Chicago World's Fair drew rave reviews. Its popularity soared further when Esther Williams performed in a string of MGM 'aqua musicals' in the 1940s. 7 August 2008. Wolfgang Rattay

A SHOT AT GLORY

India's Rajyavardhan Singh Rathore unloads spent shells during the men's double trap shooting final at the Asian Games in Doha. Rathore, a Commonwealth Games champion and Athens Olympics silver medallist, helped India to win the team silver medal behind China. 5 December 2006. Caren Firouz

ABOVE Australian Lauryn Ogilvie scores a hit on a target clay on her way to winning the gold medal in the women's skeet singles in Bisley, England, which hosted shooting events at the 2002 Commonwealth Games. Ogilvie, who previously competed for the U.S., also won pairs gold. 2 August 2002. Ian Waldie

RIGHT Annette Woodward, Australia's oldest Olympian in 28 years at the age of 57, trains in Melbourne after being selected for the Athens Olympic team in the 25-metre pistol. Woodward, a radiographer, came out of retirement to make the team after nursing her dying husband. She finished 18th. 26 July 2004. Stuart Milligan

A SHOT IN THE DARK

ABOVE A skier is silhouetted as she passes a lamp during the women's 7.5-km (4.6-mile) sprint at a biathlon World Cup event in Khanty-Mansiysk in western Siberia. German Katrin Apel, a relay gold medallist from the 2002 Salt Lake City Olympics, won the race for her first victory in three years. 16 March 2005. Sergei Karpukhin

COURSING ACROSS COUNTRY

RIGHT Seen from the air, some of the 11,000 cross-country skiers in the Engadin ski marathon cross a frozen lake near Sils in Switzerland. The race has been an annual event on the second Sunday in March since 1969. A separate women's race, a week earlier, began in 2000. During a typical race, course-side volunteers hand out 21,500 chocolate bars, 20,000 energy tablets and 10,000 bananas to participants. 13 March 2005. Pascal Lauener

COOL RUNNINGS

Jamaicans Winston Watt and Wayne Blackwood shoot downhill during the 2005 men's bobsleigh World Cup in Cesana Pariol, Italy, the venue for the Turin Winter Olympics competition in the following year. A bobsleigh team from the Caribbean island provoked intense interest at the 1988 Calgary Winter Olympics where they crashed violently on the final run. Their exploits were later made into a Disney movie called *Cool Runnings*. 22 January 2005. Max Rossi

LUGE LOOP

Spectators' shadows are cast on the track as American Courtney Zablocki competes in the first run of the women's luge at the 2006 Turin Olympics. Zablocki missed a medal by just 0.004 seconds, finishing fourth behind a trio of Germans led by defending champion Sylke Otto, but still produced the best performance by an American woman in luge history. The final was marred by three crashes and Zablocki's team mate Samantha Retrosi was taken to hospital with concussion. 13 February 2006. Pawel Kopczynski

SKELETON START

Poland's Monika Wołowiec starts her run in the women's skeleton at the Turin Winter Olympics. The race was won by Maya Pedersen, who gave Switzerland their first gold of the Games. Britain's Shelley Rudman collected a surprise silver in her first full season of competition and former world champion Diana Sartor was fourth despite being nine weeks pregnant, a fact she kept from her coach until after the race. 16 February 2006. Jean-Paul Pelissier

SKATER IN FLIGHT

ABOVE Tong Jian of China waits to catch Pang Qing in the pairs free skating at the Salt Lake City Winter Olympics. The competition ended in scandal when French judge Marie-Reine Le Gougne admitted she had been pressured by her federation president to mark down Canadians Jamie Salé and David Pelletier in order to ensure the title went to Russia's Yelena Berezhnaya and Anton Sikharulidze. After days of arguments, the Canadians were awarded duplicate gold medals and figure skating officials set about devising a new scoring system. 11 February 2002. David Gray

AIRBORNE ELEGANCE

RIGHT Canada's Deidra Dionne practises for the aerials freestyle competition at the Turin Winter Olympic site in Sauze d'Oulx, Italy. Dionne, a bronze medallist at the 2002 Olympics, broke her neck in September 2005 when she crashed while training in Australia. After seven hours of surgery she battled through rehabilitation to return to competition for the Turin Games five months later, though she failed to reach her event final. 19 February 2006. Dylan Martinez

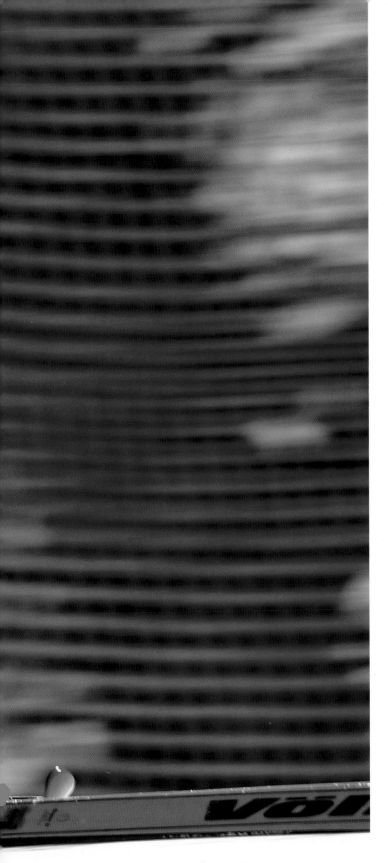

AIMING FOR A MEDAL

ABOVE Norway's silver medallist Ole Einar Bjørndalen shoots during the men's 12.5-km biathlon pursuit at the 2006 Turin Olympics. Bjørndalen, who had won a gold and two silvers at the 1998 Nagano Olympics, was a sensation at the 2002 Salt Lake City Games when he captured all four titles in the space of nine days. But he was hampered by a sinus problem in Turin and had to settle for two silvers and a bronze. 18 February 2006. Jean-Paul Pelissier

SUPER-G ON MONO-SKI

LEFT Tyler Walker of the U.S. skis during his men's super-G at the ninth Paralympic Games in Sestriere, Italy, where he finished sixth. Walker, who had both legs amputated below the knee as a child because of a congenital disorder, became the first mono-ski champion at the World X Games in January 2007, when his event made its debut at the annual extreme sports event in Colorado. 14 March 2006. Tony Gentile

THE PARALYMPIC GAMES

The Paralympic Games is the elite multi-sport event for athletes with physical disabilities, visual disabilities, cerebral palsy and for amputees. Governed by the International Paralympic Committee, the Games take place every four years following the Olympic Games. The name comes from the Greek word 'para' (meaning 'alongside' or 'beside'), referring to the event running parallel to the Olympic Games. The modern Paralympics evolved from a 1948 sports competition for injured British war veterans, organized by Sir Ludwig Guttmann. Four years later, competitors from the Netherlands were invited. By 1960, an Olympic-style event was established. Nearly 4,000 athletes competed at the 2004 Games in Athens. China topped the medals table ahead of Britain and Canada. Events held for the first time at Athens included five-a-side blind football and women's sitting volleyball.

OPPOSITE LEFT ABOVE Double amputee Oscar Pistorius of South Africa, who runs with carbon fibre blades attached to his legs, competes in the men's 400 metres at the British Grand Prix athletics meeting at Don Valley in Sheffield, northern England. Pistorius successfully appealed to the Court of Arbitration for Sport after the world governing athletics body banned him from its competitions because it maintained the blades gave him an unfair advantage. However, he failed to record a qualifying time for the 2008 Beijing Olympics but ran in the Paralympics the following month, winning three gold medals. 15 July 2007. Eddie Keogh

OPPOSITE LEFT CENTRE Venezuela's Fernando Ferrer (left) and his guide compete in the men's 4x100 metres T11–T13 final during the 2008 Beijing Paralympics. Athletes compete in 26 different sports divided into six categories of disability. 16 September 2008. Jason Lee

OPPOSITE LEFT BELOW A woman athlete competes in the final of the 5,000 metres at the Athens Paralympics. 21 September 2004. Yannis Behrakis

OPPOSITE RIGHT A guide adjusts the hands of a blind athlete before the men's 100 metres final at the Athens Paralympics. 22 September 2004. Yannis Behrakis

ABOVE Colombian swimmer Robinson Martinez (bottom) trains in California for the Athens Paralympics. 21 May 2004. Eduardo Munoz

ICEBREAKERS

LEFT Pittsburgh Penguins' Sidney Crosby skates past an adoring fan during the first period of the NHL game against the Toronto Maple Leafs in Toronto. Hailed as ice hockey's next big player by 'The Great One' himself, Wayne Gretzky, Crosby lived up to the hype, becoming, at 19 years and five months, the youngest player voted to start the All-Star Game since fan balloting began in 1986. 18 April 2006. Mike Cassese

LEFT A mock Stanley Cup is wheeled into a shopping mall during a staged funeral procession for the cancelled NHL season in Edmonton. In a dispute over salary caps, the league locked out its players in September 2004. Five months later, still unable to reach an agreement with players, the NHL cancelled the remaining schedule and became the first North American professional sports league to lose an entire season to a labour dispute. 5 February 2005. Dan Riedlhuber

MOURNS THE DEATH OF THE
2004-05
NHL SEASON
K-ROCK

RIGHT Celebrating Edmonton Oilers fans cast shadows on the ice behind Carolina Hurricanes' goaltender Cam Ward after the Oilers' Ryan Smyth scored during the third period of Game 6 in the NHL Stanley Cup finals in Edmonton, Alberta. Two days later the Hurricanes beat the Oilers in Game 7 to win their first cup and rookie Ward was named Most Valuable Player of the playoffs. 17 June 2006. Andy Clark

RIGHT Pittsburgh Penguins defenceman Noah Welch hits Anaheim Ducks forward Travis Moen into the boards during an NHL game in Anaheim, California, which the home team won 3–2. The Ducks opened the 2006–7 season with an NHL record of 16 games without a loss in regulation time before falling to the Calgary Flames. But the California team regained their momentum and advanced to the playoffs for the second straight season. 6 November 2006. Mike Blake

TAKE OFF

ABOVE Russia's Dmitry Ipatov soars from the ski jumping hill as a watching official huddles under an umbrella to protect herself from heavy rain during practice for the second stop of the Four-Hills tournament in Garmisch-Partenkirchen, Germany. The event was shortened to one jump because of strong winds and poor conditions. Unseasonably warm weather and rain disrupted winter sports events across Europe in 2006–7, prompting ski federations to turn their thoughts to the prospect of global warming. 1 January 2007. Kai Pfaffenbach

REFLECTIONS ON ICE

LEFT An athlete warms up at the 2006 Olympic speed skating venue, the Oval Lingotto, during practice for a World Cup event in Turin. The colours on the ice are reflections from a giant television screen. At the Turin Olympics, the hall rang to the cheers of Italians as Enrico Fabris pushed the home team to a gold medal in the team pursuit before winning another gold in the 1,500 metres. 'Enrico, you are part of Italian sports history now,' Prime Minister Silvio Berlusconi told Fabris, who also collected a 5,000 metres bronze. 8 December 2005. Max Rossi

SAILING TO VICTORY

LEFT America's Cup challenger Luna Rossa Challenge from Italy sails before semi-final race six against BMW Oracle Racing of the United States at the Louis Vuitton Cup off Valencia, Spain. Luna Rossa completed a 5–1 win over a team who had been considered favourites to advance to the final. 20 May 2007.
Victor Fraile

RIGHT Nicorette and Skandia jostle for position in large swells outside Sydney Heads after the start of the 2004 Sydney-to-Hobart yacht race. Sweden's Nicorette won line honours in the 60th annual 628-nautical-mile race, after the starting fleet of 116 yachts had been devastated by gale-force winds and huge seas. Skandia capsized in the Tasman sea after losing her keel. In 1998 six sailors died and five boats sank on one of the world's roughest stretches of water. 26 December 2004. David Gray

RIGHT America's Cup challenger Emirates Team New Zealand's bowman works on the bow before the start of the rescheduled Round Robin 1 Flight 2 race against Mascalzone Latino Capitalia Team of Italy at the Louis Vuitton Cup off Valencia. Team New Zealand went on to defeat Luna Rossa in the final to earn the right to challenge Alinghi in the America's Cup. 20 April 2007. Heino Kalis

INDOOR ENDURO

Motorbike riders Samuli Aro from Finland and Spaniard Ivan Cervantes in action at the VI Enduro Indoor International of Barcelona at the city's Sant Jordi stadium. Both men helped manufacturer KTM to win a host of world titles. As its name indicates, enduro racing is a test of riders' stamina and is staged off road in rugged natural terrain, often through forests. Indoor racing artificially replicates those conditions. 14 November 2004. Albert Gea

WILD WATER

Athletes warm up during the first day of World Cup canoe and kayak racing at the
Athens Helliniko complex. The wild water facility for the 2004 Olympics, where
German Birgit Fischer won her eighth gold at the age of 42, was hailed as one of
the world's best competition venues. Athens, however, struggled to find long-term
uses for many of its Olympic venues and in 2007 the Helliniko site was leased to a
consortium who planned to turn it into a fun park. 8 July 2005. Yiorgos Karahalis

SOLBERG SOARS

ABOVE Subaru Impreza driver Petter Solberg of Norway goes airborne in the Tandalo stage on the second day of the Rally of Italy in Sardinia. Frenchman Sébastien Loeb took the championship lead with victory in Sardinia. The Citroën driver went on to take the world title for the second successive year after winning a record 10 rallies, hitting a bull in Argentina and postponing his honeymoon at a crucial stage of the season. 30 April 2005. Giampiero Sposito

DEFYING THE DESERT

RIGHT Bleached animal bones highlight the hostile terrain of the United Arab Emirates Desert Challenge as Stéphane Peterhansel of France steers his Mitsubishi on the fourth leg in Moreed. Peterhansel won the event in 2002 and 2003. The former skateboarding champion has won a record nine titles in the Dakar Rally, considered the toughest and most dangerous challenge in world motor sports. In 2007 he won for a third time in the car category, after six victories on two wheels. The 2008 rally was called off after four French tourists were killed in Mauritania the previous month and the race was rescheduled for South America in 2009. 13 November 2005. Eric Gaillard

THE TRAVELLING CIRCUS

ABOVE Michael Schumacher and his crew in Ferrari red are reflected in the glass of the stands as he makes a pit stop during the Spanish Formula One Grand Prix. The German driver won the Barcelona race for the fifth time in his career and the third year in a row. He retired at the end of 2006 as the most successful driver in Formula One history with a record seven titles and 91 race wins. 4 May 2003. Albert Gea

OPPOSITE ABOVE Renault's Fernando Alonso of Spain celebrates winning his second successive Formula One world championship after finishing runner-up to local hero Felipe Massa of Ferrari in the Brazilian Grand Prix. Schumacher was fourth in his farewell race. 22 October 2006. Bruno Domingos

OPPOSITE BELOW Abdel Rouf, a member of the Bahrain Royal Arab Stud, watches Minardi driver Patrick Friesacher of Austria during Formula One practice. Bahrain hosted the first Grand Prix in the Middle East in 2004 at a new, $150-million circuit. 2 April 2005. Wolfgang Rattay

FORMULA ONE DRAMA

ABOVE Ferrari Formula One driver Felipe Massa of Brazil navigates past a corner on the Marina Bay street circuit during the 2008 Singapore Grand Prix, the first Formula One race staged at night. Massa, who started the race in pole position, slumped to last after a terrible pit stop when he was given the green light to rejoin the race even though the fuel hose was still connected. He finished out of the points in 13th place. 28 September 2008. Tim Chong

OPPOSITE ABOVE A Renault team mechanic marks a Michelin tyre before the 2006 U.S. Grand Prix at Indianapolis. The 2005 race descended into chaos when only six cars started after Michelin discovered its tyres were unsafe and could not be used through the final high-speed banked corner. Fans booed and jeered and some threw objects on to the track as the 14 cars with Michelin tyres peeled off into the pit lane rather than take up their starting positions after the parade lap. 29 June 2006. John Gress

RIGHT Spaniard Fernando Alonso is reflected in a fireman's helmet during free practice for the 2006 French Grand Prix at Magny-Cours. Alonso, in a Renault, finished second behind seven-times champion Michael Schumacher, driving a Ferrari, who made history by becoming the first driver to win the same Grand Prix eight times, lapping all but the top seven drivers. It was the 100th French Grand Prix since Renault won the first race at Le Mans. 14 July 2006. Jean-Paul Pelissier

FAST TRACK

BELOW American Jimmie Johnson celebrates his victory at the 48th Daytona 500 on the roof of his confetti-covered Chevrolet at Daytona Beach, Florida. The race was marred by a record 11 cautions for accidents which eliminated several of the front-runners. NASCAR's biggest race has a prize purse of more than $18 million. In 2007, former Formula One driver Juan Pablo Montoya of Colombia finished 19th in the race after switching to a career in U.S. stock car racing. 19 February 2006. Mark Wallheiser

OPPOSITE Tony Stewart spins his car in celebration after winning the 2006 NASCAR race at the Atlanta Motor Speedway in Hampton, Georgia. Stewart set himself up as the favourite to win the 2007 Daytona 500 with good results in the build-up but crashed out of the race on lap 152 after a collision with fellow leader Kurt Busch. Instead, Kevin Harvick took victory by just 0.02 seconds after overtaking Mark Martin on the final lap. 29 October 2006. Steve Schaefer

TWO-WHEEL SPEED

RIGHT Honda MotoGP rider Marco Melandri of Italy glances backwards during the second practice session of the Italian motorcycling grand prix at the Mugello race track. The race was won by another Italian, Valentino Rossi, who lost his opportunity to win a sixth successive championship when he crashed during the final race in Valencia. As a result American Nicky Hayden claimed his first world championship on a Honda. 2 June 2006. Max Rossi

BELOW Ducati MotoGP rider Casey Stoner of Australia loses control of his motorcycle during a free practice for the Catalan Motorcycle Grand Prix at the Circuit de Catalunya racetrack in Montmeló, near Barcelona. Stoner, who finished third, was named Young Australian of the Year in 2007 after winning the world championship. 6 June 2008. Albert Gea

OPPOSITE Spain's Alvaro Bautista leads the field during qualifying for the Dutch TT 125cc motorcycling race in Assen. The race, always held on the last Saturday of June, is the biggest sports event of the year in the Netherlands. Motorcycling fans, who flock to the race from around Europe, have dubbed the venue 'The Cathedral'. 23 June 2006. Paul Vreeker

MOTOCROSS STUNT

A freestyle motocross rider is silhouetted against the sky during a practice session for the Red Bull X-Fighters at the stadium X-lecia in Warsaw, Poland. It was the last event staged in the venerable venue before it was ripped down in order to build a soccer stadium. 5 September 2008. Kacper Pempel

DESERT RIDERS

RIGHT Grant Robertson (left) from Australia, Stefano Candida (centre) from Italy and Ali al Shanfari from the United Arab Emirates ride the Ruba al Khali stage on the third day of the UAE Desert Challenge, near Lewa, south of Abu Dhabi. The race is regarded as the traditional warm-up for the tough Dakar Rally. 1 November 2002.
Anwar Mirza

STORM IN THE SAND

BELOW Some of the 1,000 racers in the annual Le Touquet beach race in northern France jostle for position on the 15.5-km (9.6-mile) circuit. Frenchman Arnaud Demeester, dubbed Sand-Man, became the first competitor to win the event six times with his 2007 victory, which was watched by an estimated 250,000 spectators. 18 February 2001. Bob Martin

LEAP OF FAITH

OPPOSITE Canadian John Anderson, on Gestine 36, jumps over the water during the CN International Open Cup at the 2006 Spruce Meadows Masters in Calgary, Alberta. Spruce Meadows, located in the foothills of the Canadian Rockies, hosts an annual showjumping event in the autumn. Equestrian is the only Olympic event teaming men and women with animals. It includes three disciplines: dressage, jumping and the three-day event. 10 September 2006. Todd Korol

BADMINTON'S ELITE

ABOVE England's Lucy Wiegersma, riding In the Purple, practises before the dressage section at the 2006 Badminton horse trials. Dressage is conducted over three rounds with horse and rider performing set routines in a walk, trot and canter during the first two rounds. The third round is freestyle with individually choreographed routines performed to music. Badminton, in Gloucestershire, England, is one of five international elite three-day events. 4 May 2006. Eddie Keogh

RECORD RACE

OPPOSITE A record crowd of 112,668 watches Smarty Jones, ridden by Stewart Elliott, gallop to an historic victory in the 2004 Preakness Stakes in Baltimore. Smarty Jones won by 11½ lengths, bettering the previous biggest winning margin of 10 lengths set by Survivor in the 1873 inaugural race. The three-year-old had already won the Kentucky Derby, first leg of the coveted Triple Crown, but his bid ended when he finished second at the Belmont Stakes to 36–1 outsider Birdstone. 15 May 2004. Gary Hershorn

FINAL FENCE

BELOW Competitors clear the last fence of the Jewson Novices Handicap steeplechase on the final day of the 2006 Cheltenham festival in Gloucestershire, England. Cheltenham is the climax of the National Hunt season, featuring the Champion Hurdle, the Queen Mother Champion Chase and the Cheltenham Gold Cup on successive days. It is particularly popular with Irish trainers and in 2007, for the first time, there were more entrants from Ireland than Britain in the Champion Hurdle. 16 March 2006. Toby Melville

THE FLYING TOMATO

A multiple exposure shows Shaun White taking the final jump to win the men's
snowboard slopestyle event at the ninth Winter X Games in Aspen, Colorado. The
American, nicknamed 'The Flying Tomato' for his unkempt red hair, won the 2006
Turin Olympics gold medal in halfpipe, an event in which riders rise up over the rim
of a half-cylinder and perform aerial tricks. The win brought White celebrity status
at home. 29 January 2005. Rick Wilking

IN PURSUIT

The British team pursuit quartet set a world record as they qualify for the final at the track cycling event during the 2008 Beijing Olympics. During a Games that proved a triumph for British cycling, the foursome went on to break the world record again in the final during a crushing victory over Denmark. Bradley Wiggins won his third Olympic gold and his second of the Beijing Games. 17 August 2008. Phil Noble

CYCLING ON TOUR

LEFT Cyclists cross a bridge on the fourth stage of the Tour of Spain cycling race from Águilas to the Mediterranean resort of Roquetas de Mar. Unheralded Spaniard Aitor González, predictably nicknamed 'Speedy', won the three-week race, which ended in Real Madrid's Bernabéu stadium. The Vuelta, as it is known in Spain, is one of cycling's three big annual stage races, along with the Tour de France and the Giro d'Italia. 10 September 2002. Marcelo del Pozo

LEFT The leading pack tackle a climb during the 163-km (101-mile) 16th stage of the 2002 Giro d'Italia from Conegliano to Corvara. Mexican Julio Perez Cuapio won the stage while Australian Cadel Evans took the leader's pink jersey. The Giro was inspired by the Tour de France and designed, like the French classic, to increase a newspaper's circulation, in this case *La Gazzetta dello Sport* which is printed on pink paper. 29 May 2002.
Stefano Rellandini

RIGHT Riders pass in front of a chemical plant during the 150.5-km (93.5-mile) first stage of the 2004 Tour of Qatar cycle race in Doha. Saunier Duval team rider Francisco Ventoso of Spain won the stage and took the gold leader's jersey. The Tour, across a flat desert around the hinterlands of Qatar, is one of the many sports transplanted from Europe to the Middle East, where there is no tradition of cycling. Doha hosted the 2006 Asian Games and plans to bid for the 2016 Olympics. 2 February 2004. Jacky Naegelen

RIGHT A man watches the pack go by on the fifth stage of the Tour of Spain, from Alcázar de San Juan to Cuenca. Spanish climbing specialist Roberto Heras won what would have been a record fourth victory when the Vuelta ended in Madrid, but was later stripped of the title and banned for two years after testing positive for the banned blood booster erythropoietin (EPO) and Russian Denis Menchov was crowned champion instead. 31 August 2005. Dani Cardona

SPANISH EURO TRIUMPH

ABOVE Spain's Carles Puyol (left) and team mate Sergio Ramos (right) compete
for the ball with Italy's Luca Toni during their Euro 2008 quarter-final at the Ernst
Happel Stadium in Vienna. Italy packed their defence in what appeared to be a
deliberate attempt to force a penalty shootout on a day with ominous connotations
for the Spanish. Spain has lost three quarter-final shootouts in major competitions
held on 22 June (the 1986 and 1996 European championships and the 2002 World
Cup). This time they made no mistakes after the scores were tied 0–0 following
extra time. Spain held their nerve to win the shootout 4–2 with Arsenal's Cesc
Fàbregas striking the decisive penalty. 22 June 2008. Tony Gentile

RIGHT Spanish striker Fernando Torres scores the winning goal in the Euro 2008
final at the Ernst Happel Stadium in Vienna, beating Germany's Jens Lehmann with
Philipp Lahm unable to come to his goalkeeper's assistance. Torres's goal, from a
clever pass by Xavi, gave Spain a 1–0 victory and their first major title for 44 years.
They were deserved winners under veteran coach Luis Aragonés after a consistently
entertaining tournament, finally shrugging off the unwanted title of perennial
under-achievers on the big stage. 29 June 2008. Christian Charisius

ABOVE AS Roma captain Francesco Totti gestures in frustration after missing a scoring opportunity during their Champions League Group F soccer match against Dynamo Kiev at Rome's Olympic stadium. 19 September 2007. Tony Gentile

ABOVE LEFT Spanish playmaker Cesc Fàbregas, the best and brightest of Arsenal's new generation, acknowledges a goal against the north London club's arch-rivals Tottenham Hotspur at White Hart Lane. 15 September 2007. Kieran Doherty

LEFT Italy's goalkeeper Gianluigi Buffon glances up during the penalty shootout in the 2008 Euro championship quarter-final against Spain at the Ernst Happel stadium in Vienna. Spain eliminated the world champions 4–2. 22 June 2008. Tony Gentile

LEFT BELOW Barcelona's Lionel Messi celebrates his second goal against Atlético Madrid during a Spanish First Division soccer match at Vicente Calderón stadium in Madrid. The Argentine helped his team to a 6–0 win. 20 May 2007. Sergio Perez

BELOW Manchester City's Brazilian import Robinho presses his hands together during a Premier League match against Portsmouth at the City of Manchester stadium. Robinho inspired City to a 6–0 win. 21 September 2008. Nigel Roddis

ABOVE AC Milan's Kaká looks to the heavens after his side beat Liverpool 2–1 in the 2007 Champions League final in Athens through twin strikes from Filippo Inzaghi. 23 May 2007. Kai Pfaffenbach

ABOVE RIGHT Bayern Munich's Franck Ribéry acknowledges his penalty in the last minute of extra time which gave his side a 1–0 win over TSV 1860 Munich in a 2008 German Cup quarter-final in Munich. 27 February 2008. Michael Dalder

RIGHT Barcelona's Samuel Eto'o celebrates his goal against Real Sociedad during their Spanish First Division soccer match at Anoeta stadium in San Sebastian. Barcelona won 2–0. 5 May 2007. Felix Ordonez

RIGHT BELOW Chelsea's Michael Ballack blows a kiss as he celebrates scoring against Sheffield United during their English Premier League soccer match at Stamford Bridge in London. 17 March 2007. Alessia Pierdomenico

BELOW Liverpool's Fernando Torres scores against Derby County during a Premier League match at Anfield, Liverpool. Torres and fellow Spaniard Xabi Alonso each scored twice in a 6–0 demolition. Nigel Roddis

THE FALL GUY

ABOVE Portugal's Cristiano Ronaldo sits on the pitch while France coach Raymond Domenech gesticulates during their 2006 World Cup semi-final in Munich. Ronaldo was jeered during the match by fans convinced he persistently dived in an attempt to fool referees that he had been fouled. They booed again shortly after Zinedine Zidane had converted the winning penalty when Ronaldo fell theatrically to the pitch in a blatant dive which was ignored by referee Jorge Larrionda. 5 July 2006. Alex Grimm

DROGBA TAKES FLIGHT

OPPOSITE Chelsea's Didier Drogba soars over Levski Sofia goalkeeper Bozhidar Mitrev after a challenge during their Champions League group match at Stamford Bridge in London which ended 2–0 for the home side. Ivory Coast international Drogba provoked a media storm in March 2006 when he told a television interviewer: 'Sometimes I dive.' He later said his imperfect English had given the wrong impression and denied diving. European governing body UEFA vowed to crack down on the practice, saying players found guilty would be banned for at least two games. 5 December 2006. Dylan Martinez

ENGLAND'S ASHES

ABOVE The end of an unforgettable day at The Oval in London as the England captain Michael Vaughan holds the tiny urn containing the Ashes, the symbol of cricket supremacy between the old country and its former colony Australia. England lost the Ashes in 1989 and never looked like winning them back until 2005, when the nation was transfixed by one of the great sporting contests. In the following year, Australia took emphatic revenge with a 5–0 series whitewash at home. 12 September 2005. Russell Boyce

LIVERPOOL'S COMEBACK

RIGHT Liverpool soccer captain Steve Gerrard is surrounded by a sea of red after his team's astonishing comeback in the 2005 European Champions League final against AC Milan in Istanbul. The English team were seemingly dead and buried at halftime when they trailed the Italian giants 3–0. Midfielder Gerrard gave his side a sliver of hope with a headed goal then Vladimír Šmicer and Xabi Alonso levelled the scores. Jerzy Dudek saved from Andrea Pirlo and Andriy Shevchenko in the penalty shootout to clinch victory. 25 May 2005. Dylan Martinez

ABOVE Italian fencer Aldo Montano is thrown in the air by supporters after winning the gold medal in the men's sabre final at the Athens Olympic Games. 14 August 2004. Tony Gentile

ABOVE LEFT Manchester United players celebrate with the soccer Champions League trophy following their victory over Chelsea at the Luzhniki stadium in Moscow in the first all-English final. United won on penalties. 22 May 2008. Eddie Keogh

LEFT U.S. captain Paul Azinger shows the Ryder Cup to fans after his side overcame the European team to win the 37th Ryder Cup championship at the Valhalla Golf Club in Louisville, Kentucky. 21 September 2008. Jeff Haynes

LEFT BELOW Team CSC rider Carlos Sastre of Spain shares a toast with team manager Bjarne Riis of Denmark following his victory in the 95th Tour de France. 27 July 2008. Bogdan Cristel

BELOW Boston Red Sox players exult after defeating the Colorado Rockies in Game 4 to win Major League Baseball's World Series in Denver. 28 October 2007. Mike Blake

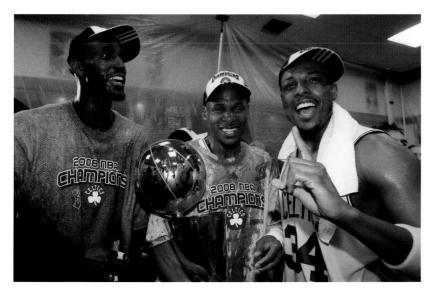

ABOVE Boston Celtics' Kevin Garnett, Ray Allen and Paul Pierce (left to right) celebrate with the Larry O'Brien trophy after defeating the Los Angeles Lakers in Game 6 to win the NBA basketball finals 4–2 in Boston. 17 June 2008. Brian Snyder

ABOVE RIGHT Sébastien Loeb of France (right) and co-driver Daniel Elena from Monaco rejoice after winning the Mexico rally, third round of the FIA world championship, in León. 2 March 2008. Henry Romero

RIGHT Matthias Steiner of Germany poses after winning the super-heavyweight weightlifting gold at the 2008 Beijing Olympics. He is holding a photo of his late wife Susann, who died in a car crash the previous year. 19 August 2008. Alvin Chan

RIGHT BELOW Australia cricket captain Ricky Ponting (second left) holds the Ashes trophy aloft in Sydney amid a spray of champagne from a bottle held by team mate Shane Warne following Australia's 5–0 victory over England. 5 January 2007. David Gray

BELOW Spain's goalscorer Fernando Torres and team mate Sergio Ramos (centre left and right) lift the winners' trophy after defeating Germany 1–0 in the Euro 2008 final at the Ernst Happel stadium in Vienna. 29 June 2008. Kai Pfaffenbach

TO THE VICTOR THE SPOILS

ABOVE Captain Cafu bows his head and holds the soccer World Cup aloft after Brazil win the trophy for a record fifth time in the 2002 final against Germany. After a difficult qualifying campaign, Brazil played like liberated men in the tournament jointly hosted by Japan and South Korea. A rejuvenated Ronaldo scored both goals in the final while Ronaldinho and Rivaldo dazzled in midfield and Cafu, playing with Roberto Carlos at the back, was the rock on which opposition attacks foundered. 30 June 2002. Dylan Martinez

RIGHT Fabio Cannavaro acknowledges the applause after leading Italy to a penalty shootout victory in the 2006 World Cup final over France in Berlin. The teams had been tied 1–1 after extra time. The steadfast Italian defender won FIFA's World Player of the Year ahead of French captain Zinedine Zidane, who was sent off in the final, and Brazilian playmaker Ronaldinho. 9 July 2006. Dylan Martinez

BELFAST TELEGRAPH SATURDAY DECEMBER 3 2005
62 SPORT
GEORGE BEST
1946 - 2005

Heroes and Zeroes

Champions/ Celebrities / Fallen Idols

A mourner watches George Best's funeral cortege pass through the streets
of Belfast. Widely regarded as the best soccer player ever to emerge from the
British Isles, Best relished but was eventually consumed by the pop star lifestyle,
alcohol addiction leading to his premature death in 2005 at the age of 59.
3 December 2005. Fran Veale.

DAVID BECKHAM

Soccer and show business formed the ultimate alliance in January 2007 when David Beckham announced he had signed for the Los Angeles Galaxy at a weekly wage of one million dollars. It seemed a marriage made in a Hollywood heaven for the marketing men and a coup for Major League Soccer in its unending battle to sustain a sport which barely registers with the average American sports fan. Cynics might argue that Los Angeles was the ideal location for the former England captain and his ambitious wife, the one-time pop idol Victoria who has never replicated the success she briefly enjoyed with the Spice Girls in the late 1990s.

At the age of 31, Beckham was the best-known and most photogenic footballer in the world. But he had passed his sell-by date with Real Madrid, where his commercial value had overshadowed his dwindling contribution on the field.

A move to AC Milan on loan before the start of the 2009 Major League season was also more about marketing than football.

In his prime with Manchester United and England, Beckham's defining skill was his ability to strike a sumptuous pass, free kick or penalty with his right foot. Despite periodic appearances in central midfield, he always looked more comfortable on the right, where his crossing could be fully effective and his lack of pace less exposed.

Although Beckham's fame ultimately exceeded his ability he remained a model professional, his commitment to the sport unaffected by the glare of publicity he commanded throughout the world and the jet set life he so obviously relished. Given the latter, his ultimate career choice was perfect.

OPPOSITE, ABOVE LEFT A fan watches Beckham on a giant screen at the Euro 2004 qualifier against Slovakia in Middlesbrough. 11 June 2003. Jeff J. Mitchell

OPPOSITE, ABOVE RIGHT David and Victoria Beckham arrive in Rome for the wedding of actors Tom Cruise and Katie Holmes. 17 November 2006. Tony Gentile

OPPOSITE, BELOW LEFT Beckham celebrates scoring against Azerbaijan in England's World Cup qualifier at St James' Park, Newcastle. 30 March 2005. Darren Staples

OPPOSITE, BELOW RIGHT Beckham gestures after Real's Primera Liga match against Deportivo la Coruña at Coruña's Riazor stadium. 7 January 2007. Miguel Vidal

RIGHT Beckham leaves after a promotional event in Tokyo. 29 December 2006. Toru Hanai

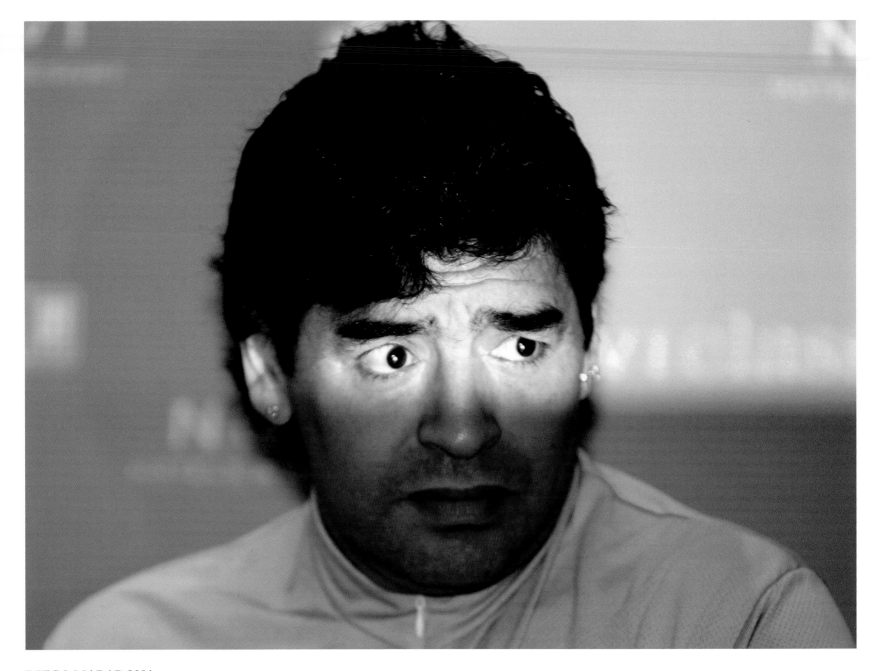

DIEGO MARADONA

Thousands kept a silent vigil in the streets of Buenos Aires in 2004 as Diego Maradona fought a lonely and apparently losing battle in a private hospital. Grotesquely overweight, with a heart weakened by years of cocaine abuse, the little Argentine who had dazzled and delighted throughout the 1980s was close to death.

Desperate times demanded desperate measures. After his discharge, Maradona underwent a stomach-stapling operation in a Colombian hospital and, against all the odds, was present in Germany to cheer on his old team in the 2006 World Cup. His rehabilitation seemed complete two years later when he was named as the national coach, although in the previous year he had been admitted to hospital again for the effects of excessive drinking, eating and cigar smoking.

Maradona had emerged from a Buenos Aires slum to conquer the world. Stocky and powerful with a low centre of gravity and the ability to accelerate suddenly from a standing start, he made his professional debut with Argentinos Juniors shortly before his 16th birthday. After the 1982 World Cup he moved to Europe, playing first for Barcelona and then Napoli. He enjoyed both his most notorious and his finest moments at the 1986 World Cup, where he scored illegally against England with his left hand then added a second legitimate goal after an astonishing run through his bewildered opponents with the ball seemingly attached to his left foot.

Argentina won the Cup but Maradona's life was already spinning out of control and he was banned for 15 months in 1991 after a positive test for cocaine. He returned seemingly restored to full vigour at the 1994 World Cup but tested positive for a cocktail of stimulants and never represented his country again.

OPPOSITE Maradona listens to reporters' questions after arriving in Novi Vinodolski, Croatia, to play a charity match. 15 June 2005. Nikola Solic

ABOVE Maradona waves an Olympiakos shirt bearing his name during a league game against Iraklis in Athens. 16 January 2005. John Kolesidis

RIGHT, TOP TO BOTTOM A cigar-smoking Maradona at an Argentine first division match in Buenos Aires. 19 February 2006. Marcos Brindicci. Maradona, wearing a Boca Juniors shirt, thanks fans at his farewell match in Buenos Aires. 10 November 2001. Enrique Marcarian. A fan outside the Buenos Aires clinic treating Maradona for heart and breathing problems. 21 April 2004.
Marcos Brindicci

ZINEDINE ZIDANE

Tough, resilient, supremely skilled and fiercely devoted to family and friends, Zinedine Zidane was the world's pre-eminent midfielder for the best part of a decade with Juventus, Real Madrid and France. But he never forgot his working-class roots in Marseille where his Algerian immigrant father Smail toiled in a warehouse to bring up his family. After spells with Cannes and Bordeaux, Zidane moved to Juventus, then Real Madrid. A once-in-a-lifetime player with mesmerizing footwork and an explosive shot, he was equally adept in the air. He also had an occasionally violent temper and was sent off for stamping in the first round of the 1998 World Cup. But he returned to help France win, scoring from two headers in the final against Brazil, and was part of the 2000 European championship-winning side.

Past his best but still able to turn a match on its head, Zidane made his final appearance for France at the 2006 World Cup. In the final against Italy he converted a penalty and narrowly missed with a header when, with time running out, his temper flared and he was sent off for head-butting Marco Materazzi.

ABOVE Zidane chases the ball past two Greek players during France's Euro 2004 quarter-final in Lisbon. 25 June 2004. Jean-Paul Pelissier

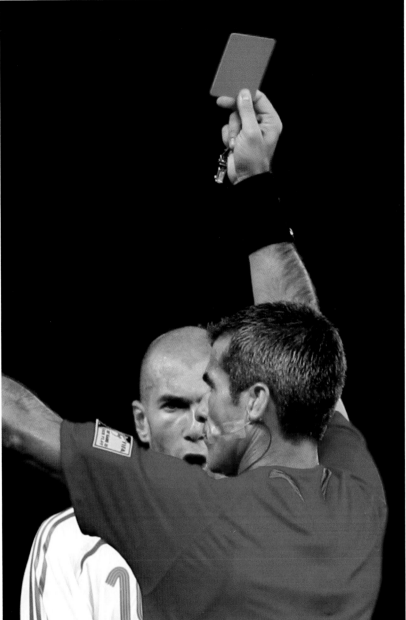

TOP Zidane plays soccer with children in Corso on a charity visit to Algeria.
12 December 2006. Louafi Larbi

ABOVE French President Jacques Chirac receives Zidane at the Élysée Palace in
Paris, the day after the World Cup final. 10 July 2006. Philippe Wojazer

ABOVE Referee Horacio Elizondo shows Zidane a red card during France's 2006
World Cup final against Italy in Berlin. 9 July 2006. Jerry Lampen

RONALDO

At the turn of the century Ronaldo's still unfulfilled career hung in the balance. A striker of breathtaking ability worthy of mention in the same breath as Pelé, he was World Player of the Year in 1996 and 1997 and a sensation at the 1998 World Cup as Brazil strode imperiously to the final against hosts France. Yet on the morning of the match he suffered a mysterious fit and during the game he was a listless ghost at the French feast during a 3–0 defeat.

Following a knee injury in 1999, the prognosis was bleak. But after an 18-month convalescence Ronaldo returned to football, moved to Real Madrid and was selected for the 2002 World Cup. The tournament was a triumph for Ronaldo and Brazil. He scored eight goals in seven games, including both goals in the 2–0 final win over Germany, to equal Pelé's record of 12 World Cup goals.

Four years later Ronaldo became the all-time World Cup goal-scoring record holder, with his 15th goal against Ghana, beating German Gerd Müller's previous mark. But the fires were now burning low, he was clearly overweight and there were only intermittent flashes of his old, irresistible dynamism.

OPPOSITE, CLOCKWISE FROM TOP Turkish players watch Ronaldo score during a World Cup semi-final in Saitama. 26 June 2002. Ruben Sprich. Ronaldo celebrates after a goal against Germany in the World Cup final in Yokohama. 30 June 2002. Dan Chung. Ronaldo tries to beat Costa Rica goalkeeper Erick Lonnis in a World Cup game in Suwon. 13 June 2002. Petar Kujundzic. Ronaldo fights for the ball in a World Cup qualifier against Chile in Santiago. 6 June 2004. Sergio Moraes

BELOW Dejection for Ronaldo after Brazil lose to France in a World Cup quarter-final in Frankfurt. 1 July 2006. Alex Grimm

CRISTIANO RONALDO

A complete footballer, Cristiano Ronaldo combines the trickery and speed of a great winger with the appetite and instincts of a striker accomplished enough to score 42 goals in 49 games for Manchester United in the 2007–8 season.

Ronaldo's bewitching range of skills propelled United to their second Premier League and Champions League double and he was a clear winner of the Ballon d'Or European footballer of the year award in December 2008.

Born in Funchal, Madeira, on 5 February 1985, Ronaldo attracted the attention of football scouts from the age of 10 before joining Sporting Lisbon. He was on the point of joining Arsenal in 2003 before United enticed him to go north by offering him £12.5 million, three times more than the north London club.

Ronaldo's detractors have accused him of persistent diving in an attempt to win penalties. He also enraged England fans for his role in the 2006 World Cup quarter-final against Portugal when Wayne Rooney was sent off for stamping on a Portuguese defender. Ronaldo complained vociferously to the referee and television replays showed him winking to the Portuguese bench as Rooney left the field.

After the Cup, Ronaldo was linked in the media with Real Madrid but eventually signed a five-year extension with United in April 2007.

ABOVE Ronaldo gestures towards the Reading fans after scoring for Manchester United during their English Premier League soccer match at the Madejski Stadium in Reading. 19 January 2008. Eddie Keogh

RONALDINHO

Like so many Brazilians before him, Ronaldinho learned his skills in beach football. He quickly made his name at the Porto Alegre club Gremio. His ball skills and a flair for scoring spectacular goals attracted worldwide attention after he made his national debut in 1999 and he decided to try his luck in Europe with Paris Saint-Germain.

After top-scoring at the 1999 Confederations Cup, Ronaldinho joined Ronaldo and Rivaldo at the 2002 World Cup in Japan and South Korea, where he played a leading part in Brazil's successful campaign. He also provided one of the tournament's enduring images with an audacious free kick which drifted over a frantically back-pedalling England goalkeeper David Seaman in the quarter-finals.

Ronaldinho joined Barcelona in 2003 and in his first season inspired the Catalan club to 17 consecutive matches without defeat and to second place in the league. The following season they went one better and in December 2004 Ronaldinho was named FIFA player of the year, an award he won again in 2005.

Barcelona claimed European club football's greatest prize in 2006 when they beat Arsenal 2–1 in the Champions League final. But in the World Cup later that year Ronaldinho, in common with his team mates, was uncharacteristically subdued.

After appearing overweight and uninterested at Barcelona, Ronaldinho recaptured his enthusiasm and goal-scoring touch when he transferred to AC Milan 2008.

BELOW A jubilant Ronaldinho after scoring for Barcelona against Werder Bremen in a Champions League group match in Barcelona. 5 December 2006. Albert Gea

TIGER WOODS

Once in a generation, an athlete arrives with skills and charisma in such abundance that they transcend their sport. Baseball produced Babe Ruth, cricket unveiled Don Bradman and soccer revealed Pelé. People with little interest in sport knew their names, much as they knew Pablo Picasso was a painter. Today golf has Tiger Woods, the most famous athlete in the world and on course to overhaul Jack Nicklaus's record of 18 major titles.

The son of a black American Vietnam War veteran and a Thai mother, Woods paraded his skills at the age of three on the Mike Douglas television show. His late father Earl had no doubts over his son's genius. Tiger, he proclaimed, could become a new messiah. Sensibly, Tiger concentrated on golf, and went on to become the best in the world in all facets of the game. He is the longest driver, the most accurate with the irons, commands the best approach shots and is deadly with the putter. He is also the most athletic, with a punishing fitness regime, although his body betrayed him in 2008 when he was forced to undergo reconstructive surgery on his right knee after winning the U.S. Open virtually on one leg and missed the remainder of the season.

PREVIOUS PAGES, LEFT Woods watches his shot during the first day of the Champions tournament in Shanghai. 10 November 2005. Aly Song

PREVIOUS PAGES, RIGHT Woods celebrates after making a birdie on the 18th hole during the final round of the U.S. Open golf championship at Torrey Pines in San Diego. 15 June 2008. Matt Sullivan

OPPOSITE, CLOCKWISE FROM TOP LEFT Woods hits his driver off the seventh tee at the Buick Invitational tournament in San Diego. 27 January 2006. Mike Blake. Woods receives the traditional winner's green jacket from former champion Vijay Singh of Fiji at the Masters. 8 April 2001. Gary Hershorn. Young fan David Dennison watches the practice round at the 101st U.S. Open at Southern Hills, Tulsa. 11 June 2001. Mike Segar. Woods hugs caddy Steve Williams after winning the British Open at Hoylake, his first victory since the death of his father Earl. 23 July 2006. Robert Galbraith

RIGHT Woods hits his second-hole tee shot during the 2006 Masters second round at Augusta National. 7 April 2006. Mike Blake

MICHAEL SCHUMACHER

'Flawed' and 'genius': as the chequered flag went down on Michael Schumacher for the final time at the Brazilian Grand Prix in 2006 and the assessments began, these were the words most freely used. There was no doubting the magnitude of Schumacher's achievements. He was Formula One champion a record seven times and set other records that may never be beaten, including most race victories, fastest laps, pole positions and races won in a single season. According to *EuroBusiness* magazine, he became the world's first billionaire athlete in 2005.

But Schumacher's methods have sometimes aroused disquiet and even anger since he made a sensational debut for Jordan in the 1991 season. In 1994, he became the first German to win the championship after a controversial collision with Briton Damon Hill in the final race in Australia. He took a one-point lead over Jacques Villeneuve into the final race of the 1997 season at Jerez, where there was another collision as the Canadian tried to overtake. Schumacher, who retired from the race, giving Villeneuve the title, was deemed to be at fault and disqualified from the championship. At the 2006 Monaco Grand Prix, enraged rivals accused the German of cheating when he stopped his car at the penultimate corner in qualifying in a blatant attempt to block them.

On the plus side, Schumacher was a supremely dedicated professional who poured his talents and energy into making the Ferrari team as good as it could possibly be. Before his arrival no Ferrari driver had won the championship since Jody Scheckter in 1979 and the Italians were widely derided by their rivals.

He is also a devoted family man who treasures his privacy, and has given generously to charity. In retirement he has dabbled in motorbike racing while making it clear he does not contemplate a second career.

OPPOSITE Schumacher looks in his Ferrari's rearview mirror in the pit lane during practice for the Monaco Grand Prix. 31 May 2003. Pascal Deschamps

BELOW The Ferrari crew practise their pit stop manoeuvres at the Sepang circuit in Malaysia. 20 March 2003. Bazuki Muhammad

LEFT Schumacher walks in the paddock during a free practice session at the Jerez race track. 17 September 2004. Marcelo Del Pozo

BELOW LEFT Schumacher sprays champagne on cheering fans as he celebrates winning the Italian Grand Prix at Monza. 14 September 2003. Dylan Martinez

BELOW Schumacher jumps for joy on the podium after winning the Malaysian Grand Prix at Sepang. 21 March 2004. Zainal Abd Halim

OPPOSITE ABOVE Schumacher drives in free practice for the Italian Grand Prix at Monza. 3 September 2005. Chris Helgren

OPPOSITE BELOW Schumacher shakes hands with Renault's Fernando Alonso before his final race in Brazil. 22 October 2006. Sergio Moraes

LEWIS HAMILTON

Lewis Hamilton moved from sixth to fifth on the final lap of the final race of the 2008 season in São Paulo to become Formula One's youngest world champion at the age of 23.

The sport's first and only black driver, with his roots in the Caribbean island of Grenada and a childhood on a working-class housing estate in Britain, had been supported by McLaren for more than a decade. But nothing else in his background remotely suggested that he might one day emulate drivers such as Michael Schumacher and Ayrton Senna. Hamilton's parents divorced when he was two, and he was bitten by the motorsports bug as a youngster when he stepped into a child's go-kart on a hard-earned family holiday in Spain.

In his maiden 2007 season, Hamilton racked up nine podiums in a row and ended the season as overall runner-up by a single point after blowing his chance to become the first rookie champion. A year later he became the first British champion since Damon Hill in 1996.

ABOVE Hamilton talks with team mate Fernando Alonso of Spain after winning the United States Grand Prix in Indianapolis. 17 June 2007. Carlos Barria

RIGHT Hamilton celebrates as he drives past his pit crew after winning the British Grand Prix at the Silverstone race track in England. 6 July 2008. Eddie Keogh

VALENTINO ROSSI

The son of former 250cc grand prix winner Graziano, flamboyant Italian Valentino Rossi has been almost single-handedly responsible for raising the profile of his sport with titles in all four classes. In addition he embraced the challenge of moving from the powerful Honda team to under-performing Yamaha in 2004, when he demonstrated emphatically that man, not the machine, was the key factor by taking his fourth consecutive top-category world title with nine victories and five pole positions.

After coming up through the ranks with go-karts and mini-bikes, Rossi finished ninth in the 125cc series with Aprilia in his first grand prix series in 1996 at the age of 17. In the following year he won the title with 11 wins from 15 races. Rossi moved up to the 250cc class in 1998 and won the title in 1999.

The process was repeated when he raced a works-supported Honda 500cc bike in 2000, finishing second to American Kenny Roberts on a Suzuki, then winning in 2001 before the 500cc championship was replaced by the MotoGP. Rossi swept to victories in the next two seasons on a full factory machine engineered by Jerry Burgess, finishing in the top three in each of the 16 races in 2003 before making his momentous decision to move to Yamaha.

After winning five titles in a row, Rossi – nicknamed 'The Doctor' for his calculated, clinical approach to racing – was dethroned by Honda's American Nicky Hayden in 2006. Australian Casey Stoner won the 2007 title but Rossi bounced back in the following year, winning his third world title for Yamaha to become the second man after Giacomo Agostini to regain the championship after a two-year gap.

The charismatic Rossi, who has signed a contract with Yamaha until 2010, has had test drives with Ferrari, suggesting he is considering a future on four wheels. He discounted a move to Formula One but has talked about a possible switch to the World Rally Championship.

ABOVE Rossi prepares for a free practice session at the Masaryk circuit in Brno. 20 August 2004. David W. Cerny

RIGHT Rossi rides down the final straight on his way to British Grand Prix victory at Donington Park. 24 July 2005. Toby Melville

YAO MING

Yao Ming has become a celebrity in two countries with his own fan club and a personal website devoted to his life and exploits in the U.S. National Basketball Association. One of the tallest players in the world at 2.28 metres (7 feet 6 inches), Yao is a popular figure in the United States with his unaffected good humour and on-court prowess. In China he is revered as an example of the country's growing significance in the international sporting community.

Born in the vibrant, bustling city of Shanghai, Yao played for China at the 2000 Sydney Olympics, joining Wang Zhizhi and Menk Bateer in a trio dubbed 'The Walking Great Wall'. He debuted in the Chinese league at the age of 17 and was the Most Valuable Player in the Chinese league in 2000–1. Yao was the number one overall draft pick for the Houston Rockets in 2002 and the first international player without college experience to be selected first overall.

Yao carried the Chinese flag at the opening ceremony for the 2004 Athens Olympics, took the Olympic flame into Tiananmen Square as part of the 2008 torch relay, and held the flag again at the Beijing Olympics opening ceremony. Despite recent surgery on a stress fracture in his foot, he took the court in Beijing to help China reach their third men's basketball quarter-final with 25 points and 11 rebounds in a 59–55 win over Germany.

KOBE BRYANT

Charges of raping a teenaged Colorado hotel employee in 2003 seemed to spell certain ruin for Kobe Bryant, an outstanding shooting guard in the Los Angeles Lakers although forced to live in the immense shadow of Shaquille O'Neal until the latter was traded to the Miami Heat.

Bryant denied rape but admitted adultery at an emotional news conference. Vanessa Laine, his wife of two years and mother of his daughter, stood by her man and he was supported by his team mates. But women's groups were outraged and sponsors, including McDonalds and Coca Cola, fled. After a late decision to drop charges, Bryant paid his accuser an undisclosed sum in a civil suit.

Bryant's on-court reputation had also been tarnished in a book by coach Phil Jackson outlining the Lakers' 2003–4 season, in which he said Bryant was uncoachable. But Bryant fought back. He captivated the fans when he scored 81 points in one game in January 2006, second only to Wilt Chamberlain's 100-point record. After his infamous feuds with O'Neal he also became more of a team player, taking the leader's role by concentrating on assists as much as shots. In 2008 he was named the NBA Most Valuable Player for the first time in his career and helped the U.S. to win Olympic gold. Off court he stayed out of trouble and the endorsements started to trickle back, including a commercial for Nike.

RIGHT Bryant outjumps his opponents in an NBA game against the Houston Rockets in Los Angeles. 16 December 2006. Lucy Nicholson

OPPOSITE ABOVE Yao Ming stands for the national anthems before a world basketball championship game against Slovenia in Sapporo. 24 August 2006. Toru Hanai

OPPOSITE BELOW Yao (second from right) fights for a rebound during a Houston Rockets game against the Lakers in Los Angeles. 7 January 2005. Lucy Nicholson

MICHAEL JORDAN

Arguably the best player ever to step on to a basketball court, Michael Jordan is indisputably the most famous. During his peak with the Chicago Bulls in the mid-1980s and early 1990s Jordan appeared to defy gravity, earning him the sobriquets 'Air Jordan' and 'His Airness'. Inspired by Jordan's athleticism, non-stop hustling and extraordinary scoring feats, the Bulls won three NBA championships in a row, before Jordan unexpectedly retired after the murder of his father in 1993 to enjoy a brief, undistinguished flirtation with professional baseball.

He returned to the Bulls, recaptured his old form and produced the play of the century in game six of the 1998 finals when he stole the ball from Karl Malone, dribbled upcourt and scored the goal that gave the Bulls another hat-trick of championships.

Jordan was a marketing phenomenon, and a spokesman for such major brands as Nike and Coca Cola. He was on the cover of *Sports Illustrated* a record 49 times

and named the greatest sportsman of the 20th century by the sports channel ESPN. He retired as a player after the 2003 season with a lifetime average of 30 points a game. His extensive business and endorsement contracts had made him one of the wealthiest athletes in the world. *Forbes* magazine put his personal income from Nike at $25 million a year in 2004, adding that his brand generated an estimated $500 million per annum for the shoe company.

ABOVE Jordan smiles during a news conference in Hong Kong on his first Asian tour. 21 May 2004. Bobby Yip

SHAQUILLE O'NEAL

Shaquille O'Neal, the pre-eminent centre of his time, was a personality made in the city of dreams. After moving from Orlando to the Los Angeles Lakers for $120 million in 1996, he took up an acting and music career that he pursued with the same application he gave to his sport, cutting rap albums and featuring in movies. In the same year he was a member of the U.S. gold medal-winning team at the Atlanta Olympics.

Although O'Neal teamed up with teenager Kobe Bryant, the Lakers continued to promise more than they produced until Phil Jackson took charge in 1999. Jackson's triangle offence featuring O'Neal and Bryant took the Lakers to consecutive NBA titles in 2000, 2001 and 2002.

After repeated attempts to get the salary increases he felt his abilities deserved, O'Neal was traded to the Miami Heat in 2004. He raised his game at the right moments to help the Heat deliver an NBA championship two years later, his fourth title in seven seasons, before he was traded to the Phoenix Suns.

RIGHT O'Neal (right) and Philadelphia 76ers' Dikembe Mutombo reach for the ball during the NBA Finals in Philadelphia. 10 June 2001. Mike Blake

BARRY BONDS

Barry Bonds's statistics are as impressive as his bodybuilder's physique. In 2007 he broke Hank Aaron's career record for home runs, finishing the season seven ahead on 762. He holds the record for most walks (2,558) and in 2001 he scored a record 73 home runs.

But controversy has surrounded Bonds since the turn of the century when he began to consistently hit homers in unprecedented numbers. In 2000 he struck a career-best 49 and in the next year he broke Mark McGwire's single-season record by three. Three 45 home-run seasons followed.

Bonds, godson of the wonderful San Francisco Giants player Willie Mays, had been slim and athletic at the start of his career. Now muscles bulged from his chest and arms, the result, he said, of intensive weight training.

Persistent rumours of steroid use gathered force when a federal raid on Victor Conte's BALCO laboratory, a manufacturer of previously undetectable steroids, turned up the name of Bonds on a list of clients. Bonds admitted taking substances supplied by Conte but denied he had ever knowingly taken banned performance-enhancing drugs.

However, the authorities were closing in and in 2008 Bonds, having parted company with the Giants at the end of the previous season, pleaded not guilty in a federal court to charges that he had lied about past steroid use. He was committed for trial in 2009.

LEFT A spectator taunts Bonds during the Giants' National League game against the Phillies in Philadelphia. 7 May 2006. Gary Hershorn

ABOVE St Louis Cardinals' slugger Mark McGwire extends his hitless streak to 29 at bats in Milwaukee. McGwire, who has never tested positive for steroids, refused under oath to answer questions about steroid use during a U.S. Congressional hearing on the subject and was snubbed by Hall of Fame voters in 2007 despite having hit 583 home runs during his career. 4 July 2001. Allen Fredrickson

ROGER FEDERER

Beautifully balanced and possessing an infinite variety of shots, Roger Federer has probably the most aesthetically pleasing game in the history of tennis. A gloriously fluid serve, balletic grace around the court and a quick-witted ability to improvise under pressure prompted twice grand slam champion Rod Laver to dub Federer 'a genius'.

'He is only in the middle of his career,' Laver enthused. 'If he keeps going the way he is, then he will be the best player ever.'

Federer enjoyed a golden year in 2004, winning three of the four grand slam tournaments, including his first U.S. singles title. He was equally dominant in 2006, with only the French Open on clay again eluding his grasp.

Truly great champions confront and overcome adversity at some stage in their careers. In 2008 Federer, weakened by a viral infection, was beaten in the semi-finals of the Australian Open. In Paris, he folded against defending champion Rafael Nadal, winning only four games and losing his third consecutive final at Roland Garros to the Spaniard. Nadal then won a magnificent five-set final at Wimbledon and took over as world number one in August, ending the Swiss master's record reign of 237 weeks in a row at the top. Federer, his pride stung, swept aside Andy Murray in New York to become the first man to win five consecutive U.S. Opens. But if he is to fulfil Laver's prophecy, he must find a similar answer to the formidable challenge presented by the relentless Nadal.

OPPOSITE Federer serves to Lleyton Hewitt in their semi-final at the U.S. Open in New York. 10 September 2005. Lucy Nicholson

ABOVE LEFT Federer keeps his eye on the ball during the Australian Open in Melbourne. 14 January 2003. David Gray

TOP LEFT Federer shakes hands with Spain's Rafael Nadal after winning their Wimbledon final in London. 6 July 2003. Ian Hodgson

TOP RIGHT Federer kisses the men's U.S. Open trophy after beating Andy Roddick in the final in New York. 10 September 2006. Shaun Best

ABOVE RIGHT Federer holds the runner-up trophy after losing to Rafael Nadal in their Wimbledon final in London. 6 July 2008. Kevin Lamarque

PREVIOUS PAGES, LEFT Federer plays a shot to Colombia's Alejandro Falla during the French Open in Paris. 31 May 2006. Philippe Wojazer

PREVIOUS PAGES, RIGHT Federer drops to his knees as he celebrates his win over Andy Roddick in the Wimbledon final in London. 4 July 2004. Kevin Lamarque

RAFAEL NADAL

Rafael Nadal's tireless athleticism and unquenchable spirit generate a unique excitement when the muscular Spaniard with the piratical bandana steps on to a tennis court. Regardless of the state of the match, Nadal chases down every ball and competes tenaciously for each point, hurtling from one side of the court to the other.

His whole-hearted commitment was handsomely rewarded in 2008. Nadal became only the third man in the open era to win the French Open and Wimbledon titles in the same year, was ranked world number one for the first time and, for good measure, took the Beijing Olympics gold medal.

A natural right-hander, Nadal was persuaded by his uncle and coach Toni to play left-handed in order to gain maximum power from his two-handed backhand. It was Nadal's forehand, though, that became the most potent weapon in modern tennis. A shot of ferocious power and vicious top-spin has made Nadal supreme on clay, with four consecutive French Open titles at Roland Garros.

Signs that Nadal had developed an all-round game capable of winning on any surface came in early 2008 when he reached the semi-finals of the Australian Open for the first time. He swept Roger Federer aside in Paris, conceding only four games, and then ended the Swiss maestro's five-year reign as Wimbledon champion in the longest and most dramatic final ever staged on the Centre Court grass.

OPPOSITE Nadal hits a return shot to Björn Phau of Germany during their match at the U.S. Open in Flushing Meadows, New York. 25 August 2008. Kevin Lamarque

BELOW Nadal celebrates after defeating Roger Federer in their Wimbledon final in London. 6 July 2008. Alessia Pierdomenico

WILLIAMS SISTERS

Compton, California, with its gang violence and drug-related murders, was the bleak environment in which Richard Williams vowed that his daughters Venus and Serena would conquer the game of the white middle classes. Williams coached from text books and videos. He instilled mental toughness and played the media game for all it was worth. Venus and Serena, he said, were the next two female Michael Jordans.

The family moved to Florida and into the tutelage of professional coaches. The sisters' power and athleticism were exceptional for teenagers and after entering the professional ranks Serena won the family's first grand slam at the age of 17 with victory in the U.S. Open. Venus made a sensational start to the new century. She won the U.S. and Wimbledon singles, the singles gold at the Sydney Olympics, and teamed with Serena to win the Olympic doubles title as well. The following year was equally successful. Venus won the U.S. and Wimbledon titles again. She did not drop a set in the U.S. tournament, defeating Serena 6–2 6–4 in the final. Then it was Serena's turn. Starting with the French Open in 2002, the sisters met in five grand slam finals, all won by Serena.

Then in 2003 their elder sister Yetunde Price was murdered in California. The emotional turmoil and a series of injuries led to a prolonged form slump, relieved in 2005 when Venus beat Lindsay Davenport in the longest Wimbledon women's final.

They have had problems with motivation and fitness, but at their best they are still untouchable, as Serena demonstrated in the 2007 Australian Open final, when she made Russian Maria Sharapova look like a nervous schoolchild. Their 2008 Wimbledon final in gusting winds was a classic, with Venus absorbing a ferocious assault from her younger sister to win a fifth singles title on her favourite grass court.

PREVIOUS PAGES, ABOVE LEFT Serena (left) and Venus Williams confer during a doubles match against Elena Dementieva and Vera Zvonareva in Hong Kong. 6 January 2005. Bobby Yip

PREVIOUS PAGES, BELOW LEFT Serena Williams celebrates winning a point against Svetlana Kuznetsova in the China Open final in Beijing. 26 September 2004. Andrew Wong

PREVIOUS PAGES, RIGHT Venus Williams jumps for joy after beating Lindsay Davenport to win the Wimbledon title in London. 2 July 2005. Kieran Doherty

OPPOSITE Serena Williams serves to compatriot Ashley Harkleroad during the JP Morgan Chase tournament in Carson, California. 9 August 2006. Lucy Nicholson

RIGHT Venus Williams is seen during her match against Maria Kirilenko of Russia at the Sony Ericsson Open tennis tournament in Key Biscayne, Miami. 24 March 2007. Carlos Barria

BELOW Venus (left) and Serena Williams answer questions from children on a visit to a Washington tennis centre. 8 December 2005. Jason Reed

BELOW RIGHT Serena Williams wears tennis 'boots' before her quarter-final against Amélie Mauresmo at the Australian Open in Melbourne. 25 January 2005. Stuart Milligan

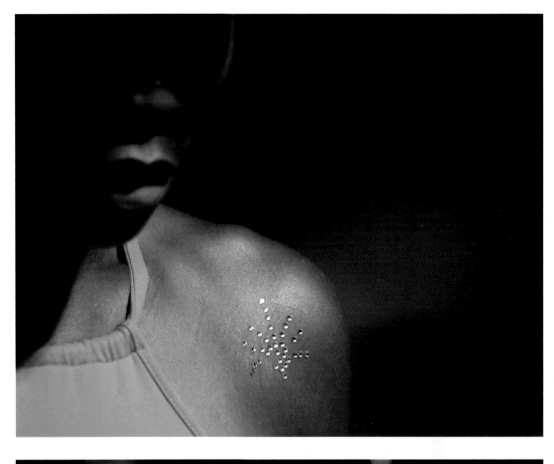

ANDRE AGASSI

A driven parent, a talented offspring and a childhood dominated by remorseless practice: it is a familiar story and one not always followed by a happy ending.

A tennis racket was the young Andre Agassi's constant companion as his father Mike, an Olympic boxer for Iran, transferred his dreams to his son's shoulders. Andre hit thousands of balls in practice and at the age of 13 was sent to Nick Bollettieri's famed academy. Bollettieri recognized an outstanding talent but, predictably, Agassi rebelled, adopted the American punk fashion styles of the early 1990s and seriously considered giving up the game.

But with the innate good sense that characterized his career, Agassi realized he had a unique gift and turned professional aged 16. He still wore his hair long but on the court he was totally focused, displaying the extraordinary reflexes and counter-punching skills honed by his endless years of practice.

Agassi's natural affinity with clay courts took him to the French Open finals in 1990 and 1991. He initially shunned the grass of Wimbledon, saying that he did not intend to adhere to the All England Club's dress regulations requiring all-white clothing. The year after his 1991 debut, though, Agassi won his first grand slam title at Wimbledon. By the end of his career, which finished with an emotional farewell at the 2006 U.S. Open, he had become only the fifth male player to win the grand slam singles titles in Australia, Paris, London and New York.

At his peak, after a slump in the late 1990s and before chronic back problems forced him to quit, Agassi was the total professional and a splendid ambassador for the game. After a failed marriage with the movie actress Brooke Shields he also found personal happiness by marrying the German grand slam champion Steffi Graf.

OPPOSITE ABOVE LEFT Agassi blows
kisses to the crowd after losing to
Benjamin Becker at the U.S. Open
in New York. 3 September 2006.
Kevin Lamarque

OPPOSITE ABOVE RIGHT Agassi signs
autographs after his quarter-final
win over Sébastien Grosjean at the
Australian Open in Melbourne.
27 January 2004. David Gray

OPPOSITE BELOW LEFT Agassi bows
to the crowd after his final U.S. Open
match, a loss to Benjamin Becker,
in New York. 3 September 2006.
Brendan McDermid

OPPOSITE BELOW RIGHT Agassi talks
to the media after arriving at his
charitable foundation's benefit concert
in Las Vegas. 7 October 2006.
Tiffany Brown

RIGHT Agassi serves to Tomas Berdych
in the third round of the U.S. Open in
New York. 3 September 2005. Shaun Best

PETE SAMPRAS

Tennis fans who prefer erratic brilliance to sustained excellence found Pete Sampras boring. But that was not a criticism that much bothered the American serve-and-volley expert who won a record 14 grand slam tournaments before he retired in August 2003.

Tall and athletic, Sampras had a classical first serve which inspired the nickname 'Pistol Pete'. His second serve could be just as devastating, earning him frequent aces, and he followed up with the best overhead and forehand in the game. His game was ideally suited to Wimbledon's grass courts, where he won a record-equalling seven titles. He shared the U.S. Open record of five titles with Jimmy Connors.

Great players flourish most when they encounter great rivals and Sampras was fortunate to play in the same era as Andre Agassi. The pair met in Sampras's first grand slam final and 12 years later Agassi was again on the opposite side of the net when Sampras won his final grand slam title in the U.S. Open.

MARTINA NAVRATILOVA

Czech emigrant Martina Navratilova transformed herself from a chubby teenager into a finely-honed athlete who dominated the women's game in the 1980s. She won her 18th and final grand slam singles title in 1990, a triumph that proved only a prelude to an astonishing second act in a remarkable career.

In 2000, aged 44, Navratilova returned to competitive doubles. Partnering Leander Paes, she won the 2003 Australian and Wimbledon mixed doubles titles. At the age of 46 years and eight months she was the oldest ever grand slam champion. In the following year, she was controversially given a wild card for the Wimbledon singles but responded by winning her first-round match in straight sets, becoming the oldest player to win a singles match in the open era. Finally, in 2006, even the tireless Navratilova had had enough and announced her impending retirement. She lost her last match at Wimbledon, playing in the mixed doubles, but ended her career in triumph when she partnered Bob Bryan to the U.S. Open title.

OPPOSITE Sampras runs for a return during
his second round match with Juan Ignacio Chela
at the Australian Open in Melbourne. 17 January 2002.
Mark Baker

BELOW Navratilova serves during a mixed doubles
match at the U.S. Open in New York. 5 September 2005.
Ray Stubblebine

LANCE ARMSTRONG

Three years before the first of his record seven Tour de France wins, Lance Armstrong was given less than a 50 percent chance of recovering from testicular cancer which had spread to his brain and lungs. Privately, the doctors were even more pessimistic. But Armstrong endured surgery and harrowing chemotherapy with defiance and stoicism. He afterwards described his ordeal as 'the best thing that ever happened to me'.

Nothing had ever come easy to the tough, fiercely determined Texan whose father had walked out on his mother Linda when Armstrong was only two. He took the surname of his stepfather while Linda devoted her life to caring for her talented son. Armstrong made his name as a triathlete then joined the U.S. Olympic cycling development programme. He became the national amateur champion in 1991, world champion in 1993 and achieved his first Tour stage win in the same year.

After making a full recovery from cancer, Armstrong transferred his burning will to live to preparing with an unsparing rigour for the Tour de France. Unlike most of his rivals, he devoted himself exclusively to the Tour and was rewarded with seven wins from 1999 to 2005 before retiring.

Inevitably in a sport plagued by a series of drugs scandals, Armstrong has been accused of taking performance-enhancing substances. He denied reports that he had used the blood-booster erythropoietin (EPO) after retroactive testing of samples taken during the 1999 Tour.

In 2008, Armstrong announced he would make a comeback at the age of 37 with the Astana team to compete in the 2009 Tour and promote a global cancer awareness campaign.

LEFT Armstrong and the pack cycle past the Pyrenees on the Tour's 16th stage from Mourenx to Pau. 19 July 2005. Eric Gaillard

ABOVE Armstrong passes the Arc de Triomphe in Paris after winning his seventh Tour de France. 24 July 2005. Philippe Wojazer

TOP Armstrong cycles in the pack on the final stage of the Tour de France from Corbeil-Essonnes to Paris. 24 July 2005. Thierry Roge

ABOVE Armstrong wins the 17th stage of the Tour from Bourg-d'Oisans to Le Grand Bornand. 22 July 2004.
Wolfgang Rattay

TOP RIGHT A fan waves to Tour riders during the eighth stage between Sallanches and L'Alpe d'Huez. 13 July 2003. Eric Gaillard

ABOVE RIGHT Armstrong leads his team to victory in the time trial fourth stage from Tours to Blois. 5 July 2005.
Jacky Naegelen

BELOW Six-year-old William Douglas
encourages Armstrong during the
Tour of Georgia in Rome, Georgia.
21 April 2005. Tami Chappell

FLOYD LANDIS

Just as he seemed out of contention for the 2006 Tour de France, an astonishing win in the final mountain stage elevated Floyd Landis from 11th place to third. On 23 July, he acknowledged the applause on the Champs Élysées as he rode home to succeed Lance Armstrong as champion. He was the third American to win the world's greatest endurance race after Armstrong and Greg LeMond.

Landis had grown up in Pennsylvania as a member of the socially conservative Mennonite sect. His father was opposed to his eldest son's passion for cycling but eventually relented when it became clear that nothing was going to deter young Floyd. Landis's persistence paid off when he was recruited by Armstrong to race in his U.S. Postal team in three Tours, and the 2006 race appeared to be his ultimate reward when a stunning 120-km breakaway attack reversed his fortunes the day after he had slumped from first to 11th overall in the mountains.

Then the rumours started. Landis pulled out of a Danish race, and the news subsequently emerged that he had tested positive for excessive amounts of the male sex hormone testosterone. After the second urine sample confirmed the result, Landis was sacked by his Phonak team and became the first man in the 105-year history of the race to lose his title for doping. He was also banned for two years and Phonak were disbanded.

The race had begun without nine riders, including the 1997 winner Jan Ullrich and Giro d'Italia champion Ivan Basso, who were withdrawn by their teams because they had been implicated in a Spanish doping investigation.

LEFT Fans applaud Landis on the Tour de France 17th stage from Saint-Jean-De-Maurienne to Morzine. 20 July 2006. Eric Gaillard

ABOVE Landis attends an arbitration hearing in Malibu, California. The Court of Arbitration for Sport dismissed his appeal against a two-year doping ban. 22 May 2007. Max Morse

HANSIE CRONJE

The immediate reaction was disbelief, summed up by the headline 'RUBBISH!' in a South African newspaper. According to Delhi police transcripts, South Africa cricket captain Hansie Cronje had held conversations with an Indian bookmaker which clearly indicated he had been involved in match-fixing.

Scepticism extended well beyond South Africa's shores. Cronje, captain of the multi-racial team representing the new rainbow republic, had a fixed public image as an upright, principled character who wore a wrist band inscribed with the letters WWJD (What Would Jesus Do?).

It quickly transpired that not all was as it seemed, not only with Cronje but also with the game of cricket, in which gambling was rife during its formative years before the game was appropriated by the Victorians to help extend their brand of muscular Christianity throughout the world.

After emphatic initial denials, Cronje confessed that he had discussed fixing the results of matches, including the rain-affected fifth test against England at Centurion in 2000, won by the tourists after both teams forfeited an innings on the final day in order to ensure a result.

A South African government commission established that Cronje was obsessed by money. He was banned for life and after worldwide investigations two other test captains, India's Mohammad Azharuddin and Pakistan's Salim Malik, were also given lifetime bans for involvement in match-fixing.

Despite international opprobrium, Cronje evoked mixed emotions in South Africa. In 2004 he was voted the 11th greatest South African, two years after his death at the age of 32 when the aircraft he was flying in crashed into a mountain.

LEFT ABOVE Cronje prepares to testify at the inquiry into allegations of match-fixing in South African cricket. 15 June 2000. Mike Hutchings

LEFT Flowers left in memory of Cronje sit outside Newlands Cricket Ground before the 2003 World Cup in Cape Town. 8 February 2003. David Gray

COSTAS KENTERIS

An outlandish farce unfolded on the eve of the opening ceremony of the 2004 Athens Olympics as word spread that Greece's leading sprint hopes Costas Kenteris and Katerina Thanou had failed to turn up for a dope test. Kenteris, who exploded from nowhere to win the 2000 Sydney Olympic 200 metres title, had been expected to light the Olympic flame. Thanou was the 100 metres silver medallist behind Marion Jones in Sydney. Reports on Greek television throughout the night outlined an increasingly incredible tale in which the pair had taken off into the suburbs on a motorcycle before they crashed and ended up in hospital.

Kenteris and Thanou were withdrawn from the Games and suspended by the International Association of Athletics Federations (IAAF) for missing three scheduled out-of-competition dope tests in a year. Two alleged eye-witnesses to the crash were later charged with perjury and a group of doctors who examined them were charged with making false medical statements. In a low-key finale, proceedings were dropped in 2006 when Kenteris and Thanou admitted violating doping laws. Although neither athlete ever failed a dope test, suspicions had been aroused after the Sydney Games by their absence from the European athletics circuit, the meetings which athletes use to make their money and tune up for major championships.

ABOVE Kenteris crosses the line to win the 200 metres final at the Sydney Olympics. 28 September 2000. Zainal Abd Halim

CATHY FREEMAN

The identity of the person chosen to light the Olympic flame is traditionally a closely guarded secret. The appearance of Muhammad Ali at the 1996 Atlanta Games was met with initially hesitant and disbelieving applause followed by an exultant roar when, with left arm shaking uncontrollably as a result of Parkinson's syndrome, he raised the torch with both hands. Four years on at the Sydney Games there was a similarly explosive reaction when Cathy Freeman emerged to ignite the cauldron.

Like Ali, Freeman is a member of an oppressed race, the Aboriginal Australians who were hunted and killed for sport by 19th-century European settlers. Growing up in the late 20th century, that legacy remained formative. 'When we walked into new places, we were totally intimidated because we felt that, being black, we had no right to be there,' she recalled. At the 1994 Commonwealth Games in Edmonton, Freeman courted controversy by carrying the Aboriginal flag as well as the Australian flag during her victory lap after winning the 400 metres gold medal. But her defiance made her a symbol of hope and reconciliation for indigenous and non-indigenous Australians alike.

Freeman won the world title in 1997 and again two years later. But in Atlanta she had finished second to the deceptively languid but undeniably gifted Frenchwoman Marie-José Perec, and a battle royal was in prospect on home territory.

The pressure was immense. Australia's once proud track record had receded into distant memory and Freeman was the only realistic hope to win her country's 100th athletics gold medal.

In the event, it was Perec who succumbed to the pressure, fleeing Sydney with a series of unlikely excuses, including an unidentified intruder in her hotel room. Freeman duly delivered gold on a tumultuous night at the Olympic stadium. Mission completed, she continued to compete after the Games but never recaptured her original passion and dedication and opted to retire in 2003.

LEFT Freeman prepares to run the 400 metres final at the Sydney Olympic Games. 25 September 2000. Mark Baker

JUSTIN GATLIN

Those brave souls striving against the odds to retain faith in the credibility of track and field thought they had found their man when Justin Gatlin emerged as the latest American track sensation.

Gatlin was serious and modest, the latter quality especially prized in the ego-ridden world of international sprinting. He also spoke eloquently about his abhorrence of drugs, after a positive test for an amphetamine was excused on the grounds it was medication for Attention Deficit Disorder.

At the 2004 Athens Olympics Gatlin clocked 9.85 seconds in the 100 metres, the second fastest time in Games' history at that time. The following year he won the world title in Helsinki by the widest margin in the history of the championships and added the 200 metres to follow compatriot Maurice Greene into the record books as the only man to win the world 100–200 double.

However, in July 2006 Gatlin tested positive for unusually high levels of the male sex hormone testosterone after a relay race in Kansas. He was banned for four years and was unable to defend his title at the Beijing Olympics.

RIGHT Gatlin celebrates winning the 100 metres final at the Athens 2004 Olympic Games.
22 August 2004. Richard Heathcote

MICHAEL JOHNSON

Michael Johnson was the best sprinter in the world for a decade, untouchable over 200 and 400 metres in major championships. His 19.32 second win in the 1996 Atlanta Olympics 200 metres final, taking nearly a third of a second off his previous world record, remains one of the truly epic track and field performances. He had already won the 400 metres, the first stage of an ambitious and unprecedented Olympic programme involving eight races in seven days.

Johnson concluded his career by winning the 400 metres gold at the 2000 Sydney Olympics. He had already added the 400 metres world record to his collection at the 1999 Seville world championships and when he decided to retire after Sydney there was nothing left to achieve.

ABOVE Johnson watches a replay of his heat at the U.S. Olympic trials in Sacramento. 15 July 2000. Gary Hershorn

RIGHT Johnson wins his 400 metres heat at the Sydney Olympics. 22 September 2000. Jerry Lampen

MARION JONES

Attractive, articulate and gloriously talented, Marion Jones was the face of the 2000 Sydney Olympics. Eight years later she spent the Beijing Games in jail after admitting taking performance-enhancing drugs.

Jones's spectacular fall from grace began in Sydney, where she won three sprint gold medals and two bronzes, featured on the covers of *Vogue*, *Time* and *Newsweek*, and secured multi-million-dollar contracts. But cracks in the glossy Jones facade emerged during the Games with the news that her husband C.J. Hunter, the world shot put champion, had tested positive four times for huge amounts of nandrolone during the previous year.

Jones publicly supported Hunter at a joint news conference but the pair soon separated and Jones went on to have a son by sprinter Tim Montgomery, who broke the world 100 metres record in 2002.

In the following year the pair were linked with the infamous BALCO laboratory, which manufactured and distributed illegal drugs. They courted further controversy by training with Charlie Francis, the former coach of Ben Johnson who was banned for life from coaching in Canada after Johnson tested positive for steroids at the 1988 Seoul Olympics.

Although Jones and Montgomery steadfastly denied using prohibited substances, the Court of Arbitration for Sport banned Montgomery for two years in 2005 after agreeing there was sufficient evidence that he had taken drugs.

Two years later Jones was sentenced to six months in prison for lying to federal prosecutors. She was stripped of all her results, medals and prize money won after 1 September 2000. Montgomery was later jailed on heroin dealing and cheque fraud charges.

ABOVE LEFT Jones runs in the 4x100 relay at the Team Challenge in Munich. 8 August 2004. Alexandra Beier

ABOVE RIGHT Jones kneels after winning the 200 metres final at the Sydney Olympics. 28 September 2000. Gary Hershorn

RIGHT Jones addresses the media outside the U.S. Federal Courthouse in White Plains, New York. At left is her mother, Marion Toller. 5 October 2007. Shannon Stapleton

USAIN BOLT

Usain Bolt electrified the Bird's Nest stadium in Beijing with the most spectacular 100–200 double in the history of the Olympic Games.

The languid Jamaican, who describes his hobbies as 'doing nothing and relaxing', had stunned the sporting world when he reduced the world 100 metres record to 9.72 seconds at the start of the 2008 season. The shock was all the greater as Bolt was a 200 specialist competing in the 100 for only the fifth time in his professional career. He was both the tallest and, at 21, the youngest world record holder in the modern era.

Although there could be no real doubt that Bolt would double up in Beijing, he still delayed a decision on the 100 until after the Games had started. In the final he unwound from the blocks, bounded away from the field and flew through the finish line in 9.69 seconds, despite slowing down and glancing left and right in the final 20 metres.

If anything, the 200 final was even more astonishing as statisticians had expected Michael Johnson's 1996 Atlanta Olympics record of 19.32 to last at least 25 years. Bolt made a great start, ran a perfectly balanced bend and held on to clock 19.30.

Johnson, who commented on the race for the BBC, said the 200 was 'simply incredible. This guy is Superman II.'

LEFT Bolt celebrates winning the men's 200 metres final during the Beijing 2008 Olympic Games. Bolt set a new world record of 19.30 seconds. 20 August 2008. Dylan Martinez

BELOW Bolt lies on the track after winning the men's 200 metres final in Beijing. 20 August 2008. Kim Kyung-Hoon

KENENISA BEKELE

Kenenisa Bekele is the most accomplished all-round distance runner the world has seen, performing with equal aplomb on the track, indoors and in the cross-country.

Bekele made his initial reputation in the world cross-country championships, winning six long-course (12 kilometres) and five short-course (four kilometres) titles. He succeeded fellow Ethiopian Haile Gebrselassie as the world 5,000 and 10,000 metres world record holder and went one better than his illustrious mentor by completing the 5,000–10,000 double at the 2008 Beijing Olympics. Gebrselassie won consecutive 10,000 titles.

Bekele has also won three world 10,000 metres titles and one world indoor 3,000 gold. He is the world indoor record holder over 5,000 and 2,000 metres.

On 4 January 2005 tragedy struck Bekele when his 18-year-old fiancée Alem

Techale collapsed and died while on a training run with him. Bekele was grief-stricken for weeks before returning to competition with an emotional world cross-country double in Saint-Galmier, France.

ABOVE Bekele is followed by Eliud Kipchoge of Kenya and team mate Edwin Cheruiyot Soi in the men's 5,000 metres final during the Beijing 2008 Olympic Games. The runners finished first, second and third respectively. 23 August 2008.
Dylan Martinez

PAULA RADCLIFFE

For more years than she would care to remember, Paula Radcliffe epitomized the gallant British loser, leading for lap after lap in major championship 10,000 metres finals only to be overtaken in the final 400 metres by a posse of light-footed Africans. Until 2002, when she graduated to the marathon, all Radcliffe had to show for her efforts was a silver medal won at the 1999 Seville world championships.

Her life was to change dramatically in 2002 when she won the London marathon in two hours 18 minutes 56 seconds, the fastest debut by a woman. She went on to win world cross-country, Commonwealth and European track gold medals, then captured the world marathon record with a 2:17:18 run in Chicago. In 2003 she reduced the record to 2:15:25 with a brilliant solo run in London. All was set fair for the 2004 Athens Olympics.

Radcliffe carried a heavy burden of expectation as the fastest woman in the field and one of Britain's few gold medal hopes. She ran from the front as usual but never looked happy in the stifling heat and humidity, and after slipping to fourth she suddenly pulled out with about four kilometres (2½ miles) remaining. A distraught Radcliffe sat weeping by the roadside and was eventually accompanied by her parents and trainer-husband Gary Lough to the finish line. Radcliffe competed in the 10,000 metres but again failed to finish.

Showing the grit and determination that have characterized her career, she was soon back in training and won the New York marathon later in the year and the 2005 Helsinki world championships gold medal.

Unfortunately fate had not finished with Radcliffe. A stress fracture three months before the 2008 Beijing Olympics curtailed her training and she finished 23rd in the race. Undaunted, Radcliffe immediately set her sights on the 2012 London Games when she will be 38, the same age as Beijing champion Constantina Tomescu.

BELOW Radcliffe cries as she retires from the marathon in the Athens Olympic Games. 22 August 2004. Yannis Behrakis

HERMANN MAIER

Downhill racer Hermann Maier has all the attributes necessary for success in a sport as dangerous as it is exciting. Aggressive, strong and fearless, Maier possesses an admirable work ethic and complete dedication. He has also coped with reverses which would have daunted a less resilient spirit. Sent home from the Austrian ski academy in Schladming because he was deemed too frail to succeed, Maier took up bricklaying in the summer and worked as a ski instructor in the winter.

After a series of successes in regional races he finally made the powerful Austrian ski team and won his first World Cup race, a super-G in Garmisch-Partenkirchen in Germany. A spectacular crash in the downhill at the 1998 Nagano Olympics did not prevent Maier winning the giant slalom and super-G titles and he ended the season by winning the overall World Cup title. He won the overall World Cup again in 2000, 2001 and 2004.

Maier's career had appeared over when he narrowly escaped death in a motorcycle accident in August 2001. A compound fracture of his right leg was serious enough for doctors to consider amputation. Instead Maier underwent reconstructive surgery and hours of physiotherapy, and although the 2002 Salt Lake City Olympics were out of the question, he returned to competition in January 2003.

ABOVE Maier removes his race bib after finishing second in a World Cup super-G in Val Gardena, Italy. 17 December 2004. Dylan Martinez

JANICA KOSTELIĆ

Pain and Janica Kostelić are lifetime companions. The only woman to win four Olympic Alpine skiing gold medals broke her leg at the age of 11. Two years later she broke an ankle. Then, aged 17, she damaged her right knee in a career-threatening injury which required five hours' reconstructive surgery. By the time she won her fourth gold medal at the 2006 Turin Olympics, Kostelić had survived 11 operations on her fragile knees and the loss of her thyroid gland.

The Croatian's exceptional resilience was forged in extraordinary times. As Yugoslavia disintegrated into civil war, Kostelić's father Ante, a former skier and handball exponent, drove Janica and her older brother Ivica hard – literally. Ante ferried his children around European ski resorts in his car, which doubled at night as the family's sleeping quarters. Janica and Ivica, with little else to distract them, practised endlessly.

The rewards came during eight days at the 2002 Salt Lake City Olympics when Janica won gold medals in the combined, slalom and giant slalom and finished second in the super-G.

Fate had one further test for Kostelić. In 2003 she found herself increasingly struggling for breath. Eventually she collapsed and was air-lifted to hospital, where an over-active thyroid gland was diagnosed (coincidentally the same complaint suffered by twice Olympic 100 metres champion Gail Devers, still competing in 2007 at the age of 40). After surgery Kostelić returned to dominate her sport and in Turin she became the first woman to win the combined title for a second time.

BELOW Kostelić embarks on a practice run for a World Cup downhill race in St Moritz. 19 January 2006. Wolfgang Rattay

YEVGENY PLUSHENKO

Yevgeny Plushenko has pushed back the barriers in figure skating since he became the youngest male skater to receive a perfect score of 6.0, a landmark achieved at the age of 16. He was the first man to perform a quadruple toe loop-triple toe loop-triple loop jump in competition and has landed quadruple lutz jumps in practice.

After starting his career at the age of four he won the 1997 junior world championship at the age of 15. In the following year he was third in the senior championship.

Plushenko was coached by Alexei Mishin, who coincidentally trained his great rival Alexei Yagudin, the 1998 world champion. The pair came head-to-head at the 2002 Salt Lake City Olympics, where it was Yagudin who prevailed after finishing first in the short programme. Plushenko, fourth in the short programme, rallied with a dazzling display in the free programme to the music from 'Carmen' but could not overhaul Yagudin for the gold. Yagudin's retirement paved the way for Plushenko's triumph at the 2006 Turin Olympics.

OPPOSITE Plushenko performs in the short programme at the European championships in Turin. 26 January 2005. Tony Gentile

CINDY KLASSEN

Medals flocked Cindy Klassen's way at the 2006 Turin Games, albeit in speed-skating with its proliferation of events over various distances. Winning bronze medals in the 3,000 and 5,000 metres, silvers in the 1,000 and team pursuit, and a gold in the 1,500, she equalled American Eric Heiden's 1980 record of five Olympic speed-skating medals and became the first Canadian to collect six Olympic medals after her bronze at the 2002 Salt Lake City Olympics. Unsurprisingly Klassen was named 'woman of the Games' by International Olympic Committee president Jacques Rogge.

A descendant of Mennonite immigrants to Manitoba, Klassen was a member of the Canadian youth ice hockey team but turned her attention to speed-skating when she was not selected for the 1998 Nagano Olympics.

She sustained a potentially career-ending injury at the start of the 2003–4 season when her right forearm was sliced to the bone, cutting through 12 tendons, a nerve and an artery. But despite losing the feeling in two fingers, Klassen's skating was unaffected.

ABOVE Klassen races in the 1,000 metres at the Turin Winter Olympics. 19 February 2006. Jerry Lampen

MICHAEL PHELPS

Seventeen races over nine days in Beijing yielded a record eight gold medals and seven world records for the U.S. swimming phenomenon Michael Phelps.

'He's not from another planet,' commented British freestyler Simon Burnett. 'He's from the future.'

Phelps and his quest for eight titles, one more than Mark Spitz at the 1972 Munich Olympics, dominated the build-up to the Beijing Games. Less than a year earlier, the American had despaired when a fractured wrist curtailed his training, but in the end he emerged even stronger after extensive work with the kickboard.

In the fourth of his Beijing finals, the 200 metres butterfly, Phelps's goggles leaked so badly that he could not see the end of the pool. He equalled Spitz's seven golds by out-touching Californian-born Serbian Milorad Čavić to win the 100 metres butterfly by one-hundredth of a second.

With Phelps swimming the butterfly leg in the 4x100 metres medley, the U.S. completed a sweep of all three men's relays, despite a late challenge from Australia, and shaved 1.34 seconds off the world record they had set at the Athens Olympics.

Ambition achieved, Phelps promised to race at the 2012 London Olympics. 'My whole goal is to change the sport of swimming in a positive way,' he said. 'I think it can go even further.'

BELOW Phelps touches the starting block before a training session at the Athens Olympic Aquatic Centre. 12 August 2004. David Grey

RIGHT Phelps swims to a world record and gold medal next to Nikolay Skvortsov (right) of Russia and Takeshi Matsuda (left) of Japan in the men's 200 metres butterfly final at the National Aquatics Centre during the Beijing 2008 Olympics. 13 August 2008. Wolfgang Rattay

FRANKIE DETTORI

The effervescent, Italian-born jockey Frankie Dettori – a crowd favourite with his flamboyant leaping dismount – hails from exotic stock. His mother was a trapeze artist and his uncle a circus clown. More relevantly, his father Gianfranco was Italy's leading jockey. He was given a palomino pony at the age of eight and left school at the age of 13 to pursue a racing career, moving to Britain and joining trainer Luca Cumani at Newmarket two years later.

Dettori made racing history and a bookmaker's nightmare on 28 September 1996 by winning all seven races on the card at Ascot. He had no inkling himself that he was going to achieve the unthinkable. 'I could have an each-way chance in the first and I may win the third,' he said on the morning of the meeting. Instead he rode Wall Street, Diffident, Mark of Esteem, Decorated Hero, Fatefully, Lochangel and Fujiyama Crest to consecutive victories which were later dubbed the 'Magnificent Seven'.

In 2006, Dettori again sent the bookmakers into a spin by riding five winners at Goodwood for cumulative odds of 779–1.

LEFT Dettori leaps from Papineau after winning the Gold Cup race at Royal Ascot in England. 17 June 2004.
Peter MacDiarmid

STEVE REDGRAVE

'Anyone who sees me go anywhere near a boat again, ever, you've got my permission to shoot me.' Memorable words from an exhausted Steve Redgrave when asked if he would be rowing at the 2000 Sydney Olympics after winning his fourth Olympic gold at the 1996 Atlanta Games. But, as history records, Redgrave reconsidered at leisure and went on to win a fifth gold medal in Sydney before finally retiring.

Briton Redgrave, a large man 1.96 metres (6 feet 5 inches) tall, won his first Olympic gold at the 1984 Olympics in the coxed four. With Andy Holmes he won the coxless pairs in 1988, teamed with Matthew Pinsent to win the same title in Barcelona and Atlanta and made his farewell in the coxless four with Pinsent, Tim Foster and James Cracknell in Sydney.

Redgrave, who was diagnosed with diabetes in 1997, had a ferocious work ethic. He competed for Britain in bobsleigh and ran three London marathons for charity, but was more than happy to give up the never-ending grind of training. 'I hated training,' he said. 'It was a means to an end.'

ABOVE Tim Foster, Matthew Pinsent, Steve Redgrave and James Cracknell (left to right) celebrate winning Olympic gold in the coxless four in Sydney. 23 September 2000. Andy Clark

ELLEN MACARTHUR

Born in the land-locked British county of Derbyshire in a nation of famous seafarers, Ellen MacArthur was fascinated by the ocean as a child and sailed her own dinghy at the age of eight. She pursued her vocation with a single-minded passion even when the battle to find a sponsor seemed hopeless. The retail group Kingfisher came to her rescue in 1998 and were immediately rewarded for their investment when MacArthur won her class in the solo Route du Rhum race that year. MacArthur, a fluent French speaker, became a heroine in France and then an international celebrity when she finished second in the 2000–1 Vendée Globe round-the-world solo race aged 24. In 2005 she sailed into the record books when she completed a solo round-the-world voyage, often in atrocious weather, in record-breaking time.

ABOVE MacArthur sails into Falmouth, Cornwall, after breaking the solo round-the-world record. 8 February 2005. Stephen Hird

MICHELLE WIE

Michelle Wie, the willowy American with the whiplash drive, was at the age of 12 the youngest person to qualify for a LPGA event. At 13 she was the youngest to make the cut. A week before her 16th birthday she signed multi-million dollar professional contracts. Wie expressed her desire to follow players such as Babe Zaharias and Annika Sörenstam by competing on the men's tour. 'I belong on the LPGA, I belong on the PGA. I think I belong on both,' she said.

The painful reality at the end of 2008 season was very different. After struggling with wrist injuries in 2006 and 2007, Wie, who had played in eight PGA events through sponsors' invitations, had failed to make the cut once. She had not won once on the women's tour or won a 72-hole stroke play event at any level.

OPPOSITE Wie hits her tee shot on the fifth hole in the Sony Open second round in Honolulu. 16 January 2004. Lucy Pemoni

ABOVE Tyson flexes his biceps after the weigh-in for his title fight against Lennox Lewis in Memphis. 6 June 2002. Jeff J. Mitchell

OPPOSITE ABOVE Tyson playfully bites his son during a news conference in Tunica, Mississippi. 20 February 2003. Peter Jones

OPPOSITE BELOW Tyson sits on the canvas after being knocked out by Briton Danny Williams in their heavyweight fight in Louisville. 30 July 2004. Peter Jones

MIKE TYSON

By the start of the new century, Mike Tyson was no longer the feared and respected fighter of his prime but had become little more than a travelling freak show. After his life unravelled following a rape conviction he had demonstrated similar lack of discipline in the ring, biting Evander Holyfield's ear and trying to break South African Francois Botha's arms. Still there was no doubting Tyson's crowd-pulling potential, and he was greeted by large crowds when he walked the streets of London in 2000 on a brief visit during which he recorded knockouts against mediocre opposition.

Lennox Lewis was a different proposition. A fight scheduled for Nevada was cancelled when the state boxing commission refused to grant Tyson a licence. The fight finally went ahead in Memphis on 8 June 2002, when Lewis exposed Tyson with a commanding victory in eight rounds. The American was never to be taken seriously as a fighter again.

Tyson filed for bankruptcy in 2003 after squandering the millions he had earned. He was knocked out by a journeyman Briton Danny Williams in 2004 and in the following year he quit during a fight with the equally unheralded Kevin McBride.

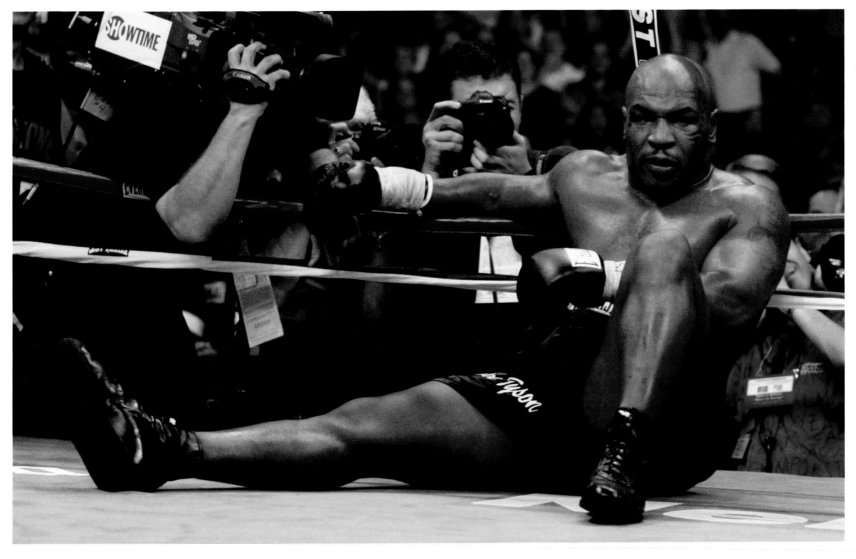

LENNOX LEWIS

Lennox Lewis fought hard and long for the respect he craved and ultimately deserved when he retired in 2004 as one of only three men after Gene Tunney and Rocky Marciano to retire as world heavyweight champion. The Briton had lost only two of 44 professional fights in 14 years as a professional after winning the 1988 Seoul Olympic super-heavyweight title for Canada.

Born in east London, he moved to Canada with his mother Violet at the age of nine and his soft but distinctive Canadian accent was one reason he failed to win popular acclaim when he returned to Britain. Instead the people's choice was the muscular but limited Frank Bruno, whose career had been carefully stage-managed. Lewis also failed to impress the Americans, who found him too passive for their liking, preferring to craft points victories rather than excite the crowds with a flurry of punches.

Despite the reservations on both sides of the Atlantic, Lewis gradually accumulated an impressive record. After signing with a British promoter, Lewis became the World Boxing Council champion by default when American Riddick Bowe threw the belt into a dustbin. He lost the title two years later to Olivier McCall in the second round of their fight at Wembley.

In 1999 Lewis became the undisputed world champion when he outpointed the fading Evander Holyfield and in 2002 he confirmed he was the best heavyweight of his era by stopping Mike Tyson in the eighth round of a one-sided fight in Memphis. Having disposed of the old generation he then beat the best of the new by stopping Ukrainian Vitali Klitschko before deciding to retire at the age of 38. 'One of the reasons I am retiring is because I respect boxing so much,' he said. 'It's time for the younger generation to have their chance.'

OPPOSITE Lewis shadow boxes during a workout in Tunica, Mississippi, ahead of his fight against Tyson. 5 June 2002. Jeff J. Mitchell

RIGHT Lewis has his hands taped before a workout at a Mississippi casino. 5 June 2002. Jeff J. Mitchell

BELOW Vitali Klitschko takes a hit from Lewis during their title fight in Los Angeles. 21 June 2003. Fred Greaves

MUTTIAH MURALITHARAN

The son of a confectioner from Kandy, Muttiah Muralitharan is one of the most successful yet controversial cricketers to play the game.

At first glance, Muralitharan appears to consistently break the fundamental rule of bowling, namely the requirement to deliver the ball with a straight arm. From a front-on action, with eyes bulging, the Sri Lankan flicks the ball from a supple wrist. His stock delivery is the off-spinner, whipping into the batsman's body. He has also mastered the doosra, the ball which spins away from the batsman without a discernible change in action.

Muralitharan's relationship with the Australians has been fraught. They were openly unhappy with his action after their first encounter in 1993 and in the 1995 Boxing Day test at Melbourne he was no-balled by Australian umpire Darrell Hair. The Australian crowds were also openly hostile and at one stage Muralitharan announced he would no longer tour the continent, a decision he later rescinded.

Muralitharan's career was rescued by the International Cricket Council (ICC), the game's ruling body. After extensive tests, photographs and analysis, the ICC concluded that Muralitharan did not bend and straighten his arm illegally at the point of delivery. It concluded, instead, that his action created 'the optical illusion of throwing'.

Throughout the furore, Muralitharan has continued to accumulate a prodigious number of wickets. He followed Shane Warne to 700 test wickets and, provided a fragile shoulder stands the strain, could conceivably become the first player to capture 1,000 victims.

ABOVE Muralitharan practises in the nets at Old Trafford, Manchester, before the third test against England. 11 June 2002. Ian Hodgson

SHANE WARNE

A bleached blond with a well-chronicled fondness for the good things of life, Shane Warne turned leg-spin bowling into pure theatre. His delivery from outside leg stump to beat and bowl former England captain Mike Gatting in 1993 was rated the ball of the century. At the end of the decade he was the only current player ranked by the Wisden cricket almanac as one of the five greatest players of the 20th century.

From a relaxed amble to the crease, Warne would spin the ball prodigiously from a vigorous body action. He bowled with unremitting accuracy, infinite variety and high intelligence. Before he retired in 2007 after Australia had regained the Ashes from England with a 5–0 series whitewash, Warne had become the first bowler to reach 700 test wickets. He took a test hat-trick, was man-of-the-match in a World Cup final, and was almost single-handedly responsible for the revival of the subtle art of spin bowling when it appeared fast bowlers were destined to rule forever.

Like all great athletes, Warne's true calibre was revealed at its best in adversity. When England won the Ashes in 2005 in a series rated by common accord as the best ever, Warne at times seemed to be playing the home side on his own. Up to the final passages of play in the final test at The Oval, Warne still commanded centre stage and still looked as if he could wrest the game back for Australia with a master class of spin bowling.

Warne's exploits also hit the news pages. He was banned for a year after testing positive for a weight-reducing drug, which could also be used to mask steroid use, and his marriage broke up after a series of affairs. Because of his indiscretions he was never a serious contender as Australia test captain, a job in which he would surely have excelled.

BELOW Warne tosses a ball during training in Mumbai ahead of a warm-up match for Australia's test tour. 28 September 2004. Arko Datta

ROBERT HOYZER

In January 2005, 25-year-old German referee Robert Hoyzer admitted fixing soccer matches for financial gain. In a scandal that severely embarrassed the 2006 World Cup hosts, Hoyzer said he had taken bribes from a Croatian mafia circle based in Berlin. The betting fraud amounted to two million euros. Hoyzer was sentenced to two years five months in jail while another former referee, Dominik Marks, was given an 18-month suspended sentence. Berlin-based Croatian Ante Sapina was found guilty of running the operation and sentenced to two years 11 months.

ABOVE Hoyzer referees a German Cup match between Paderborn and Hamburg whose result he was subsequently proven to have influenced for his own financial gain. 21 August 2004. Marc Koeppelmann

PIERLUIGI COLLINA

With his distinctive bald head and prominent eyes, Italian referee Pierluigi Collina was instantly recognizable and universally respected as he patrolled the pitch. He refereed the 1996 Olympic Games final between Nigeria and Argentina and was chosen at the 1998 World Cup to officiate in the highly charged fixture between the Netherlands and neighbours Belgium. The multi-lingual Collina was then entrusted with the dramatic Champions League final between Bayern Munich and Manchester United in 1999 and the Euro 2000 qualification playoff between old rivals England and Scotland.

He crowned his career when he refereed the 2002 World Cup final between Germany and Brazil. His commanding display, at the end of a tournament which had produced plenty of controversy over refereeing standards, showed exactly why he was so widely respected among players as well as officials.

LEFT Collina reacts as Barcelona players complain about Chelsea's fourth goal during a Champions League match in London. 8 March 2005. Dylan Martinez

LUIZ FELIPE SCOLARI

Brazilian Luiz Felipe Scolari not only bears a disconcerting resemblance to the American film actor Gene Hackman but also possesses a similarly uncompromising demeanour.

In Scolari's case it is no act. A pragmatist in a nation of soccer romantics, Scolari took charge of Brazil in 2001 when the national team were in danger of missing qualification for the World Cup the following year. Brazil ground out the results and travelled to Japan and South Korea without Romario, after Scolari rejected calls to select a striker he regarded as past his best. His judgment was vindicated when Rivaldo, Ronaldinho and a rejuvenated Ronaldo took Brazil to their fifth World Cup victory. Scolari then decamped to Portugal where he coached his new charges to the Euro 2004 final, which they lost to Greece. In 2008 Scolari, who had been previously linked with the England coaching job, took charge at Chelsea.

LEFT Scolari pictured during training at Stamford Bridge, London, home of Chelsea Football Club. 11 August 2008. Tony O'Brien

ALEX FERGUSON

Alex Ferguson, born and raised in Glasgow where he was a toolmaker in the Clyde shipyards before forging a professional soccer career, is the most successful manager practising his craft in the Premier League.

Ferguson made his name as a manager at Aberdeen and took over Manchester United in 1986, where he abolished a drinking culture that had got out of hand and reconstructed the youth team. Success was slow, but the arrival of volatile Frenchman Eric Cantona in 1992 and the emergence of David Beckham from the youth team transformed the club's fortunes.

Beckham was at the heart of the club's 1999 Premier League, FA Cup and European Cup triumphs. In 2008 a new generation headed by Portuguese Cristiano Ronaldo took United to another league and European Cup double, increasing Ferguson's tally to 20 major trophies at the club.

LEFT Alex Ferguson salutes the crowd after Manchester United's English Premier League match against West Ham at Old Trafford in Manchester. 3 May 2008. Nigel Roddis

GUUS HIDDINK

Guus Hiddink, the prototype of the modern professional soccer manager with his constant changes of address, learned his trade with PSV Eindhoven before taking a talented Netherlands side to fourth place in the 1998 World Cup. After a brief spell with Real Madrid, Hiddink demonstrated his ability to maximize slim resources by taking South Korea to the same spot four years later at the first Asian World Cup. His achievements with South Korea, who had not won a match in four previous tournaments, were recognized by a grateful nation when he was given honorary South Korean citizenship, while the World Cup stadium in Gwangju was renamed the Guus Hiddink stadium.

By 2006 Hiddink had transferred his allegiance to Australia, where he guided the Socceroos to the second round in their first World Cup appearance for 32 years. He then moved to Russia as head coach, guiding his latest charges to the Euro 2008 semi-finals.

RIGHT Hiddink gestures during a friendly soccer match between Australia and the Netherlands in Rotterdam. 4 June 2006. Jerry Lampen

JOSÉ MOURINHO

A brooding, handsome Portuguese habitually dressed in an expensive coat, José Mourinho was the perfect representative for the new Chelsea built through the largesse of Russian billionaire Roman Abramovich.

After spells at Benfica and União de Leiria, Mourinho moved to Porto and quickly established himself as the most successful soccer club coach in Europe, winning the championship in 2003 and 2004, the Portuguese and UEFA Cups in 2003, and the European Cup in 2004.

Confirmed as manager of Chelsea in June 2004, Mourinho went on to command a higher profile than most of his players. He fully justified his sobriquet as 'the special one' by taking the west London club to successive Premier League titles in 2005, their first for 50 years, and in 2006.

Tension was growing between Mourinho and Abramovich, however, and after failing to win a third league title in 2007 Mourinho left Chelsea, moving in 2008 to Italian champions Inter Milan.

RIGHT Inter Milan coach Mourinho gestures during a friendly soccer match against Bayern Munich in Munich. 5 August 2008. Michaela Rehle

TONY LA RUSSA

A dogged baseball player of limited talent, Tony La Russa earned a law degree from Florida State University but never practised. Instead he brought his intensity and drive to management.

La Russa's analytical approach to the game has led him to be dubbed 'the thinking man's manager'. He has managed the Chicago White Sox, the Oakland Athletics and, since 1996, the St Louis Cardinals. In 2004 he became the sixth manager to win pennants with both American and National League teams. Two years later he became the first manager to win multiple pennants in both leagues and one of only two to win the World Series with teams in both leagues. He is also one of only three managers to be named Manager of the Year in both of baseball's major leagues.

LEFT La Russa attends a Cardinals workout for the series playoffs against the New York Mets in New York. 10 October 2006. Mike Segar

PHIL JACKSON

As an American coming of age in the 1960s, Phil Jackson naturally gravitated to the counter-culture, taking as his guidebook the hippie bible *Zen and the Art of Motorcycle Maintenance*. Partly as a result he became known as 'The Zen Master' after becoming the most successful basketball coach of his time.

Jackson graduated from playing to coaching in the NBA. He was head coach of the Chicago Bulls from 1989 to 1998 and the Los Angeles Lakers from 1999 to 2004, returning in 2005. With the peerless Michael Jordan at their heart, the Bulls won six NBA championships under Jackson in nine years. At the Lakers he drew the best out of Shaquille O'Neal and Kobe Bryant, who took the Lakers to three successive championships.

LEFT Jackson questions the referee during the Lakers' NBA game against the Portland Trail Blazers in Portland. 13 December 2003. Steve Dipaola

JOHN BUCHANAN

Cerebral, bespectacled, with a fondness for the literary works of the Chinese warlord Sun Tzu, John Buchanan is a very long way from the stereotypical image of an Australian sports coach.

The former university lecturer had a modest playing record before taking Queensland to their first Sheffield Shield triumph after decades of disappointment and duly succeeded Bob Simpson and Geoff Marsh in charge of the world's most successful national cricket team.

Buchanan's holistic approach, including off-field activities such as boot camps and poetry readings, did not win universal approval; Shane Warne remarked that he thought a coach was something to transport a team to and from training. However, Buchanan's record stands up to scrutiny. At one stage his team had won 15 out of 15 tests and after losing the Ashes to England in 2005, Australia crushed their oldest opponents 5–0 in the following series. Buchanan resigned after Australia won a record third successive World Cup in 2007.

RIGHT Buchanan (right) juggles balls with Steve Waugh during a workout in Port of Spain, Trinidad. 15 April 2003. Andy Clark

CLIVE WOODWARD

Clive Woodward's place in English rugby folklore is secure. For Woodward's singular achievement was to coach the England side that overcame decades of southern hemisphere superiority to win the 2003 World Cup through a last-minute drop kick by Jonny Wilkinson.

As a player Woodward represented England and the Lions during the 1980s. After retirement he entered business, where he realized he wanted to bring the lessons he had learned from the commercial environment to the world of sport.

Woodward learned his trade as a club rugby coach and took over the national side in 1997. He immediately set about transforming the culture of English rugby, insisting on a fully professional environment for his players. The finest England XV yet assembled responded by beating New Zealand and Australia on their home territory in 2003 then winning the World Cup.

RIGHT Woodward holds rugby balls during a World Cup training session in Melbourne. 21 October 2003. Kieran Doherty

The Spirit of Sport

Dreams / Passion / Offbeat and Global Sports

A silhouette of a soccer player is projected on to a wall decorated with graffiti by World Cup fans in Dortmund, Germany. 13 June 2006. Andrea Comas

SPORTS EDUCATION IN CHINA

Hungry for success, China has 300,000 children training rigorously in sports academies across the country. Future winners are plucked from kindergarten by scouts and drilled in gymnastics, table tennis, swimming, volleyball, badminton, weight-lifting and soccer. Beijing's famed Shishahai sports school has moulded dozens of international champions, including martial arts movie star Jet Li. Work starts at 6.30 a.m. and ends around 9 p.m. after a full day of practice and studying. Critics denounce the system as cruel, but the centres, modelled on Soviet sports schools, have helped the 2008 Olympic hosts to secure some 1,700 medals at Olympics, world championships and world cups since 1949. All photos by Reinhard Krause

BELOW Young Chinese gymnasts perform handstands at the Shishahai academy, the biggest sports boarding school in Beijing.

OPPOSITE ABOVE LEFT A boy grimaces as he exercises in the gymnastics hall of the Shishahai academy.

OPPOSITE ABOVE RIGHT Concentration is etched on the face of a young gymnast as he practises on the rings.

OPPOSITE BELOW Children hoping to continue China's Olympic success beyond the 2008 Beijing Games practise in the Shishahai gymnasium. All photos 21 December 2004.

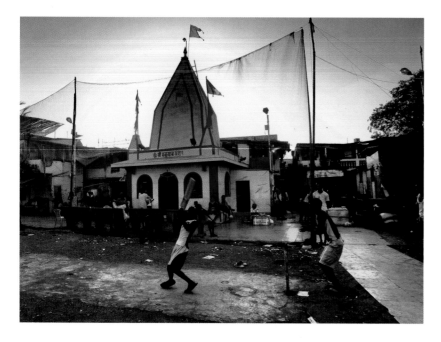

STREET CRICKET IN INDIA

TOP Indian children play cricket in front of a temple in Mumbai. Youngsters in cricket-mad India, the world's second most populous nation, can be found playing improvised matches in almost every street of every city and town. 23 May 2005. David Gray

SOUTH AFRICAN SOCCER DREAMERS

ABOVE Aspiring soccer heroes train in Johannesburg. For the teenagers at the African Stars Soccer Academy, and thousands more across the country, the dream is to be part of the 'Bafana Bafana' national team at the 2010 World Cup on home soil. 30 April 2004. Mike Hutchings

CUBAN BOXER IN TRAINING

A 13-year-old Cuban boy lifts a 15-kg (33-lb) weight during his boxing training session at an Old Havana neighbourhood gym. Cuba's state system has produced a steady stream of Olympic boxing champions. 12 August 2003. Claudia Daut

BASKETBALL IN DIVIDED KOSOVO

BELOW Kosovo Albanian boys play basketball in the snow near the ethnically divided town of Mitrovica. When all-Serb team Bambi joined the Kosovo league, playing against the Albanian majority, their coach's car was blown up. 8 February 2005.
Hazir Reka

KABUL PALACE KICKABOUT

BOTTOM In front of an old palace in Kabul, damaged during the civil war, Afghans gather for a kickabout. Soccer is hugely popular in Afghanistan but suffered under the Taliban, which imposed a litany of restrictions on games. 29 August 2006.
Ahmad Masood

SOCCER IN AN ENGLISH HEATWAVE

BELOW Two young men play soccer on a patch of dried-up ground in Gerrards Cross, Buckinghamshire, during a summer heatwave of record temperatures and lack of rain in England. 26 July 2006. Toby Melville

COURTYARD SOCCER IN ABIDJAN

BOTTOM Barefoot Ivorian boys play soccer in a courtyard in Abidjan with a makeshift goalmouth painted on the wall. The world's most popular sport needs nothing more than a ball and an open space. 26 October 2005. Thierry Gouegnon

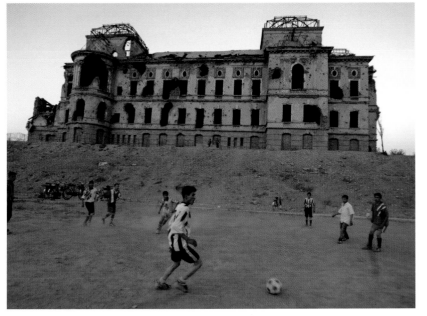

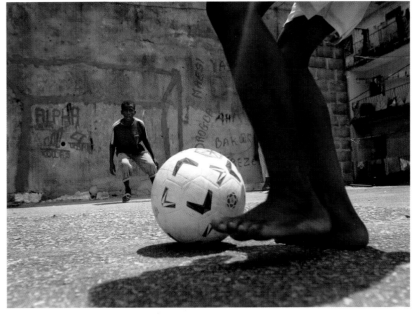

CHINESE GOLF BOOM

TOP A young Chinese golf player practises at Chaoyang Kosaido Golf Club in Beijing. The Chinese people have embraced golf with gusto and courses are springing up all over the country. 20 July 2006. Claro Cortes IV

BOXING IN UGANDA

ABOVE American athlete Michael Johnson, winner of five Olympic gold medals, watches boys box at the Community Based Aids Programme boxing club in Kampala, Uganda. Johnson visited the project to celebrate five years of support from the Laureus Sport for Good Foundation. 26 October 2006. Euan Denholm

CUBAN BASEBALL PASSION

TOP A Cuban boy plays baseball near the light tower at the entrance to Havana's bay. Baseball was introduced to Cuba 150 years ago by U.S. sailors loading sugar and has become a national passion on the Caribbean island. 25 November 2005. Claudia Daut

FOOTBALL IN NEW YORK

ABOVE Children play football in Stuyvesant Square while enjoying record winter temperatures in New York. Though soccer is played by many American children, the homegrown game of football, along with baseball and basketball, remain the most popular spectator sports in the U.S. 6 January 2007. Lucas Jackson

CAVE BASKETBALL IN CHINA

Two ethnic Miao children play basketball in a school playground inside a huge cave in a remote village in Ziyun county in southwest China. The village of Zhongdong, which means 'middle cave', is built in an enormous, natural cave, carved out of a mountain over thousands of years by wind, water and seismic shifts.
12 February 2007. Jason Lee

SOCCER BEHIND THE BARRIER

Though there is officially no Palestinian state, FIFA recognizes the national team as Palestine and offered to pay for the refurbishment of the main soccer stadium in the Gaza Strip after the pitch was hit by an Israeli warhead in 2006. The conflict with Israel has hindered the development of the Palestinian professional game. The Palestinians use stadiums in Syria, Jordan and Egypt for matches for security reasons but have sometimes found their players unable to get to games abroad because of travel restrictions. The team labour in the lower reaches of FIFA's world rankings and have touted for recruits in Latin America, where many countries have communities of Palestinian and other Arab descent.

LEFT Palestinian players warm up for a friendly match beside a stretch of Israel's separation barrier which divides the West Bank village of Abu Dis. 9 June 2006. Yannis Behrakis

ABOVE A Palestinian fan watches the friendly game in Abu Dis just a few hours before the World Cup kickoff in Germany. 9 June 2006. Yannis Behrakis

THE DREAMS OF A TEENAGED BULLFIGHTER

Miguel Angel Delgado has the face of a choirboy and the build of a child yet he moves in the bullring with a calm assurance that belies his 16 years. Delgado started training at the age of eight at the Écija bullfighting school in southern Spain, one of a growing number of schools catering to boys and girls who dream of wearing the sequined 'suit of lights' in the country's bullrings. Some aficionados complain the schools churn out little bullfighting clones, ill-prepared for the cut-and-thrust of the circuit, but Delgado has attracted praise for his maturity and calmness. If he rises to the top of the pile, he could charge 100,000 euros ($125,400) for each appearance in the bullring. All photos by Marcelo del Pozo

BELOW LEFT Delgado dresses in his hotel room before going to Pinilla bullring to fight in Écija, southern Spain.

BOTTOM LEFT Beside an improvised shrine in his hotel room, Delgado adjusts his outfit before the bullfight.

BELOW Delgado (left) stands in the arena next to other apprentices.

BOTTOM After killing a bull and being given its ear as a trophy, Delgado is carried out of the ring in triumph.

OPPOSITE The teenager drives a sword into a bull at Pinilla bullring. All photos 17 June 2006.

PASSION AND CONTROVERSY IN THE BULLRING

Bullfighting is a national symbol in Spain and arouses deep emotions both for and against. The cachet enjoyed by matadors endures and leading fighters command huge fees: El Juli (opposite above left) was said to have turned down 150,000 euros for one appearance in Seville. Yet there is also a vocal and increasingly militant anti-bullfighting camp, and the sport has come under pressure in forums such as the European Parliament for infringing animal rights regulations.

OPPOSITE Spanish matador Fernando Cepeda prepares to drive his sword into a bull during a bullfight in Las Ventas bullring in Madrid. 19 May 2005. Victor Fraile

BELOW El Juli, one of Spain's top young matadors, gets ready to perform a pass during a bullfight in Seville's Maestranza bullring. 11 April 2004. Marcelo del Pozo

BOTTOM Francisco Marco manoeuvres in front of a fighting bull in Pamplona during the San Fermín Festival, when thousands of people run through the winding streets to the bullring early each morning, dodging six bulls which have been let loose. Fifteen people have been killed since 1924. 8 July 2003. Damir Sagolj

BELOW Salvador Cortés holds his prize, the ears of a bull he has just fought and killed during a bullfight in Seville, as he is acclaimed by fans. 28 April 2006. Marcelo del Pozo

BOTTOM Matador Miguel Abellán performs a pass as a bull does a somersault after getting its horn stuck in the ground during a bullfight in Seville. 29 April 2006. Marcelo del Pozo

FESTIVE BULL-TAMING IN INDIA

OPPOSITE Indian villagers try to catch a bull during the Jallikattu bull-taming festival in the village of Palamedu, 500 km (310 miles) southwest of the city of Chennai. Injuries are common in the annual event, which is held as part of southern India's harvest festival of Pongal. Daredevil participants try to catch a bull and run with it for 50 metres (160 feet) to win prizes including television sets, bicycles and cash. Breath tests are conducted and anyone found to have been drinking alcohol is barred from running. 15 January 2006. Babu

BRAZILIAN RODEO

BELOW A cowboy loses his hat as he competes in the bulldogging event at the Barretos Rodeo in Brazil. Barretos, in western São Paulo state, hosts one of the largest rodeos in the world. It has swollen from a get-together of bachelor cowboys into a mega-event drawing U.S. riders, country music stars and 1.2 million visitors during 10 hot and dusty days of raucous competition. Brazil's 1,300 rodeo festivals pull in more than 25 million visitors per year – five times the attendance at soccer games – and are spurring an economic bonanza. The region of Barretos now earns $150 million a year, or around three times the revenue of Rio de Janeiro's world-famous Carnival. 25 August 2006. Paulo Whitaker

THE MANLY SPORTS OF MONGOLIA

The Naadam festival, Mongolia's national games, took on special significance in 2006 as the country marked 800 years since Genghis Khan united disparate tribes to form the Mongol Empire. In district centres across the vast nation, nomadic herders who make up nearly half of Mongolia's 2.7 million people congregated into stadiums for the annual pageant featuring what are known as the country's 'three manly sports': archery, bareback horse racing and wrestling. Mongolians say Naadam, the biggest event in the national calendar, is also about pride in the country's independence after centuries of rule under the Manchus, followed by decades of Soviet domination overcome in 1991.

TOP LEFT A rider passes a rainbow at Khui Doloon Khudag village on the eve of the Naadam festival. 10 July 2003. Claro Cortes IV

ABOVE LEFT Young Naadam wrestlers wait for their matches in Ulan Bator. 11 July 2003. Claro Cortes IV

TOP A wrestler trains for Naadam at a camp in the grasslands town of Suuj. 5 July 2006. Nir Elias

ABOVE Wrestlers take an outdoor shower at the end of a training session in Suuj. 5 July 2006. Nir Elias

BELOW Mongolians train at the Suuj
camp. There are no weight divisions
so big wrestlers more often win.
5 July 2006. Nir Elias

SUMO CEREMONY

ABOVE A sumo wrestler throws ceremonial salt before facing off in the first officially sanctioned Grand Sumo tournament in the United States in two decades. The giant wrestlers were treated like rock stars when Japan's ancient sport arrived at America's gambling and entertainment mecca of Las Vegas. 9 October 2005. Steve Marcus

RIGHT Japan's Kotomitsuki (top) heaves Tochinonada flat on to the sacred sumo ring at the New Year Grand Tournament in Tokyo. Historians say sumo began as entertainment for the gods, but there was nothing divine about a series of violent outbursts by some of the sport's heavyweights that tarnished its image in 2006. 17 January 2005. Toru Hanai

OIL WRESTLING IN TURKEY

A young oil wrestler pins his rival to the grass as the referee signals for the end of their match in the 645th annual oil wrestling tournament in Sarayici, western Turkey. Wrestlers, clad in leather trousers and smeared with olive oil, grapple with one another in a sport dating back to the middle ages. Putting a hand down the opponent's trousers to get a better grip is a common tactic. 2 July 2006. Fatih Saribas

ONE-LEGGED AFGHAN WRESTLING

BELOW Afghan boys play Ghursay, a type of traditional Afghan wrestling, in Kabul. Players hold up one leg and attempt to push over their opponents while trying to reach a target on the ground. 17 February 2006. Ahmad Masood

BOLIVIAN WOMEN TAKE TO THE RING

BOTTOM Bolivian Aymara Indian female wrestlers are helped by experienced wrestler 'Mister Atlas' (left) to prepare for a bout in El Alto. To the horror of Bolivian machos, women have made a successful incursion into the professional wrestling ring. 19 December 2004. David Mercado

INDIAN WRESTLER'S RESPITE

BELOW A wrestler performs a headstand in a clay pit near the river Ganges in the eastern Indian city of Kolkata. 15 November 2006. Parth Sanyal

BARE-KNUCKLE FIGHTING

BOTTOM Fist-fighters slug it out in the annual Venda bare-knuckle tournament in Gaba village, Limpopo province, South Africa. Volunteers ranging from five-year-old boys to pensioners are randomly chosen to fight until one of them is knocked out or surrenders. 28 December 2006. Siphiwe Sibeko

SCOTTISH HIGHLAND GAMES

Soldiers take part in the tug-of-war at the Braemar Highland Games in the Grampian Highlands, the grand finale to the Games season. Athletes from throughout Scotland gather on the first Saturday of September to compete in traditional events such as caber-tossing, hammer throwing, highland dancing and bagpipe playing, watched by Britain's royal family. 6 September 2003. Jeff J Mitchell

INDIAN POLE EXERCISE

An Indian boy practises traditional pole mallakhamb at a training centre in Mumbai. The centuries-old sport involves performing exercises and poses on a wooden pole. Devotees say that it boosts all-round fitness, increases agility, builds muscle and improves mind and body coordination, and it has become a fashionable leisure pursuit in both Delhi and Mumbai. 26 September 2004. Arko Datta

LEFT An elderly Indian from Brazil's Surui nation looks through a traditional Cokar headdress, made with macaw feathers, during the sixth Indigenous Nations' Games in Palmas. 6 November 2003.

INDIGENOUS SPORTS IN BRAZIL

From the Amazon rainforest, the open plains of the south and the coastal regions of the northeast, Brazil's diverse tribes congregate for the annual Indigenous Nations' Games to take part in unique events such as the 'toras' run, a relay race in which competitors shoulder a section of a tree trunk weighing up to 60 kg (130 lb). Singing, dancing and storytelling are part of the festival. The Indian population numbered an estimated six million when Portuguese explorers first landed in 1500 in what would become Brazil. Over the centuries, they have suffered enslavement, extermination campaigns, disease and neglect and by 2000 numbered about 734,000 in around 230 tribes, according to government figures.

All photos by Paulo Whitaker

BELOW LEFT Members of Brazil's Yawalapiti nation compete against another tribe in the tug-of-war at the sixth Games. 6 November 2003.

BOTTOM LEFT Members of Brazil's Matis nation, who live along the border with Peru, watch the Games in Palmas. 6 November 2003.

BELOW A child from the Kayapo tribe practises with a bow and arrow. 6 November 2003.

BOTTOM Xerente women train for the relay race carrying sections of tree trunks, called 'toras,' at the seventh Indigenous Nations' Games in Porto Seguro, Brazil. 24 November 2004.

OPEN-AIR BILLIARDS IN TIBET

Ethnic Tibetans play billiards below a rain-threatening sky in Dangxiong County, Tibet. A battered billiard table is a common sight even in the smallest village in Tibet, where it is said one in six people play the game. The sport is popular across the region, and has been one of the disciplines in the Asian Games since 1998. 29 June 2006. Jason Lee

THE GAY GAMES IN CHICAGO

Brought together under the slogan 'participation, inclusion and personal best', 12,000 athletes descended on Chicago in July 2006 for the seventh Gay Games, eight days of events mixing aerobics and same-sex ballroom dancing with traditional sports. Seventy nations were represented, including some where gay relationships are outlawed. The U.S. government eased immigration restrictions for non-citizens with HIV to attend. The event was one of two in North America due to a schism among organizers; Montreal hosted the first World Outgames with around 13,000 participants. The Gay Games movement was started in 1982 by Tom Waddell, a U.S. decathlete at the 1968 Mexico City Olympics. All photos by John Gress

TOP LEFT U.S. wrestlers Jake Whitehill (left) and Calvin Malone relax on the mat during a break. 17 July 2006.

ABOVE LEFT Janis Verrusa (right) of the U.S. laughs with compatriot Kathy Brennan before the Physique competition of the Games. 18 July 2006.

TOP RIGHT American Will Cater (left) and Arik Pou of the Philippines embrace between wrestling bouts at the seventh Games. 17 July 2006.

ABOVE Frenchman Michel Jacq-Hergoualdh, 63, keeps an eye on the pre-judging for the Games' Master Physique event. 18 July 2006.

OPPOSITE Americans Jay Kobayashi (front) and Bradley Erickson perform a figure skating routine inspired by the film *Brokeback Mountain*. 19 July 2006.

BUILDING THE BODY BEAUTIFUL

Bodybuilders believe their sport deserves a place at the Olympics but critics argue it is riddled with performance-enhancing drugs and is more akin to a beauty contest. Seven-times Mr Olympia Arnold Schwarzenegger, who went on to become the governor of California, has admitted using steroids during his bodybuilding career and said in 2007 he thought it likely that some contestants were still using banned drugs.

LEFT Male competitors wait backstage at the world fitness championships in the Greek town of Kavala. 5 November 2006. Grigoris Siamidis

BELOW LEFT In high heels and thongs, women compete at the world fitness championships in Kavala. 5 November 2006. Grigoris Siamidis

MR AFGHANISTAN

Bodybuilders apply tanning lotion as they prepare to compete for the title of
Mr Afghanistan in Kabul. Bodybuilding is the most popular sport in Afghanistan
after soccer according to the sport's guardians, who organized the country's first
Mr Afghanistan contest in 2005. Forty-eight bodybuilders flexed their muscles
and showed off oiled torsos to compete for the title, which went to a 23-year-old
businessman. Gyms have mushroomed since the days of Taliban rule. 18 September
2006. Ahmad Masood.

A BREEDING GROUND FOR BOXING CHAMPIONS

For decades Mdantsane, a township of about half a million inhabitants just outside East London, regarded itself as South Africa's home of boxing and a breeding ground for champions. The township has produced more than 10 world champions since South Africa was readmitted into the international sporting fraternity. Trainer Mzi Mnguni converted his old hardware store into a gym and used his own cash to buy all the equipment, including punchbags, gloves and protective gear. Even so, the basic facilities contrast starkly with state-of-the-art studios in Johannesburg, which are luring away the best boxers.

OPPOSITE AND BELOW Boxers train at the Eyethu Boxing Club in Mdantsane township. 25 April 2006. All photos by Siphiwe Sibeko

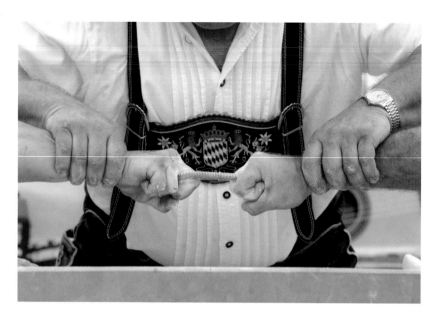

FINGER WRESTLING IN BAVARIA

In Bavarian beer cellars, men keep up the centuries-old tradition of finger wrestling. Using only their middle fingers for the tug-of-war they attempt to pull their opponent belly-first across the table. To strengthen their fighting fingers, some contestants train by hauling loaded carts up a hill or pulling a heavy lorry. The strain exerted in competition can induce nosebleeds.

ABOVE Two entrants in the Bavarian finger-wrestling championships wait for the referee to start their match in Mittenwald. 20 July 2003. Alexandra Beier

RIGHT A finger wrestler tries to drag his opponent over the table in the Bavarian village of Pflugdorf. 27 August 2006. Alexandra Beier

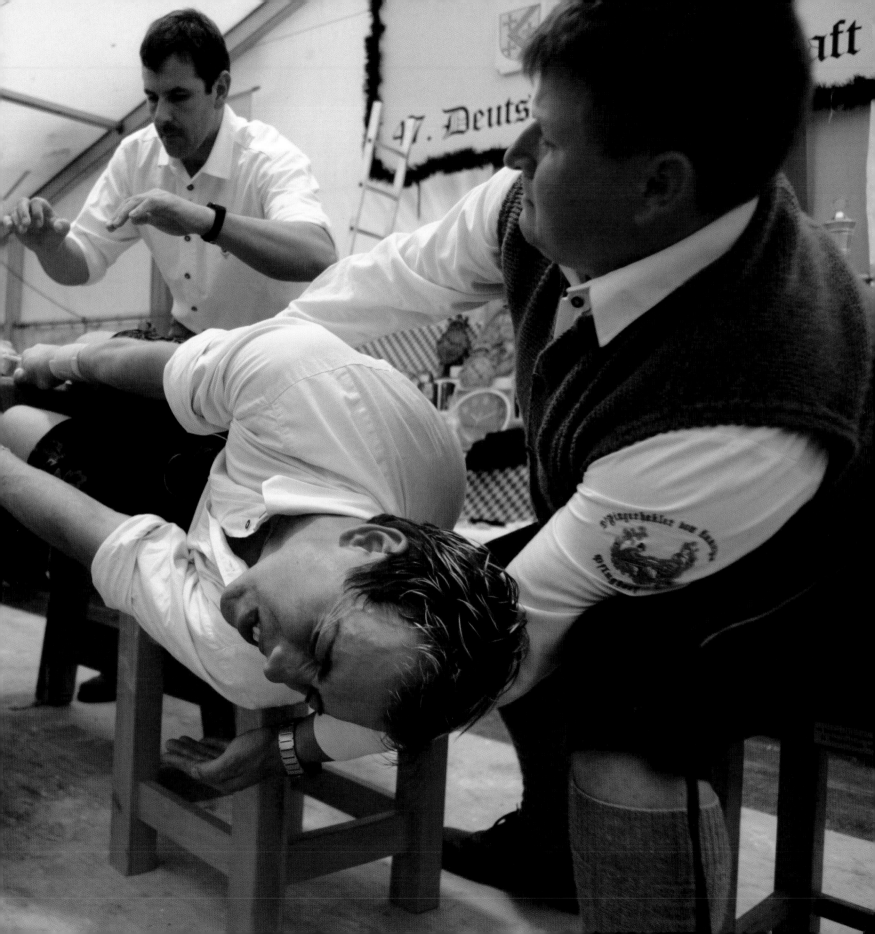

AFGHANISTAN'S NATIONAL SPORT

There are few hard and fast rules in buzkashi, regarded by many as Afghanistan's national game, but the idea is simple. First the carcass of an animal, perhaps a calf, sheep or goat, is placed inside a chalk circle on the pitch. Two teams of horsemen throng round the dead animal, their horses nervously jostling each other, the riders hanging down from the saddles. When one rider gets a grip on the carcass he gallops away with it hanging at his side. His aim is to make it once around the stadium and deposit the animal back in the chalk circle to score, fighting off rival horsemen who try to seize the animal or block his route home.

OPPOSITE Afghan chapandaz, or horse rider, Sultan Mahmood practises his skills in Kabul. 27 February 2004. Ahmad Masood

RIGHT In Mongolia, where the game is also played, horsemen tussle over a goat skin at the Altai Eagle Festival in Sagsai. 1 October 2006. Zeev Rozen

RIGHT BELOW Afghan men compete in Kabul. Buzkashi was rarely seen in the capital under Taliban rule, partly because civil war closed routes to the north where the game is most popular. 3 November 2006. Ahmad Masood

THE PALIO IN SIENA

To some it is just a trumped-up horse race, a multi-coloured tourist attraction. To the people of Siena, the Palio is the very essence of existence, the lifeblood of the Italian town. Each 2 July and 16 August, almost without fail since the mid-1600s, 10 riders have hurtled bareback around Siena's shell-shaped central square in a desperate bid to win the Palio, a silk banner depicting the Madonna and child. For the 75 or so seconds it takes horse and rider to lap three times around the sloping square's hard-packed earth, Siena is caught in the grip of a monstrous frenzy. The action is alarming, with jockeys, known locally as 'assassins' or 'mercenaries', free to ram and beat their rivals as they charge headlong around the course, inches from spectators and in constant danger of careering into the barriers that force them round the two absurdly tight right-angle turns.

TOP LEFT A priest blesses a horse and rider with the traditional exhortation 'Vai e torna vincitore' ('Go and return a winner'). 16 August 2006. Stefano Rellandini

ABOVE LEFT Selva parish jockey Alberto Ricceri embraces his horse after winning the 2006 Palio. 16 August 2006. Stefano Rellandini

TOP Luigi Bruschelli of Istrice parish rides during the last day of practice for the Palio. 1 July 2008. Stefano Rellandini

ABOVE The flag of the Lupa parish is waved in front of Siena's Cathedral before the race. 2 July 2004. Daniele La Monaca

BELOW Siena's Piazza del Campo is packed with spectators on the last day of practice for the Palio. 15 August 2006. Stefano Rellandini

ELEPHANT POLO

The Himalayan kingdom of Nepal is the venue for the annual World Elephant Polo Championship, an event dreamed up by two Britons over drinks while on holiday in St Moritz. Rules are the same as for horse polo, with a few important changes: elephants must not lie in the goalmouths, pick up the ball with their trunks or stand on it. Mahouts slap their legs on the elephants' sides to give directions and the players sit behind, wielding a stick at least two metres long. Men must control the stick with one hand but women can use both, a rule that threw referees at Thailand's King's Cup into confusion when the Screwless Tuskers team of Thai ladyboys arrived to play in the 2003 tournament. After some discussion, they were allowed to play as women but lost to Australia.

LEFT Elephants are prepared for the eight-team world polo competition in the Meghuli Forest in southern Nepal. 30 November 2006. Gopal Chitrakar

BELOW Scottish team Angus Estates (in blue and black) play National Park of Nepal in the 2006 final in Chitwan. The Scots won 8–6. 1 December 2006. Gopal Chitrakar

EAGLE HUNTING IN KAZAKHSTAN

The people of eastern Kazakhstan have been hunting with golden eagles since the days of Genghis Khan. The tradition of a winter hunt is now preserved by a handful of families who have passed their skills from generation to generation. Clad in fur hats and embroidered tunics similar to those worn by their nomadic ancestors, the hunters, or berkutchi, take the eagles to the foothills of the Tien Shan mountains, where they hunt foxes. The eagles dive at speeds up to 300 kph (185 mph), using their razor-sharp talons to strike prey. People travel from all over the world to witness the majesty of the hunt. For visitors from central Asia, it is a rare chance to reconnect with their ancestors. All photos by Shamil Zhumatov

OPPOSITE ABOVE LEFT An eagle has its head covered by a leather cap before a hunt near the town of Taldykorgan, Kazakhstan. 23 January 2004.

OPPOSITE ABOVE RIGHT A Kazakh hunter rides with an eagle during a traditional two-day hunting competition near Taldykorgan. 24 January 2004.

OPPOSITE BELOW A golden eagle catches a fox during a hunting festival in Chengelsy Gorge, 150 km (93 miles) east of Almaty. 11 February 2006.

BELOW A Kazakh female hunter releases her eagle in Taldykorgan. The eagles have wingspans of up to two metres (6ft 6in). 23 January 2004.

SPORTING NOVELTIES

ABOVE An orang-utan raises his arm after knocking out his fellow primate at a kickboxing match in Bangkok. Many of the apes in such events are imported illegally from the jungles of Malaysia and Indonesia, where fewer than 30,000 orang-utans are thought to remain. Environmentalists say that if the current rate of decline continues the species could become extinct in 20 years. 15 November 2003. Sukree Sukplang

OPPOSITE Kenyan jockeys race ostriches during the Jockey Club of Kenya's celebration of 100 years of thoroughbred horse racing at Ngong racecourse in Nairobi. The ostriches weigh between 180 and 200 kg (400–450 lb) and reach speeds of nearly 50 kph (30 mph). Other events at the Ngong celebrations included goat racing, helicopter rides and a fashion show. 31 October 2004. Radu Sigheti

HORSE RACING ON ICE

BELOW Skiers are towed by horses at speeds of up to 50 kph (30 mph) in the skikjöring event at the centenary White Turf meeting on a frozen lake at the glitzy Swiss ski resort of St Moritz. Over three consecutive Sundays, thousands of spectators sip champagne in lakeside marquees to watch the skikjöring, a 2.7-km (1.7-mile) race unique to the Engadine region of Switzerland, as well as other flat and trotting horse races. The skikjöring driver displaying the greatest courage, strength and stamina and gaining the most points over the three races is crowned King of the Engadine. 4 February 2007. Siggi Bucher

MUD FLAT RACING

RIGHT Jockeys race their horses through shallow water during the traditional horse-race meeting in Duhnen on the German North Sea coast near Cuxhaven. In 2006 some 30,000 spectators watched the annual event, held since 1902. The races begin when the ebbing tide exposes the mud flats. 6 August 2006. Christian Charisius

EXTREME CYCLING IN MEXICO

A Mexican cyclist jumps with his mountain bike during the extreme cycling contest known as the Red Bull Down Taxco, in the city of that name, in the Mexican state of Guerrero. In 2005 dozens of daredevil competitors from all over the world took part in the competition, which saw riders racing downhill through the cobbled streets of Taxco, often flying high and sometimes diverting through the rooms and passages of houses on the route. Some cyclists found the downhill flight too much and were reduced to carrying their machines in front of large crowds who cheered Swiss mountain-biker René Wildhaber to victory. Such extreme events have gained great popularity among young people in many parts of the world, assisted by the patronage of the Red Bull drink brand. 20 August 2005. Luis Cortes

WOMEN RACERS

LEFT Laleh Seddigh is reflected in a mirror of her racing car before the start of the Arjan rally outside Tehran. Seddigh was the first Iranian woman to compete against men in any sport since the Islamic revolution. Supported by her industrialist father, Seddigh fought against convention to become an elite performer in the male-dominated world of motorsport. Impressive in any context, her achievement is all the more remarkable in Iran, an Islamic theocracy where restrictions are imposed on women. 10 June 2005. Damir Sagolj

ABOVE Carla Barajas, 19, rides her motorcycle across the world's most famous high-speed salt flats at Bonneville in Utah at 250 kph (155 mph) during the annual World of Speed event. The event is the scene of many attempted land speed records in various different motorsport disciplines. Barajas, number 15069, clocked sufficiently fast times to claim membership of the elite 150 MPH Club at the event. 14 September 2006. Todd Korol

SOLAR CAR RACING

ABOVE For the North American Solar Challenge in 2005, 20 competing teams from academic institutions all over North America took up the challenge to design, build and then race their own vehicles. The event was the world's longest solar car race and the first to go through both the United States and Canada, running over 4,000 km (2,500 miles) from Austin, Texas, to Calgary, Alberta. Here, Canadian Border Service Officer Lauren Lange clears driver Adam Vaccaro of the Massachusetts Institute of Technology at the Emerson West Lynne Border Crossing in Southern Manitoba, Canada. 21 July 2005. Stefano Paltera

DIY FORMULA ONE

RIGHT Zhao Xiuguo sits in his home-made model of a Formula One racing car while his brother Zhao Xiushun looks on proudly outside their home in Tangshan, Hebei Province, 180 km (112 miles) east of Beijing. The brothers, who worked tirelessly on the project, constructed the full-size replica car from pieces of scrap metal that they found. They said they were inspired to become the first Chinese owners of a Formula One racing car. 21 July 2006. Claro Cortes IV

THE WORLD OF SPEED

The World of Speed is an annual high-speed and endurance testing event held on Utah's sun-baked Bonneville Salt Flats, which have played host to land speed record attempts for decades. The Utah State Highway Department prepares and marks out a 16 km (ten-mile) stretch of straight land for speed trials and an oval track for distance races. The event features a broad selection of racing vehicles, many of them only seen at Bonneville. They include 'Lakesters', modified and street roadsters, vintage coupés, diesel trucks and hundreds of rare motorcycles. World of Speed has also featured a motorized skateboard. All photos by Todd Korol

LEFT Motorcycle racer Rod Henninger prepares to compete in the World of Speed event at the Bonneville Salt Flats, Utah. 14 September 2006.

LEFT BELOW Californians Keith Gaeth and Elaine Leach watch racers compete. 14 September 2006.

OPPOSITE ABOVE Randy Haubrich from New Hampshire takes loving care of his 1953 Studebaker. 14 September 2006.

OPPOSITE BELOW Roland Morrison races on a street luge board. 14 September 2006.

POND HOCKEY IN THE UNITED STATES

LEFT Ice hockey players and fans attend the inaugural United States Pond Hockey Championships on Lake Calhoun in Minneapolis. The weekend event featured 116 teams on 25 rinks, making it the nation's largest outdoor ice hockey tournament. The success of the 2006 event caused it to be extended to three days the following year, although the 2007 Championships had to be moved from Lake Calhoun to Lake Nokomis because the original venue did not freeze over. 21 January 2006. Eric Miller

BRITISH TOUGH GUYS

BELOW An athlete runs through flames as he competes in the Tough Guy Event in Preston, England, a biannual charity race designed to test physical and mental endurance on an obstacle course known as the Killing Fields. The course is a 12.9-km (eight-mile) combination of mud, brambles, ice cold water, underwater tunnels, smoke and climbing frames containing electric cables. Thousands of athletes strive to claim the coveted title of 'Toughest Guy in Britain.' 29 January 2006. Darren Staples

POUNDING THROUGH WADI RUM

ABOVE Horse riders from the Middle East compete in the annual 120-km (75-mile) International Endurance Race in the spectacular desert of Wadi Rum in southern Jordan. Horses are stopped for rest and medical checks at regular intervals. 14 November 2006. Ali Jarekji

GOLF IN THE NAMIBIAN DESERT

RIGHT Namibian Manfred Geinub plays a shot on a roadside desert golf track in Walvis Bay, Namibia. The nine-hole course dubbed the 'West Side Club' has no greens, tees, water or grass. Stinging sand and gusts of wind whistle through a lone row of palm trees on the edge of the forbidding Namib desert. Interest in golf is growing fast among the young people of the poor southern African nation. 16 May 2006. Howard Burditt

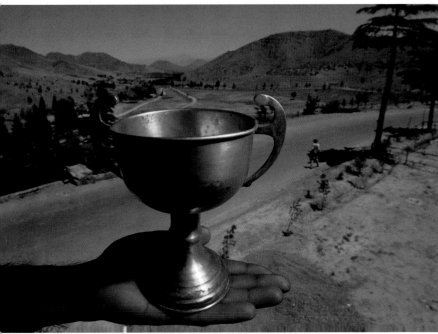

AFGHAN GOLF OPEN

In 2004 Kabul Golf Club, a battlefield in the 1990s, hosted Afghanistan's first open golf tournament in more than 30 years. The first shot of the day went to the local militia commander, applauded by his men with shouldered Kalashnikovs. Organizers hoped their tournament, contested by 40 local caddies in a picturesque valley just outside the capital, would help usher in a new era in which the only risks were from golf balls, not bullets, flying down the fairways. The club describes itself as the best – and only – course in Afghanistan. The greens are brown, the club house is a bombed-out shell and hazards include the odd spent shell and scurrying lizard.

TOP LEFT A sign marks the entrance to Afghanistan's only golf course. 26 November 2004. Ahmad Masood

ABOVE LEFT Club professional Mohammad Afzal Abdul holds the Afghan Cup. 23 May 2004. Tim Wimborne

TOP A man stands in a doorway of the bombed-out club house at the Kabul course. 29 May 2004. Tim Wimborne

ABOVE Golfers line up before the start of the tournament. 26 November 2004. Ahmad Masood

BELOW A golfer plays at the Kabul club,
which promises 'golf with attitude'.
11 November 2005. Ahmad Masood

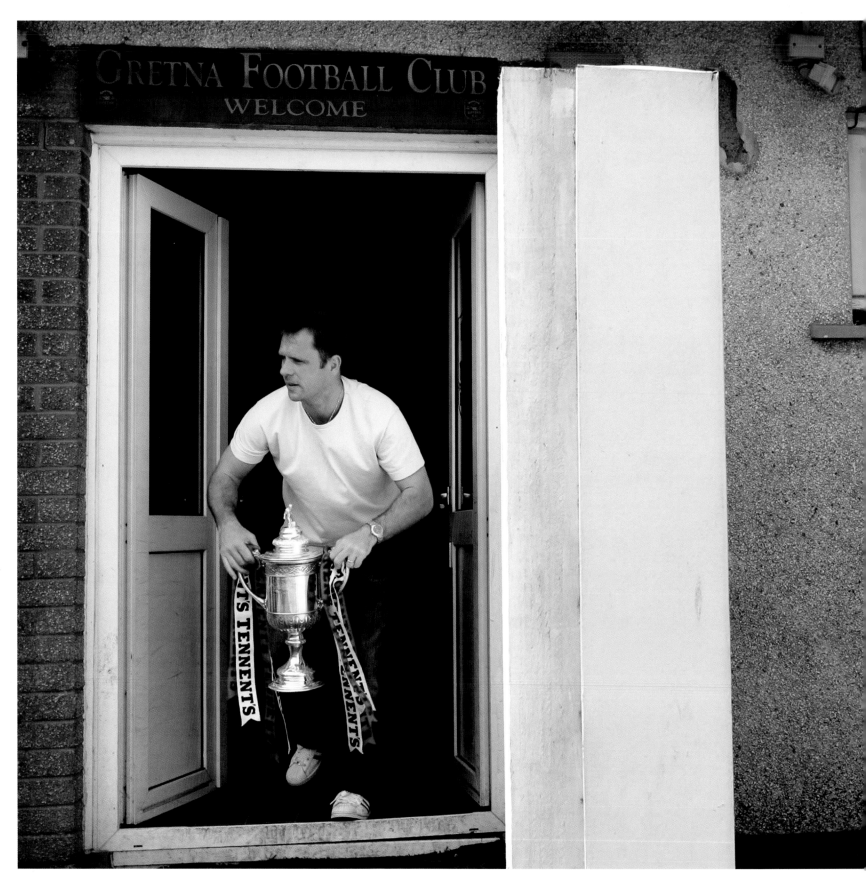

GRETNA'S CUP RUN

Virtually the entire population of the tiny border town of Gretna headed to Hampden Park when their third-division club played in the Scottish FA Cup final in 2006. Four years earlier, Gretna had been playing before crowds of 60 in a minor English league. After gaining entry to the Scottish Football League they surged through the fourth and third divisions, then reached the cup final against Hearts. Millionaire owner Brooks Mileson, who also owns a private animal sanctuary, sold cup final tickets from a cabin in the club car park and gave away hundreds to local children. Though Hearts won on penalties, there was still a happy ending for Gretna, who qualified for the UEFA Cup as Hearts had secured a Champions League spot by finishing second in the Scottish Premier League.

LEFT Gretna player John O'Neil carries away the Scottish Cup after posing for photographers at the club's Raydale Park four days before the final. 9 May 2006.
David Moir

BOSNIA UNITED

No other team in Bosnia depends more on unity than FC Guber Srebrenica. The mixed line-up of Muslims, Serbs and one Croat are still viewed with suspicion by some in the town, which had a Muslim majority before the 1992–95 war but was included in the Serb half of Bosnia in the peace accord that ended it. The amateur players are usually greeted with a torrent of nationalistic abuse when they play all-Serb teams in the country's basement league. Their biggest problem, though, says left-back Emir Jasarevic, is the referees. 'They're always against us regardless of where we play. This team is different and they can't stand it.'

All photos by Damir Sagolj

TOP LEFT Muslim and Serb players of FC Guber warm up together before a match in Srebrenica. 17 September 2006.

ABOVE LEFT The players greet a turnout of 20 supporters as they take to the pitch. 17 September 2006.

TOP Players of FC Guber (right) and FC Buducnost Pilicea wait to start their match in Bosnia's bottom league. 17 September 2006.

ABOVE Guber supporters sit on the grass to watch their team's game. 17 September 2006.

BELOW Coach Jusuf Malagic, the club's goalkeeper before the war and the man who revived the team, instructs his players. 17 September 2006.

BOTTOM Players listen to the team talk at half-time. 17 September 2006.

BELOW Stojan Milinkovic, Guber's 39-year-old Serb goalkeeper and one of five members of an extended family in the squad, saves a shot. 17 September 2006.

BOTTOM A Guber player looks from a window of the team bus after a derby match in Tabanci. 10 November 2006.

THE MUD OLYMPICS

Enthusiastic participants battle for the ball during the Mud-Soccer World
Championships on the mudflats of the river Elbe in Brunsbüttel near Hamburg.
Approximately 300 athletes take part in the so-called 'Wattolümpiade' or Mud
Olympics. Other events include volleyball, cycle racing and Nordic mud-walking.
4 June 2006. Christian Charisius

CHASING THE CHEESE

Blair Matheson wins the cheese during the Whitestone Cheese Rolling New Zealand championships at Waikaka, near Invercargill. Cheese rolling originated as a festive tradition in England. Competitors chase large cheese wheels that are rolled down a hill, and the person who reaches the cheese first gets to keep it. 6 February 2007. Simon Baker

BOG SNORKELLING

A competitor takes part in the 2006 World Bog Snorkelling Championship at Llanwrtyd Wells in Powys, mid Wales. One hundred entrants from around the world participated in the event, wearing snorkels and flippers to complete a course in a muddy trench 1.2 metres (four feet) deep. To make matters worse, conventional swimming strokes are banned. 28 August 2006. Phil Noble

HUGE SURF IN SYDNEY

Unusually large swells, not seen in the district for many months, hit Sydney's beaches in late February 2004. They were caused by strong winds combining with a low-pressure cell off the east coast of Australia.

LEFT A group of young boys crouch behind a sea-pool wall as they play in massive surf at Sydney's Narrabeen Beach. 26 February 2004. David Gray

LEFT BELOW A man prepares to brave the massive surf at Sydney's Narrabeen Beach. 26 February 2004. David Gray

MUD RACERS IN THE NETHERLANDS

OPPOSITE An exhausted participant climbs out of one of 22 energy-sapping ditches along the testing 3-km (1.8-mile) course by the meadow lands near Monnickendam in the Netherlands. In 2005 more than 200 runners took part in this traditional Dutch mud race that takes place annually at the start of the summer. 26 June 2005. Koen van Weel

WINDSURFING IN THE CANARY ISLANDS

OPPOSITE Douglas Diaz from Venezuela (left) and Tonky Frans from Bonaire Island narrowly avoid a potentially catastrophic collision during a freestyle training session at the Fuerteventura Windsurfing and Kiteboarding World Cup. This annual event, which is open to amateurs as well as professionals, plays host to a number of world championship contests. Judges rate the competitors on their adventurous jumps and daredevil moves to decide who will be the World Cup winner. 22 July 2006.

Juan Medina

EXTREME SPORTS IN LOS ANGELES

ABOVE Seventeen-year-old Rob Lorifice is separated from his skateboard as he competes at the 11th annual X Games in downtown Los Angeles. This incident happened when the rookie flew out of the quarter-pipe at the end of a Big Air ramp. More than 150 athletes compete in extreme action sports including surfing, BMX racing and rally car racing at the weekend-long annual event. 4 August 2005.

Lucy Nicholson

RIDING THE WAVE

Surfing evolved in Hawaii, where the inhabitants mastered the ancient sport of 'he'e nalu' (wave-sliding) and developed a mystical relationship with the Pacific Ocean. It became internationally popular on Waikiki Beach in the 20th century and spread worldwide, becoming a cult in California in the 1950s and 60s.

LEFT Anthony Tashnick of the U.S. gets airborne during the 2008 Big Wave Africa surfing contest at Dungeons Reef off Cape Town's Hout Bay. The event features international and local big-wave surfers taking on the reef's seven-metre (23-feet) swells. 26 July 2008. Mike Hutchings

ABOVE Hundreds of surfers take to the water in preparation for a Guinness World Record attempt for the most surfers to ride on one wave. The organizers in Muizenberg, Cape Town, claimed a record after 73 surfers, from an original 300 entries, caught and rode a wave for at least five seconds. This beat the previous record total of 53 surfers. 17 September 2006. Mike Hutchings

DRAGON BOAT RACING

Widely popular throughout Asia, dragon boat racing originated in China where, according to tradition, races are held to commemorate the death of Qu Yuan (also known as Ch'u Yuen), a famous patriotic poet closely associated with the classical age and the creation of China itself. In the year 278 BC, according to legend, Qu Yuan carried a great rock into the river Miluo and took his own life in an act of ritual suicide. Learning of this, many ordinary people in fishing boats rushed to the middle of the river first to try to save him, and then to protect his body from fish and evil spirits by splashing the water with their paddles. The modern sport inspired by that moment involves long, narrow, human-powered boats in paddling contests for which the boats are always rigged with decorative Chinese dragon heads and tails. Each boat carries a drummer, a steering helmsman and 18 or 20 paddlers.

LEFT ABOVE Competitors participate in a dragon boat race at Hong Kong's Tolo Harbour. 18 June 2005. Bobby Yip

LEFT BELOW A dragon boat race at Hong Kong's Aberdeen fishing port. 11 June 2005. Kin Cheung

OPPOSITE ABOVE Dragon boat crews paddle in a race in Sydney Harbour during Chinese New Year celebrations. 20 February 2005. David Gray

OPPOSITE BELOW A Taiwanese dragon boat leader reaches out to take the victory flag during a boat race in Taipei. 26 May 2006. Richard Chung

MARATHON RUNNING ACROSS THE WORLD

From elite athletes to charity fundraisers to club runners, people of all ages and all walks of life, all over the world, have given enormous support to public marathons and fun runs. Tens of thousands take part in the annual big-city public marathons in London, New York, Paris, Sydney, Berlin, Tokyo and Singapore, to mention but a few. For some runners, the necessary training period provides a motivation to get fit. For others, each event is a part of a carefully scheduled long-distance racing calendar. Huge crowds of spectators turn out and create a carnival atmosphere in the host city for a day. Marathon running originated in Greece, but the 42.2-km (26.2-mile) test of fitness, speed and endurance now belongs to millions of runners worldwide.

BELOW A photographer holds on to a traffic light pole at the start of the annual City to Surf fun run in Sydney. 14 August 2005. David Gray

OPPOSITE, CLOCKWISE FROM TOP LEFT The 2006 Beijing International Marathon. 15 October 2006. Grace Liang. The 2005 New York City Marathon. 6 November 2005. Seth Wenig. The 30th Paris Marathon. 9 April 2006. Victor Tonelli. The 2006 Barcelona Marathon. 26 March 2006. Albert Gea

CHINESE CHESS BREAK

ABOVE Beijing workers relax by playing Chinese chess while sitting on packages of garments awaiting shipment to Russia during the early hours of the morning. 5 May 2002. Andrew Wong

SETTING A NEW CHESS RECORD IN MEXICO

RIGHT Fourteen thousand chess enthusiasts gather to enjoy playing one of the world's most popular games and in doing so earn a place in the *Guinness Book of World Records*. The successful attempt for the most simultaneous games of chess took place in Mexico City's Zocalo plaza. 22 October 2006. Tomas Bravo

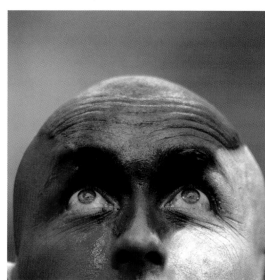

WORLD CUP FEVER

No major sports tournament stirs the passions like the month-long finals of soccer's World Cup. Held every four years on a different continent, the World Cup inspires national fervour, manifested by fans in their national colours, songs, music, poetry and loud massed support inside and outside the stadiums when games are played. The finals create a fiesta atmosphere and fans party together as if the World Cup has taken over their lives. The excitement can lead to intoxication, extreme behaviour and even tragedy. Joy and despair are shared across nationalities and colours swirl in a rare sporting cocktail.

TOP LEFT An Italian soccer fan in Milan celebrates after Italy score during their World Cup Group E match against the Czech Republic in Hamburg, Germany. 22 June 2006. Stefano Rellandini

TOP CENTRE Daniel Dressel poses with his new special German soccer hairstyle in Munich. 14 June 2006. Michaela Rehle

TOP RIGHT A fan awaits the start of the second round World Cup 2006 soccer match between Spain and France in Hanover. 27 June 2006. Alessandro Bianchi

ABOVE LEFT A journalist wears a yarmulka with the pattern of a soccer ball during a news conference in Berlin. 20 June 2006. Alexandra Beckstein

ABOVE CENTRE A Czech Republic fan waits before his country's Group E World Cup match against the U.S. 12 June 2006. Carlos Barria

ABOVE RIGHT A Portugal fan watches the World Cup 2006 semi-final between Portugal and France in Lisbon. 5 July 2006. Nacho Doce

ABOVE A soccer fan looks at a building
covered with England flags during the
World Cup. 8 June 2006. Luke MacGregor

FISHING FOR AUTOGRAPHS

Boston Red Sox pitcher Daisuke Matsuzaka signs autographs for fans during a workout session before a pre-season game against Japan's Hanshin Tigers at Tokyo Dome. In 2006, Matsuzaka pitched for Japan in the inaugural World Baseball Classic and was named the Most Valuable Player after Japan defeated Cuba 10–6 in the final. He joined the Red Sox later the same year in a record-breaking deal costing $103 million. 22 March 2008. Toru Hanai

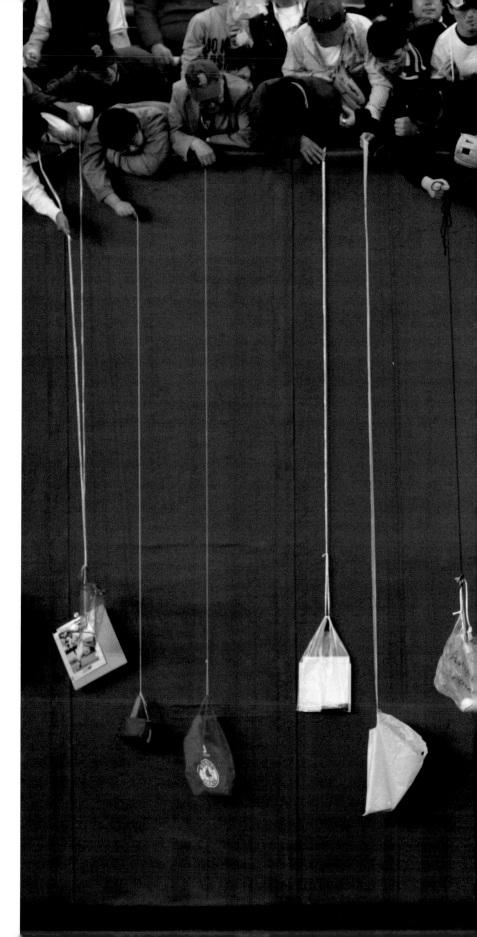

WOMEN'S SOCCER IN THAILAND

Female Thai soccer fans gather at the Rajamangala National Stadium in Bangkok to support FIFA's U-19 Women's World Championship. Soccer has grown rapidly in popularity in Thailand, where many fans, both male and female, follow the fortunes of European clubs and watch televised games beamed to them from Britain and other countries. 10 November 2004. Lee Mills

DISTRACTING THE OPPOSITION

German basketball player Dirk Nowitzki shoots a free throw for the Dallas Mavericks during their NBA Finals tie against the Miami Heat. In the background, Miami Heat fans try to distract him by holding up photographs of actor and singer David Hasselhoff after Nowitzki admitted he likes to hum Hasselhoff's song 'Looking for Freedom' during visits to the free throw line. Hasselhoff returned the compliment to Nowitzki by offering his support for the German's bid to claim the Most Valuable Player of the season award. 15 June 2006. Marc Serota

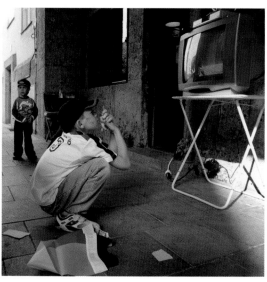

BIG-SCREEN VIEWING

For sports-lovers who cannot attend a major event because it is sold-out, there is an increasingly popular alternative: join other fans in front of a big-screen showing. The phenomenon of big-screen viewing has grown rapidly and been adopted by many international sports organizing bodies. Fan parks, set up in town squares, fields and other big open spaces, can often generate as much atmosphere as inside a stadium. At the 2006 FIFA World Cup soccer finals in Germany, up to half a million ticketless fans congregated in Berlin to share in the big-screen experience set up for them. Many soccer clubs also beam back action from their away games to their home stadium to give fans a chance to follow them when they cannot buy tickets or travel. This new habit of sports-watching has been adopted across several sports including soccer, cricket, cycling and rugby union.

OPPOSITE TOP, LEFT TO RIGHT
Paris, 22 June 2002. Charles Platiau
Austin, Texas, 24 July 2005. Jeff Mitchell
Kabul, 22 June 2002. Beawiharta

OPPOSITE CENTRE, LEFT TO RIGHT
Munich, 30 June 2006. Alexandra Beier
Turin, 28 May 2003. Claudio Papi
Saitama, Tokyo, 12 June 2006.
Toru Hanai

OPPOSITE BELOW, LEFT TO RIGHT
Accra, 22 June 2006. Yaw Bibini
Berlin, 9 July 2006. Christian Charisius
Nice, 23 June 2006. Eric Gaillard

THIS PAGE TOP, LEFT TO RIGHT
Havana, 21 March 2006. Claudia Daut
Tokyo, 13 June 2006. Yuriko Nakao
The separation wall at the West Bank
village of Abu Dis, 8 June 2006.
Ronen Zvulun

THIS PAGE ABOVE, LEFT TO RIGHT
Frankfurt, 21 June 2006. Toby Melville
Hong Kong, 14 June 2006. Bobby Yip
Epsom Downs, England, 4 June 2005.
Toby Melville

STREAKER STEALS THE LIMELIGHT

New Zealand policemen struggle to get to grips with a streaker during a rugby match on a British and Irish Lions tour. The interruption did not disrupt the rhythm of the touring side who ran out 109–6 winners against the amateurs of Manawatu, winger Shane Williams scoring five tries. The match, in Palmerston North, provided one of the highlights of a miserable tour on which the Lions lost the test series 3–0 to the New Zealand All Blacks. In recent years streakers have disrupted play on Wimbledon's Centre Court, at the Turin Winter Olympic curling competition, NHL games and the French Open men's tennis final, and an online casino has used streakers as 'human billboards' at the U.S. Open golf and the 2004 Super Bowl. 28 June 2005. David Gray

EXUBERANCE SPILLS OVER IN TURIN

Supporters of Italian soccer team Juventus invade the pitch, snatching the shorts and shirt of striker Filippo Inzaghi during a match against Atalanta at Delle Alpi stadium in Turin. The match was the final league fixture of the season. Despite defeating Atalanta 2–1, Juventus could only claim second place. The championship went to AS Roma who beat Parma 3–1 earlier in the day. The Rome club's first 'Scudetto' title in 18 years sparked a similar pitch invasion in Rome's Olympic Stadium. 17 June 2001. Stefano Rellandini

DAREDEVIL GOPHER JOINS THE RACE

ABOVE A gopher runs alongside the car of McLaren Formula One driver Lewis Hamilton of Britain during the afternoon practice session at the Canadian Grand Prix in Montreal. 6 June 2008. Christinne Muschi

MAVERICK RUNS AMOK

RIGHT Defrocked Irish priest Cornelius Horan, infamous for disrupting sporting events, grabs leader Vanderlei de Lima during the men's marathon at the Athens Olympics. The Brazilian was leading by about 45 seconds but after being held up by Horan, was only able to claim the bronze medal. De Lima later unsuccessfully appealed to the Court of Arbitration for Sport to be awarded the gold medal won by Italy's Stefano Baldini. 29 August 2004. Ruben Sprich

THE BRITISH SUMMER SOCIAL SEASON

Sporting events provide some of the highlights of the British summer social calendar. The five-day Royal Ascot horse race meeting, the Henley Royal Regatta and Wimbledon's tennis championships are all part of a tradition enjoyed by the social elite. These cherished occasions are as famous for their costumes, food and drink as the sport. Luminaries travel from all over the world to be involved, with Queen Elizabeth and Prince Phillip among the regular attendees on most days at Royal Ascot.

LEFT Race-goers await the start of the first race at the Royal Ascot race meeting in Berkshire, England. 15 June 2004. Peter Macdiarmid

TOP Spectators watch the rowing during the Henley Royal Regatta in Henley-on-Thames, Oxfordshire. The regatta has been held every year since 1839 on the River Thames, except during the two World Wars. Prince Albert became the regatta's first royal patron in 1851. 2 July 2008. Eddie Keogh

ABOVE Spectators line up to watch the Henley Regatta. 30 June 2004. Toby Melville

OUCH!

Whether it involves taking a hockey stick in the face, being set upon by a gang of aggressive defenders or crashing your motorbike at high-speed, there is no doubt that the world of competitive sport can be a painful and even dangerous place. However, such risks and sacrifices are what make sporting achievements all the more satisfying.

Bayern Munich's Mark van Bommel (right) tussles with Inter Milan's Fabio Grosso during a soccer match in Milan. 27 September 2006. Alessandro Garofalo

Hockey fans cheer as Calgary Flames' Brett Palin (left) and Vancouver Canucks' Juraj Simek fight during NHL pre-season play in Vancouver. 19 September 2007. Andy Clark

Penn State quarterback Anthony Morelli is set upon by Ohio State defenders during a football game in Columbus, Ohio. 23 September 2006. Matt Sullivan

Racing Lens' forward Eric Carrière takes it on the nose during a UEFA Cup soccer match against Groclin Grodzisk in Lens. 15 September 2005. Pascal Rossignol

Germany's Timo Wess is challenged by India's Tushar Khandker during their Field Hockey World Cup match in Mönchengladbach. 6 September 2006. Pascal Lauener

MotoGP rider Alex Barros of Brazil crashes his Yamaha during the Australian Grand Prix at Phillip Island circuit near Melbourne. 16 October 2005. Mark Horsburgh

Brazilian official Lia Mara Lourenco is treated after being pierced by a javelin during warm-ups in a São Paulo competition. 24 September 2006. Jonne Roriz-Agencia Estado

Cao Zhongrong of China falls from his horse during the show jumping event in the modern pentathlon at the 2008 Beijing Olympics. 21 August 2008. Desmond Boylan

FLYING THE FLAG

TOP A Benfica fan proudly waves his club's flag before the Portuguese Premier League soccer match against Belenenses at the Estádio da Luz in Lisbon. The match ended 0–0. 27 November 2005. Nacho Doce

ABOVE A Trabzonspor fan waves his team's colours standing in front of a Turkish flag before Trabzonspor's UEFA Cup second qualifying round soccer match against APOEL Nicosia of Cyprus. The match took place in the Turkish Black Sea city of Trabzon. 24 August 2006. Umit Bektas

ABOVE A fan sits behind a Ferrari flag at a charity soccer match between the Nazionale Piloti, including Ferrari driver Michael Schumacher, and a Greek All-Star team in Athens. 23 August 2006. Yiorgos Karahalis

TOP A mass gathering of South Korean soccer supporters watch their team's World Cup match against Portugal on a large screen in central Seoul. South Korea were joint hosts of the tournament with neighbours Japan. 14 June 2002. Noh Soon-taek

ABOVE Japanese supporters shelter from the rain under a giant sheet as they wait for the start of the World Cup Finals game between Japan and Turkey in Sendai. Turkey won the second-round match 1–0. 18 June 2002. Ian Waldie

TOP A Berlin apartment block is adorned with the flags of some of the nations competing at the 2006 FIFA World Cup in Germany. Italy went on to win the world's most important soccer competition. 12 June 2006. Pawel Kopczynski

ABOVE Portuguese and Angolan fans wait in the stands before their countries' World Cup Finals encounter in Cologne. Pedro Pauleta's fifth-minute goal proved enough for Portugal to overcome their African opponents 1–0. 11 June 2006. Albert Gea

TURNING OUT IN SUPPORT

LEFT Waiter Saturnino Gonzalez cycles on the spot holding a tray loaded with glasses to galvanize the competitors during stage eight of the Tour of Spain cycling race between Ponferrada and Lugo. 2 September 2006.
Dani Cardona

BELOW An Italy fan celebrates in the streets of downtown Frankfurt after the World Cup soccer match between Italy and Australia. A last-minute penalty from Francesco Totti helped the Italians claim a 1–0 victory in the second round en route to winning the cup. 26 June 2006.
Miro Kuzmanovic

TOP Rugby fans dressed as nuns and bishops sing and dance on the second day of the Hong Kong Sevens tournament. This annual three-day international sporting event is popular with supporters from around the world who congregate in celebration of a feast of rugby. 27 March 2004. Bobby Yip

ABOVE Romanian soccer fans react in central Bucharest while watching the Group C Euro 2008 match between Romania and France on a screen. The game in Zurich ended 0–0. 9 June 2008. Mihai Barbu

TOP Didi Senft, the tour devil or El Diablo, jumps beside a pack of riders during the fifth stage of the Tour de France cycling race between Cholet and Châteauroux. Born in Germany in 1952, Didi has been sighted on the Tour since 1993 wearing his red devil costume. 9 July 2008. Bogdan Cristel

ABOVE A supporter leans through the net to celebrate with Sevilla's Frédéric Kanouté after the Malian scored a goal against Deportivo la Coruña in a Spanish Primera Liga soccer match at Ramón Sánchez Pizjuán stadium in Seville. 20 December 2006. Alejandro Ruesga

Off the Field
Media / Marketing / Behind the Scenes

China's national flag is raised during the opening ceremony of the 2008 Beijing Olympic Games at the National Stadium, also known as the Bird's Nest. 8 August 2008. Jerry Lampen

PAGEANTRY AND POP STARS

Showbusiness meets sport in opening ceremonies which have become ever more spectacular and expensive. At every Olympic Games national pride is at stake. With billions of people watching as the curtain rises on its Games, each host city wants to put on the biggest show on earth. Pageantry and pop stars are the order of the day, as well as seemingly endless parades of athletes, massed ranks of costumed dancers and fireworks that last well into the night. Only then do the ceremonies come to the business of the swearing of the Olympic oath and lighting of the Olympic flame by a personality whose identity has been a carefully guarded secret until the last moment.

Sydney organizers chose Aboriginal runner Cathy Freeman in 2000, in a moving gesture of national reconciliation. The city's opening ceremony, which featured a band of 2,000 musicians, fire eaters and a cavalry charge by 120 stockmen, was the most watched television programme in Australian history.

The 2004 Athens opener, a three-hour pageant reviewing Greek civilization, attracted four billion viewers across the world, though a handful in the United States lodged complaints about actors portraying nude statues.

Beijing staged the most spectacular and expensive opening ceremony in Olympic history before 91,000 spectators in the National Stadium, better known as the Bird's Nest because of its complex, intertwining metal girders. Because eight is considered a lucky number in China, the four-hour show, concentrating on ancient Chinese culture, started at 8 p.m. on 8 August. It began with 2,008 drummers, featured 15,000 performers and climaxed with gymnast Li Ning appearing to run through the air before the torch-lighting ceremony.

LEFT Fireworks explode during the closing ceremony of the 2008 Beijing Olympic Games. 24 August 2008. Joe Chan

OPPOSITE TOP, LEFT TO RIGHT
Israeli athletes participate in the opening of the Maccabiah games, dubbed the 'Jewish Olympics', in Tel Aviv. 11 July 2005. Oleg Popov

Colombian dancers entertain spectators at the opening of the Central American and Caribbean Games in Cartagena, Colombia. 15 July 2006. Jose Miguel Gomez

Artists perform during the opening ceremony of the Turin Winter Olympics in Italy. 10 February 2006. Petr Josek

OPPOSITE CENTRE, LEFT TO RIGHT
Performers light up the arena with giant torches at the Asian Games in Pusan, South Korea. 29 September 2002. Bobby Yip

Theatrical group La Fura del Baus, dressed as pawns, perform at the opening of the 36th Chess Olympiad on the Spanish island of Mallorca. 14 October 2004. Dani Cardona

Chinese dancers create a field of green during the opening ceremony of the 21st University Games in Beijing. 22 August 2001. Claro Cortes IV

OPPOSITE BELOW, LEFT TO RIGHT
Actors perform during the opening ceremony of the 2008 Beijing Olympic Games. 8 August 2008. Dylan Martinez

Dancers take part in the closing ceremony at the 18th Commonwealth Games in Melbourne. 26 March 2006. Anthony Phelps

Australian Aboriginal dancers join in the opening celebrations at the Sydney Olympics. 15 September 2000. Sergio Perez

BELOW Fireworks explode during the closing ceremony of the 2008 Beijing Olympic Games. 24 August 2008. Wolfgang Rattay

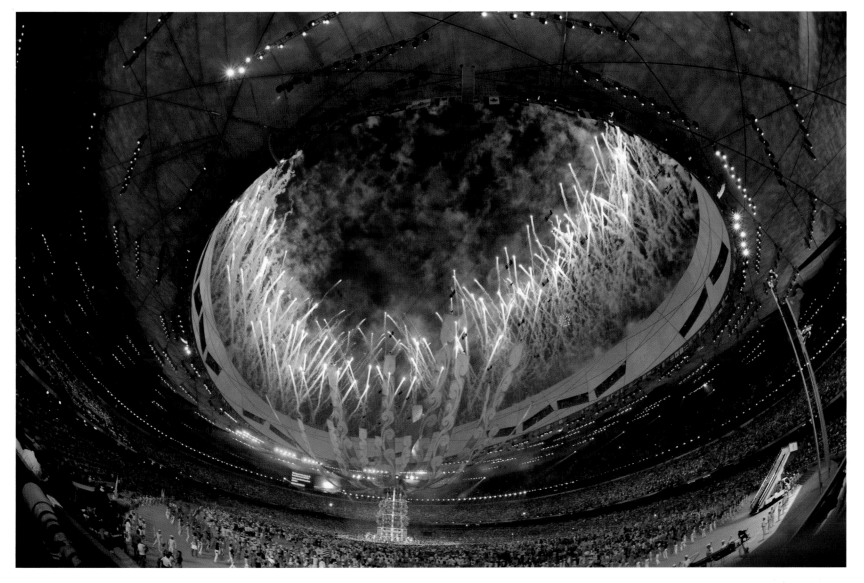

Russian tennis player Maria Sharapova looks at two of the male models chosen to act as ballboys at the WTA championships in Madrid. 11 May 2006. Andrea Comas

At the Indianapolis Motor Speedway, Americans Elizabeth Cannon and Ashley Haub wear matching stars and stripes outfits in front of a replica of a Ferrari Formula One car. 16 June 2005. Jason Reed

WORKING TO MAKE IT ALL HAPPEN

Away from the spotlight at every sporting event, an army is at work preparing courts, pitches and tracks, keeping players fed and happy and acting as ushers, interpreters, chauffeurs, score-keepers and water-carriers. Some, like the team who tend Wimbledon's manicured lawns, are paid. Others, like the tens of thousands of volunteers mobilized by every Olympic host city, work for nothing.

The threat of terrorism, political protests and crowd violence have forced sports authorities to pay increasing attention to security. Bag checks are now compulsory for players, spectators and the media at major events.

BELOW Workers dry the court in Arthur Ashe Stadium at the 2003 U.S. Open in Flushing Meadow, New York, after three days of delays due to rain. 3 September 2003. Shaun Best

OPPOSITE, CLOCKWISE FROM TOP LEFT Turkish riot police and Chinese security forces intervene as protestors try to obstruct the passage of the Olympic torch relay over Galata Bridge in Istanbul. 3 April 2008. Fatih Saribas

Workers spray a clay tennis court during the Davis Cup in Costa do Sauípe, Brazil. 9 April 2004. Paulo Whitaker

Workers mow around the bunkers at the Oakmont Country Club in Pennsylvania. 13 June 2007. Brian Snyder

A worker installs fencing to separate fans at Sarajevo's Kosevo Olympic Stadium before a World Cup qualifier between Bosnia and Serbia & Montenegro. 8 October 2004. Danilo Krstanovic

Performers line up before a match during the soccer World Cup in Berlin. 20 June 2006. Damir Sagolj

A security guard stands next to the World Cup during the 2006 final in Berlin. 9 July 2006. Alessandro Bianchi

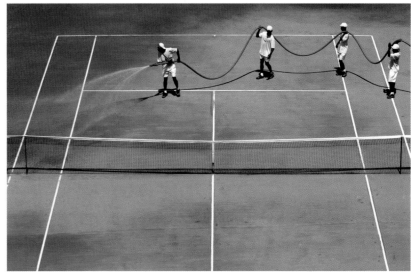

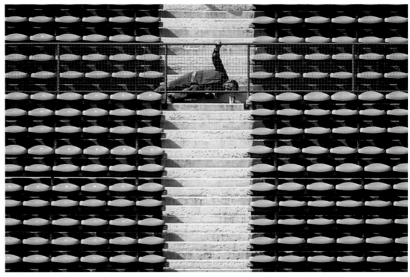

ABOVE San Diego's chicken mascot is carried off
after pretending to be hurt in an attack by the
Cincinnati Reds bullpen during a Major League
Baseball game in San Diego. 2 September 2006.
Mike Blake

RIGHT A junior cheerleader cries during the
introductions to the NFL game between the Green
Bay Packers and the Miami Dolphins in Miami.
22 October 2006. Marc Serota

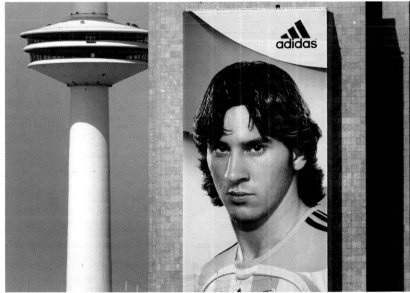

THE VALUE OF SPORTING SUCCESS

Soccer stars, golfers and tennis champions of the 21st century have become gods in the global religion of consumerism. Instantly recognizable across the world, their images appear everywhere. David Beckham's personal brand, buoyed up by his celebrity lifestyle with ex-Spice Girl wife Victoria, helped Real Madrid to move into the lucrative Asian market, where his popularity transcends his soccer skills. Part of his appeal to the Los Angeles Galaxy, the Major League Soccer club with which the Englishman signed a $250-million deal in 2007, was his potential to transform them into a global brand.

In the soccer league of superstar value, however, even Beckham has been outshone by Brazil and Barcelona forward Ronaldinho, who was declared the most commercially valuable soccer player in the world by a study in 2006. It put Ronaldinho's brand value at 47 million euros ($56.4 million) followed by Beckham

at 44.9 million euros ($53.88 million). The early years of the 21st century have seen a scramble for the hearts and wallets of Asian sports fans as markets in China and elsewhere open up. The New York Yankees baseball team sent coaches, scouts and marketing personnel to China, Brazil's leading soccer clubs signed an accord to help sport in Singapore, Japanese pitcher Daisuke Matsuzaka went to the Boston Red Sox in a record-breaking $103.1-million deal and the NBA cultivated a Chinese fan base with Yao Ming at the Houston Rockets.

No one personifies the global brand better than Tiger Woods, the multi-major golf champion whose African-American and Thai heritage, good looks and charm – combined with extraordinary sporting ability – have made him one of the most marketable icons in sport.

OPPOSITE LEFT A security officer sits in front of a billboard showing Brazil soccer player Ronaldinho in Shanghai. 8 June 2006. Aly Song

OPPOSITE RIGHT ABOVE A poster of Argentina's Lionel Messi hangs on the side of a building in Hamburg, one of the 2006 World Cup venues. 9 June 2006. Carlos Barria

OPPOSITE RIGHT BELOW An Indian couple celebrate Valentine's Day in front of a poster of Indian cricket captain Saurav Ganguly at a food pavilion in Kolkata. 14 February 2005. Jayanta Shaw

BELOW LEFT The face of France and Arsenal striker Thierry Henry looms over visitors to the China Soccer Expo in Beijing. 15 July 2004. Andrew Wong

BELOW A 65-metre (213-foot) wide poster of German goalkeeper Oliver Kahn greets travellers at Munich's airport ahead of the 2006 soccer World Cup. 29 May 2006. Michaela Rehle

BOTTOM Pedestrians in Paris walk past an advertisement featuring French Open tennis defending champion Justine Henin of Belgium. 22 May 2004. Charles Platiau

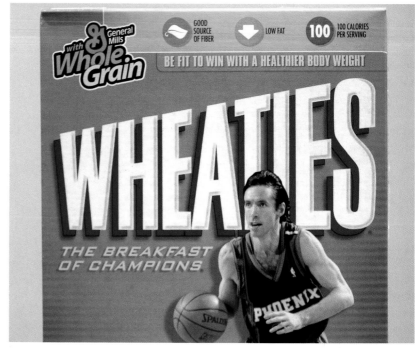

BRING ON THE MONEY

'Bring on the money,' said Maria Sharapova in 2006 when asked about her endorsement earnings. 'It is never enough. I always look for more.' Reportedly the world's highest-paid female athlete at the age of 19, the Russian 2004 Wimbledon champion has traded on her tennis talent and good looks to earn an estimated $25.4 million a year thanks to contracts to promote the goods of a string of multinational companies.

Sponsors from airlines to mobile phone companies queue up to buy association with the latest sporting phenomena. American golf prodigy Michelle Wie was earning $20 million from endorsements while still at school. However, sponsors and their cheque books can disappear just as quickly at the whiff of scandal. In

cycling, 2006 Tour de France winner Floyd Landis's Phonak team were disbanded when the Swiss hearing aid company pulled out after the American failed a dope test. NBA guard Kobe Bryant lost millions of dollars in endorsements after he was charged with sexual assault in 2003, though the charges were later dropped and his star rose again.

The money-making route is not open to everyone, however. China banned its athletes preparing for the 2008 Olympics from taking on commercial endorsements, saying they were a distraction.

OPPOSITE LEFT Images of Chinese basketball players Mengke Bateer, Yao Ming and Guo Shiqiang adorn bottles of cola in a Shanghai supermarket. 27 May 2003. Claro Cortes IV

OPPOSITE BELOW LEFT Los Angeles Lakers guard Kobe Bryant appeared on jars of hazelnut spread before the manufacturers dropped the promotion when he was charged with sexual assault. 5 August 2003. Tim Shaffer

OPPOSITE RIGHT Phoenix Suns guard Steve Nash became only the third Canadian to adorn Wheaties cereal boxes. 17 April 2006. Jeff Topping

OPPOSITE BELOW RIGHT Two Chinese men pass a huge billboard of soccer player David Beckham promoting a U.S. soft drink in Shanghai. 15 March 2002. Claro Cortes IV

BELOW Russia's 2004 Wimbledon tennis champion Maria Sharapova promotes a car at a pre-Wimbledon party in London. 22 June 2006. Leon Neil

LALIT MODI

Lalit Modi is the unabashedly aggressive entrepreneur behind the Indian Premier League Twenty20 cricket competition, the three-hour version of a sport which stretches to five days for international test matches.

Modi clashed with the Indian cricket authorities in the 1990s when he was attempting to build a sports pay channels business. Realizing he would do better to work within the system, in 2005 Modi became at the age of 42 the youngest vice-president of the Board of Control for Cricket in India and was a vocal critic of the world governing body.

Modi quickly realized the possibilities of the Twenty20 format, which was launched in 2008 with the world's leading players auctioned to eight city-based franchises: 'We want the IPL to be one of the icon brands in the world and we are going to push everything that is required to achieve that,' Modi said.

LEFT Lalit Modi (second left) accompanied by Indian industrialists Vijay Mallya (left) and Ness Wadia (right), and Bollywood actors Shah Rukh Khan (centre) and Preity Zinta in Mumbai. 20 February 2008. Punit Paranjpe

MALCOLM GLAZER

American tycoon Malcolm Glazer rocked the soccer world when in May 2005 he completed his long battle to gain a controlling stake in England's biggest club, Manchester United. Valuing the club at £800 million Glazer managed to acquire the 75 percent of shares necessary to de-list from the stock market. The Glazer takeover was bitterly contested by many fans due to concerns over the level of debt he would create. Glazer and his sons, who were appointed board directors, kept a low profile after the purchase and helped to fund new signings to generate new success for the team. This went some way to quelling the unrest. Since 1995, Glazer has also had a controlling stake in the NFL team the Tampa Bay Buccaneers. The Florida franchise had been perennial losers, but under Glazer they achieved their first Super Bowl championship in 2002.

LEFT Arsenal fans, wearing Malcolm Glazer masks, mock his takeover of Manchester United. 21 May 2005. John Sibley

ROMAN ABRAMOVICH

Russian billionaire Roman Abramovich bought English soccer club Chelsea in 2003 and immediately embarked on a spending spree unprecedented in English soccer to establish Chelsea as the top club in England and a major power in Europe. His extravagant investment in players combined with the astute tactics of Portuguese manager José Mourinho saw the club dubbed 'Chelski' by the English tabloids win Premier League titles in 2005 and 2006. Reported to be the richest man in Russia, Abramovich built up his estimated $18.5-billion fortune mostly from oil and aluminium businesses. By 2007, he had invested more than $1 billion in Chelsea, including $60 million on Ukrainian Andriy Shevchenko. Abramovich is notoriously shy of the media, but has been a regular spectator at Chelsea matches. He often visits the team dressing rooms, and has rewarded key players by allowing them the use of his luxury yacht.

RIGHT Chelsea's billionaire Russian owner Roman Abramovich (right) shakes hands with a supporter at Stamford Bridge in London. 29 September 2007. Kieran Doherty

GEORGE STEINBRENNER

New York Yankees owner George Steinbrenner is one of the most controversial figures in American sport. Steinbrenner's involvement with the Yankees began in 1973 when he headed a group of investors who bought the baseball club. Since then, success and controversy have gone hand in hand for Steinbrenner. Known for his willingness to spend huge sums on bringing the best players to his club, the man often called 'The Boss' has never been shy of making a tough decision. During his first 23 seasons in charge, he changed the Yankees' manager 20 times. While he has ruffled more than a few feathers, Steinbrenner's actions are clearly aimed at what he thinks is best for the Yankees, who won six world titles between 1973 and 2000.

RIGHT Steinbrenner responds to reporters at the Yankees minor league complex in Tampa, Florida. 17 February 2004. Peter Muhly

SEPP BLATTER

Joseph 'Sepp' Blatter is the authoritative and often-controversial president of world football's governing body, FIFA. The Swiss was elected to the role in June 1998, and survived allegations of corruption surrounding his election victories in both 1998 and 2002. He also faced criticism when he suggested women soccer players should wear tighter shorts and skimpier clothes to boost their game's popularity. But he has championed soccer in all regions of the world and worked hard on developing the game in poor countries. He has also fought to preserve the importance of international soccer in an era when the club game, buoyed up by enormous television revenues, has grown in power. He has been responsible for a number of new initiatives in world soccer including awarding a yellow card to players who perform over-zealous goal celebrations and scrapping automatic qualification to the World Cup finals for the previous winners.

LEFT Blatter attends a news conference at FIFA's headquarters in Zurich, Switzerland. 11 April 2006. Siggi Bucher

BERNIE ECCLESTONE

Englishman Bernard Charles Ecclestone rose from humble origins to become the very rich head of the multi-billion dollar Formula One racing empire. He developed F1 from a fun sport for rich playboys into a global sports business circus with high television audiences. His personal fortune is reported to be more than $4 billion. As the president and CEO of F1 Management Ecclestone has almost total control over the sport. He has promoted F1 all over the world, most recently introducing Grands Prix in China, Bahrain and Abu Dhabi. Despite selling off his 25 percent stake of the F1 business for £1 billion, Ecclestone strengthened his position in the sport by investing in the company that owns the commercial rights of F1. His famous determination has helped him overcome obstacles including a triple coronary bypass in 1999 and, more recently, a bid to oust him by three banks that own a 75 percent share in F1.

LEFT Ecclestone attends the U.S. Grand Prix in Indianapolis. 19 June 2005. Crispin Thruston

JACQUES ROGGE

International Olympic Committee (IOC) President Jacques Rogge competed for Belgium in sailing competitions at the 1968, 1972 and 1976 Olympics and also represented his country at rugby. Between 1989 and 1992 he served as president of the Belgian Olympic Committee and headed the European Olympic Committee from 1989 to 2001. He became an IOC member in 1991 and was elected as the eighth president of the world's leading sports body in 2001. An orthopaedic surgeon by profession, Rogge was knighted and given the title of Count by King Albert II in recognition of his contribution to sport. His presidency has been marked by a strong stance against performance-enhancing drugs and a commitment to making it easier for developing nations to bid for and host the Games. Rogge also promoted the Youth Olympic Games, which will be held for the first time in Singapore in 2010, and in 2008 announced he would stand for re-election as IOC president.

RIGHT Rogge at the re-opening of Sarajevo's Olympic museum. 9 February 2004. Damir Sagolj

DICK POUND

Canadian Dick Pound was the first chairman of the World Anti-Doping Agency (WADA), founded in 1999. The outspoken former International Olympic Committee vice-president took to his new task with relish although he upset a variety of people and institutions with his willingness to criticize anybody he did not think was showing the same vigilance.

During Pound's time in charge, before he was succeeded by former Australian finance minister John Fahey in 2007, WADA introduced the most significant weapon against drugs cheats since out-of-competition testing began. Non-analytical positives, evidence of doping obtained by means other than a positive urine or blood test, have resulted in bans for several prominent athletes, including triple Olympic sprint gold medallist Marion Jones.

RIGHT Pound speaks at a WADA symposium at the Olympic Museum in Lausanne. 29 January 2004. Dominic Favre-Arc

POLITICAL POINT SCORING

Cynics may say politicians show an interest in sport only when they think they can squeeze political mileage out of it. British Prime Minister Tony Blair was accused of opportunism when he invited England's cricket team to 10 Downing Street after they beat Australia in the 2005 Ashes series. There were also some raised eyebrows when he announced his allegiance to soccer team Newcastle United. American president George W. Bush seems to have a slightly more authentic interest in sport. A keen runner, Bush completed the 1993 Houston marathon. He also previously owned a share in baseball team the Texas Rangers.

ABOVE Britain's Prime Minister Tony Blair plays cricket with children at 10 Downing Street in London. 22 November 2006. Alessia Pierdomenico

BELOW U.S. President George W. Bush throws out the first pitch for the Washington Nationals at RFK Stadium in Washington, DC. 14 April 2005. Gary Cameron

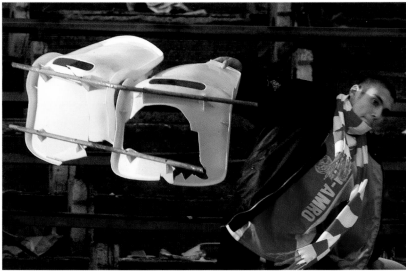

HOOLIGANISM

Hooliganism is an unfortunate blight on many sports, especially soccer. It erupts, often unexpectedly, at events all over the world. In soccer, hooliganism developed into a serious problem in the 1980s. It usually features destructive, violent and criminal behaviour by supporters, often fuelled by alcohol. Rivals gangs meet to fight and cause trouble through vandalism and wild behaviour, before, during and after matches. This behaviour has repeatedly resulted in serious injuries and death. Soccer's international ruling bodies have waged their own war on hooliganism with assistance from expert police forces, but have yet to eradicate its menace. One of the most harrowing examples occurred at the 1985 European Cup final between English champions Liverpool and Italian champions Juventus. Thirty-nine mainly Italian supporters died when a dilapidated wall collapsed after English fans broke a fence and charged at the Italians, forcing them to retreat. The incident sparked widespread fury and resulted in English teams being banned from European competition for five years, with Liverpool expelled for six. Since then, hooliganism has marred many other major soccer occasions and championships.

Aggressive behaviour is not restricted to soccer. Other sports including tennis and basketball have witnessed ugly scenes. In 2000, Los Angeles Lakers basketball fans went on a rampage through the city's streets following their team's first NBA championship title in 12 years. In 2007, the Australian Open tennis tournament was marred when fighting broke out between Croatian and Serbian supporters. Hopes that the 21st century would see an end to such violent outbursts have not been realized. In Italy in 2007, Italian soccer fans were banned from attending top matches after a policeman was killed during fighting between fans of rival Sicilian clubs. Much blame for modern hooliganism has been heaped on books and films such as *The Football Factory* and *Green Street*, which appeared to glorify thuggish behaviour, although this has been denied by the films' directors.

OPPOSITE LEFT Supporters gesture angrily at a Cardiff City v. Leeds United soccer match in Wales. 6 January 2002. Alex Morton

OPPOSITE BELOW LEFT An England soccer fan and a German riot policeman stare at each other in Stuttgart during the 2006 World Cup. 24 June 2006. Toby Melville

OPPOSITE RIGHT A CSKA Sofia soccer fan throws a seat following a 2–0 defeat by rivals Levski Sofia in Sofia. 30 September 2001. Dimitar Dilkoff

OPPOSITE BELOW RIGHT Supporters of CSKA Moskva and Vardar fight at the Skopje City stadium, Macedonia. 6 August 2003. Ognen Teofilovski

BELOW Members of the Serbian police clash with Red Star fans during a basketball game against Partizan in Belgrade. 15 June 2006. Milan Rasic

COMPUTER GAMING

Computer game manufacturers provide large revenue streams to sporting organizations in return for using the names and logos of players and teams. High-profile players including soccer star Ronaldinho are involved in games such as FIFA Street, which used the Brazilian's movements in its production. Golfing superstar Tiger Woods is another figure heavily involved in the computer game industry, putting his name to a golf game. American football coach and commentator John Madden lent his name to the most financially profitable sporting game series, which from its conception in 1990 to 2007 sold 51 million copies worldwide, more than any other sports game in history.

The $7-billion U.S. video game market has often been criticized for failing to promote physical activity in young people. It is said to be partly responsible for ever-increasing levels of childhood obesity across the world.

ABOVE Satoru Iwata, president of Nintendo (left), and Shigeru Miyamoto, senior managing director and general manager of the entertainment analysis and development division, play a game of tennis on a video screen with the new 'Wii' remote control in Hollywood, California. 9 May 2006. Robert Galbraith

VIRTUAL REFEREE

Instant video replays have been introduced into several major sports to help match officials make correct decisions on incidents that could sway the result of a game. Cricket umpires can refer decisions on run-outs, stumpings and catches to a third official who will make a judgment based on a television replay. Rugby union and rugby league referees can refer tries when they are unable to decide if the ball has been grounded correctly over the tryline, and tennis players can appeal against a line call. In 2008 Major League Baseball introduced video replays to determine whether fly balls have gone over a fence and whether home runs have been completed correctly.

BELOW Nathalie Dechy of France watches a screen declaring the result of a challenge on a serve during her match against Ana Ivanovic of Serbia at the Wimbledon tennis championships in London. Players have unlimited opportunity to challenge a line call, which is then replayed on a video screen to see if the ball was in or out, but once three incorrect challenges have been made in a set they cannot challenge again until the next set. 25 June 2008. Kevin Lamarque

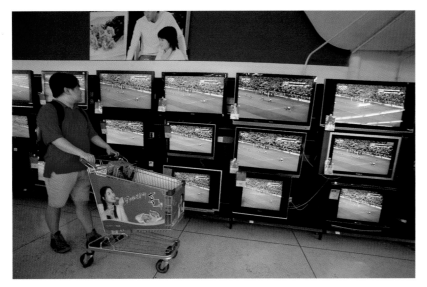

SPORT AND THE MEDIA

The huge growth and variety of the modern media, and the high stakes involved in top sport, have turned the relationship between the two into a professional and often commercial arrangement. Television, radio, the Internet and print media now deliver non-stop news on world sport all over the globe. In turn, sport has exploited this interest by introducing high levels of advertising and by charging the media for their coverage. Huge modern media companies such as Sky and Fox have invested heavily in technology and altered radically the way in which sport is televised – and the international viewer's expectations. Fans in Thailand, Malaysia and Indonesia enjoy live coverage of European soccer, with kick-offs timed to suit their lifestyles. The Australian Open tennis men's final is played in the evening to meet the demands of the European television market. The English Premier League has become the world's most lucrative soccer league with television rights sold for more than $4 billion. The money has funded the construction of modern stadiums and the recruitment of big-name international players. The media expects almost intimate access in return. Thanks to the huge modern media, sport has become a very big business.

OPPOSITE CLOCKWISE FROM TOP LEFT
Fans and a television cameraman watch the British Grand Prix at Silverstone circuit in Northamptonshire, England. 10 June 2006. David Moir

A cameraman films a surfer as he performs a re-entry at Sydney's Dee Why Beach. 16 June 2008. Tim Wimborne

American Lindsey Kildow is caught in the glare of a camera light after finishing second in a super-G Alpine ski race in St Moritz. 21 December 2004. Andreas Meier

Photographers squeeze to capture Australian golfer Nicholas Flanagan competing in the British Open at St Andrews. 13 July 2005. Eddie Keogh

A Chinese shopper watches a Euro 2008 soccer match at a supermarket in Beijing. 19 June 2008. Claro Cortes IV

BELOW Photographers surround Michael Phelps of the U.S. as he is congratulated by his mother Debbie after winning his eighth gold medal of the Games during the Beijing 2008 Olympics. 17 August 2008. Gary Hershorn

World Timeline of Sport

WORLD TIMELINE OF SPORT 2000

January

30 January UNITED STATES
Quarterback Kurt Warner guides the St Louis Rams, 200–1 long shots at the start of the season, to a 23–16 Super Bowl win over the Tennessee Titans.

March

27 March JAMAICA
West Indies cricket fast bowler Courtney Walsh dismisses Zimbabwe's Henry Olonga to become the world's leading wicket taker with 435 victims at his home ground of Sabina Park, prompting a joyous reggae party which lasts deep into the night.

June

18 June UNITED STATES
American Tiger Woods wins the U.S. Open by 15 strokes, beating the previous record at any major golf championship set by Tom Morris at the British Open in 1862.

July

9 July UNITED KINGDOM
In a rain-delayed Wimbledon final, playing in constant pain after a foot injury, American Pete Sampras recovers from dropping the first set to win a record 13th grand slam title, defeating Australia's Patrick Rafter.

23 July FRANCE
Texan Lance Armstrong becomes the first cyclist since Spaniard Miguel Indurain five years earlier to win consecutive Tours de France.

23 July UNITED KINGDOM
Tiger Woods becomes only the fifth player in history to win all four golf majors with an eight-stroke victory in the British Open at St Andrews. The American's 19-under total is the lowest score in relation to par in a major championship.

15 September–1 October AUSTRALIA
Australian Ian Thorpe wins three Olympic golds and two silvers in the pool, breaking three world records. Celebrations are muted, however, by his loss to Dutchman Pieter van den Hoogenband in the 200 metres freestyle.

15 September–1 October AUSTRALIA
American Marion Jones wins three Olympic golds and two bronzes in track and field events, but also has to endure a fraught news conference after a revelation that her shot putter husband C.J. Hunter had tested positive four times for a steroid in the previous year.

October

8 October JAPAN
German Michael Schumacher wins his third Formula One title while handing the famous Italian team Ferrari their first title for 21 years. He goes on to equal the record of nine wins in a season held by himself and Briton Nigel Mansell.

26 October UNITED STATES
The New York Yankees beat the New York Mets 4–2 in game five of the Subway Series to win their third straight Major League Baseball (MLB) World Series and their fourth in five years.

April

7 April INDIA
South Africa cricket captain Hansie Cronje and three team mates are charged with involvement in match-fixing by Delhi's joint commissioner of police after a one-day series in India the previous month. The four deny the charge.

May

24 May ISLAMABAD
Former Pakistan cricket captain Salim Malik is banned for life for match-fixing. Several team mates, including the 1999 World Cup captain Wasim Akram, are censured and fined. Hansie Cronje and former India captain Mohammad Azharuddin are also banned for life later in the year.

2 July NETHERLANDS
France win the European soccer championship to add to their World Cup, beating Italy 2–1 on a golden goal by David Trézéguet. Midfielder Zinedine Zidane, later named the World Player of the Year, is the player of the tournament.

6 July ZURICH
South Africa fails in its bid to host the 2006 soccer World Cup, losing by one vote to Germany after Oceania Football Confederation president Charlie Dempsey of New Zealand, who had been instructed to vote for South Africa, abstains.

8 July UNITED KINGDOM
Venus Williams defeats fellow American Lindsay Davenport at the Wimbledon tennis championships to win her first major. She goes on to win the Olympic gold in both singles and doubles and becomes only the seventh player to win the Wimbledon and U.S. titles in the same year.

August

20 August UNITED STATES
Tiger Woods clinches his third major of the year by winning the U.S. PGA in a three-hole playoff of escalating tension against fellow American Bob May.

September–October

15 September AUSTRALIA
Cathy Freeman lights the Sydney Olympic flame in a symbol of reconciliation between Aboriginal Australians and European settlers. She goes on to win Australia's only track gold in the women's 400 metres.

23 September AUSTRALIA
At the age of 38, British rower Steve Redgrave helps the men's coxless fours to an emotional victory and his fifth consecutive Olympic gold in as many Games.

25 September AUSTRALIA
Haile Gebrselassie of Ethiopia just holds off his great Kenyan rival Paul Tergat in the 10,000 metres after an agonizing sprint finish in the best race of the Sydney Olympic Games.

December

10 December SPAIN
Spain's tennis players land their first Davis Cup with Juan Carlos Ferrero defeating world number seven Lleyton Hewitt of Australia before King Juan Carlos and Queen Sofia in Barcelona.

WORLD TIMELINE OF SPORT 2001

January

27 January AUSTRALIA
American Jennifer Capriati, who dropped from view during her troubled teenage years, completes a remarkable comeback by beating Swiss Martina Hingis 6–4 6–3 in the final of the Australian Open tennis tournament. It is her first grand slam title.

February

18 February UNITED STATES
Dale Earnhardt dies of head injuries in a last-lap crash during the Daytona 500. He is the fourth NASCAR driver to die within a year.

April

8 April UNITED STATES
American Tiger Woods becomes the first man to hold all four golf major titles at the same time, sealing a two-stroke win in the Masters at Augusta with a birdie.

July

9 July UNITED KINGDOM
Goran Ivanišević of Croatia, three times a losing finalist, becomes the first wildcard entrant to win the Wimbledon tennis men's singles title with an emotional five-set win over Australian Patrick Rafter.

14 July AUSTRALIA
World rugby union champions Australia recover from losing the first of a three-test series to defeat the British Lions for the first time in a series.

September

9 September UNITED STATES
Twenty-year-old Australian Lleyton Hewitt wins the U.S. Open with a straight-sets win over four-times champion Pete Sampras of the United States. Hewitt finishes the year as the youngest tennis number one ever.

16 September UNITED KINGDOM
The biennial Ryder Cup team golf match between the United States and Europe scheduled to take place at The Belfry is postponed for 12 months following the September 11 attacks on the United States.

14 October JAPAN
German Michael Schumacher completes a second Formula One championship for Ferrari and a fourth overall. At the end of the 17-race series he has amassed 53 Grand Prix career victories, two ahead of former leader Alain Prost of France.

30 October UNITED STATES
Michael Jordan comes out of retirement at the age of 38 to play for the Washington Wizards in the National Basketball Association (NBA), scoring 19 points against the New York Knicks at Madison Square Garden. He finishes the season on the injured list.

25 February AUSTRALIA
Australian Don Bradman, the greatest batsman in the history of cricket, dies in Adelaide at the age of 92. Although he was dismissed without scoring in his final test innings, Bradman's average of 99.94 is still nearly 40 runs higher than his nearest rivals.

March

15 March INDIA
India end Australia's record streak of 16 consecutive cricket test victories in the second test in Calcutta despite being asked to follow on.

---

22 April SOUTH AFRICA
Boxer Lennox Lewis loses three of his four heavyweight title belts when he is knocked out by American Hasim Rahman in the fifth round. The Briton takes his revenge with a fourth-round knockout in the return bout in Las Vegas seven months later.

May

21 May SWITZERLAND
ISMM-ISL, the company that marketed soccer worldwide, collapses with debts of more than $430 million.

June

6 June ITALY
Two hundred police officers raid the hotel rooms of all 20 cycling teams after the 17th stage of the Giro d'Italia and confiscate a variety of illegal drugs. The riders retaliate by refusing to start the next stage.

29 July JAPAN
Australian Ian Thorpe finishes the world swimming championships in Fukuoka with a record six gold medals. He breaks his own world records in the 200, 400 and 800 metres freestyle and shares another world record in the 4x200 metres freestyle relay.

August

6 August CANADA
Edmonton stages the first North American world athletics championships. American Stacy Dragila, who sets seven world women's pole vault records during this year, wins the world title after a four-hour duel with Russian Svetlana Feofanova.

October

5 October UNITED STATES
Barry Bonds of the San Francisco Giants hits two homers against the Houston Astros to break Mark McGwire's 1998 Major League Baseball (MLB) single-season home-run record of 70. He finishes the year with 73.

6 October UNITED STATES
Cal Ripken, who broke Lou Gehrig's 56-year-old mark of 2,130 consecutive baseball games in 1995, closes his career at the age of 41 before former President Bill Clinton, Baseball Commissioner Bud Selig and a host of Baltimore Orioles fans.

November

4 November UNITED STATES
The Arizona Diamondbacks beat the New York Yankees 4–3 in their first baseball world series and the first to stretch into November.

27 November JAPAN
Bayern Munich, winners of the soccer Bundesliga and the European Champions League, add the World Club Cup to their trophy cabinet with an extra-time win over Argentina's Boca Juniors.

WORLD TIMELINE OF SPORT 2002

January

26 January AUSTRALIA
American Jennifer Capriati saves four championship points against Martina Hingis of Switzerland to retain the Australian Open tennis title.

February

3 February UNITED STATES
The New England Patriots win Super Bowl XXXVI, the first major sporting event staged in the United States since the September 11 attacks of the previous year, with an upset 20–17 win over the St Louis Rams.

24 February UNITED STATES
Canada beat the United States 5–2 in the ice hockey Olympic final to end a 50-year gold medal drought.

24 February UNITED STATES
Three cross-country skiers, including Spanish triple gold medallist Johan Mühlegg, are thrown out of the Games after positive tests for a new blood-boosting drug.

April

June

1 June SOUTH AFRICA
Former South Africa cricket captain Hansie Cronje dies in a plane crash, two years after he was banned from professional cricket for his part in a match-fixing scandal.

8 June UNITED STATES
Briton Lennox Lewis systematically destroys American Mike Tyson in eight rounds to retain two versions of the world heavyweight title and confirm beyond doubt he is the best fighter of his era.

July–August

21 July FRANCE
German Michael Schumacher equals Argentine Juan Manuel Fangio's record with his fifth Formula One drivers' title. His victory in the French Grand Prix at Magny-Cours gives him the championship at an earlier stage than any of his predecessors.

**25 July–4 August
UNITED KINGDOM**
Ian Thorpe picks up six gold medals and a silver as Australia dominate the Commonwealth Games in Manchester, comfortably topping the medals table ahead of England and India.

14 September FRANCE
American Tim Montgomery, the new partner of triple Olympic champion Marion Jones, sets a world 100 metres record of 9.78 seconds at the grand prix athletics final in Paris. Jones completes her first unbeaten season.

**29 September
UNITED KINGDOM**
Irishman Paul McGinley sinks a nine-foot birdie putt on the 18th to secure the Ryder Cup for Europe at The Belfry in the biennial team match against the United States.

8 February UNITED STATES
U.S. President George Bush opens the Salt Lake City winter Olympics amid unprecedented security.

8–24 February UNITED STATES
Croatian Alpine skier Janica Kostelić wins three gold medals and one silver, a record for her sport, while Norway's Ole Einar Bjørndalen also sets a record with golds in all four biathlon events.

17 February UNITED STATES
Duplicate gold medals are awarded to Canadian skaters Jamie Sale and David Pelletier after a French judge admits she had been pressured by her federation to vote for the original winners, Russians Yelena Berezhnaya and Anton Sikharulidze.

14 April UNITED KINGDOM
Moroccan-born American Khalid Khannouchi breaks his own world record in the London marathon. Briton Paula Radcliffe clocks the second fastest women's time ever on her marathon debut.

May

31 May SOUTH KOREA
Senegal provide a sensational start to the first World Cup to be staged in Asia by beating their old colonial masters and defending champions France 1–0 in the opening match.

29 June SOUTH KOREA
Turkey's Hakan Sukur scores the fastest goal in World Cup history just 11 seconds into the game against South Korea in the third-place playoff. Turkey win 3–2.

30 June JAPAN
Ronaldo, battling against injury for the past 2½ years, scores the two goals which give Brazil victory over Germany in the final for an unprecedented fifth World Cup. His eighth goal of the tournament means he equals compatriot Pelé's World Cup tally of 12.

28 July FRANCE
Lance Armstrong wins a fourth successive Tour de France title, breaking the U.S. record of Greg LeMond who won three.

September

7 September UNITED STATES
American Serena Williams, forced to miss the Australian Open with an ankle injury, completes a sweep of the other three tennis grand slam titles by beating sister Venus for a third consecutive time to win the U.S. Open.

October

13 October UNITED STATES
Britain's Paula Radcliffe shatters the world women's marathon record by 89 seconds in Chicago, reducing the mark to two hours 17 minutes 18 seconds.

WORLD TIMELINE OF SPORT 2003

January

25 January AUSTRALIA
American Serena Williams beats sister Venus to win the Australian Open tennis tournament and become the fifth woman to hold all four grand slam singles titles simultaneously.

March

2 March NEW ZEALAND
Renegade New Zealander Russell Coutts skippers Swiss yacht Alinghi to a 5–0 victory over Team New Zealand to bring the America's Cup to a landlocked European nation.

May

22 May UNITED STATES
Swede Annika Sörenstam becomes the first woman for 58 years to compete in a PGA Tour event when she takes part in the Colonial tournament in Fort Worth, Texas. She misses the cut by four shots.

June

13–27 July SPAIN
American Michael Phelps sets an unprecedented five individual world swimming records at the world championships in Barcelona, surpassing compatriot Mark Spitz who broke four, as well as contributing to three relay team world records, en route to winning seven golds at the 1972 Munich Olympics.

20 July UNITED KINGDOM
A kilted protester waving placards is dragged from the track at the British Grand Prix at Silverstone, overshadowing Brazilian Rubens Barrichello's first win of the season for Ferrari.

August

23–31 August FRANCE
American Kelli White wins the 100–200 double at the world athletics championships in Paris but then tests positive for a stimulant used to treat narcolepsy, or sleeping sickness.

24 August FRANCE
Double world cross-country champion Kenenisa Bekele of Ethiopia outsprints his mentor Haile Gebrselassie to win the 10,000 metres gold medal at the Paris world athletics championships.

28 September GERMANY
Five-times world cross-country champion Paul Tergat of Kenya sets a world men's marathon record of two hours four minutes 55 seconds in Berlin.

October

10 October AUSTRALIA
Australia's opening batsman Matthew Hayden strikes a world test record 380 against Zimbabwe in Perth. The powerful Queensland left-hander strikes 11 sixes, one short of the world record.

23 March SOUTH AFRICA
Australia cruise to a 125-run victory over India in the cricket World Cup final in Johannesburg after an unbeaten campaign, despite losing leg-spinner Shane Warne before the start of the tournament following a failed drugs test.

April

13 April UNITED KINGDOM
Briton Paula Radcliffe shatters her own world record in the London marathon, reducing her mark by one minute 53 seconds to two hours 15 minutes 25 seconds.

26 June FRANCE
Cameroon soccer international Marc-Vivien Foe collapses and dies on the pitch during a Confederations Cup semi-final against Colombia in Lyon.

July

2 July UNITED KINGDOM
Russian billionaire Roman Abramovich buys English Premier League soccer club Chelsea, in a deal worth 140 million pounds ($233 million).

24 July SPAIN
Russian swimmer Alexander Popov, 31, wins the 100 metres freestyle for a record third time at the world championships in Barcelona.

27 July FRANCE
American Lance Armstrong joins France's Jacques Anquetil and Bernard Hinault, Belgian Eddy Merckx and Spaniard Miguel Indurain as the only riders to win the Tour de France five times.

25 August UNITED STATES
American Pete Sampras retires at the age of 32 after winning a record 14 grand slam tennis titles. His perennial rival Andre Agassi won the Australian Open back in January and the best of the new American generation Andy Roddick was to take the U.S. Open title two weeks later.

September

3 September UNITED STATES
Federal agents raid the BALCO laboratory in California after scientists in Los Angeles discover a new designer steroid, THG. World 100 metres record holder Tim Montgomery, his partner Marion Jones, sprinter Kelli White and baseball slugger Barry Bonds are listed as clients.

14 September UNITED STATES
Yetunde Price, the eldest sister of tennis champions Venus and Serena Williams, is shot dead in the crime-ridden suburb of Los Angeles where the family grew up. She was 31.

12 October JAPAN
German Michael Schumacher takes the point he needs at the Japanese Grand Prix at Suzuka to break Juan Manuel Fangio's record with his sixth Formula One drivers' title.

November

22 November AUSTRALIA
England flyhalf Jonny Wilkinson drop-kicks the winning goal with his weaker right foot during the final minutes of extra time in the rugby World Cup final against Australia in Sydney.

WORLD TIMELINE OF SPORT 2004

January

6 January AUSTRALIA
Steve Waugh retires after leading the Australia cricket team to 41 victories in 57 tests, making him the most successful captain in history.

April

24 April UNITED STATES
Ukrainian Vitali Klitschko avenges his brother Vladimir's upset loss to Corrie Sanders the previous year by stopping the South African in the eighth round in Los Angeles to win the World Boxing Council heavyweight title.

25 April UNITED KINGDOM
Arsenal clinch the English Premier League title with a 2–2 draw to north London rivals Tottenham. They go on to finish the 38-game season unbeaten, the first team to do so since Preston North End in the 1888–89 season.

June

15 June UNITED STATES
Detroit Pistons upset the favoured Los Angeles Lakers with a 4–1 victory in the NBA best-of-seven finals. Defeat means the end of an era for the Lakers with coach Phil Jackson and leading player Shaquille O'Neal departing.

July

August

13–29 August GREECE
Briton Kelly Holmes, dogged by injury throughout her career, completes the 800–1,500 metres Olympic gold double in Athens.

13–29 August GREECE
American swimmer Michael Phelps wins six of the U.S. team's 35 gold medals plus two Olympic bronzes.

September

12 September UNITED STATES
Swiss Roger Federer completes his best year on the tennis circuit by winning the U.S. Open to give him victory in three of the four grand slam tournaments. He is the first man to complete the treble since Swede Mats Wilander in 1988.

17 September UNITED STATES
Barry Bonds hits his 700th career home run. Only Babe Ruth (714) and Hank Aaron (755) have ever scored more.

11 April UNITED STATES
Phil Mickelson finally fulfils his talents with victory in the U.S. Masters golf. Less happily, he teams up with Tiger Woods later in the year in an unsuccessful pairing as the United States lose 18½ to 9½ in the Ryder Cup.

12 April ANTIGUA
West Indies' cricket captain Brian Lara reclaims the world test individual batting record with an unbeaten 400 against England in the fourth test.

May

19 May UNITED STATES
American double world sprint champion Kelli White is banned after admitting taking the designer steroid THG and a variety of other prohibited drugs.

26 May GERMANY
Porto complete a golden season with a 3–0 victory over Monaco in the European Champions League soccer final in Gelsenkirchen after winning Portugal's league and Cup double.

3 July UNITED KINGDOM
Maria Sharapova wins the Wimbledon women's singles title at the age of 17 in only her second year on the tennis circuit. Russians take three of the year's four grand slam titles.

4 July PORTUGAL
Greece, who had not previously won a single game at a major soccer tournament, beat hosts Portugal 1–0 through a 57th-minute header from Angelos Haristeas to win the European championship.

25 July FRANCE
American Lance Armstrong succeeds where his distinguished predecessors Jacques Anquetil, Bernard Hinault, Miguel Indurain and Eddy Merckx failed by winning a sixth Tour de France.

13–29 August GREECE
Moroccan Hicham El Guerrouj wins the 1,500 metres Olympic gold medal at his third attempt and goes on to complete the first 1,500–5,000 double for 80 years.

18 August GREECE
Leading Greek medals hopes Costas Kenteris, the defending 200 metres champion, and Katerina Thanou withdraw from the Athens Olympics after missing a drugs test on the eve of the Games.

29 August BELGIUM
German Michael Schumacher wins his seventh Formula One world championship, finishing second at Spa-Francorchamps in Ferrari's 700th race.

October

27 October UNITED STATES
The Boston Red Sox beat the St Louis Cardinals 4–0 to win the city's first baseball World Series since Babe Ruth was sold to the hated New York Yankees in 1920.

31 October UNITED STATES
Fijian Vijay Singh becomes the first man to win $10 million on the U.S. golf tour. He joins Byron Nelson, Ben Hogan, Sam Snead and Tiger Woods as the only players to record nine victories in a year.

WORLD TIMELINE OF SPORT 2005

30 January AUSTRALIA
Russian Marat Safin keeps his volatile temper under control long enough to end Swiss Roger Federer's grand slam dream before it has properly begun. Safin knocks out Federer in the Australian Open tennis semi-finals then defeats hometown favourite Lleyton Hewitt 1–6 6–3 6–4 6–4 in the final.

6 February UNITED STATES
The New England Patriots win their third Super Bowl in four years with a 24–12 win over the Philadelphia Eagles, a ninth consecutive post-season victory to equal the record of Vince Lombardi's Green Bay Packers.

25 May TURKEY
Captain Steve Gerrard sparks an extraordinary comeback by Liverpool at the soccer European Cup final in Istanbul after AC Milan have strolled to a 3–0 lead at halftime. Liverpool fight back to level the score, then win the penalty shootout to claim the trophy for the fifth time.

14 July BRAZIL
São Paulo destroy fellow Brazilians Atlético Paranaense 4–0 in the second leg to win the Libertadores Cup and become South American soccer club champions for the third time.

22 July UNITED KINGDOM
Russian Yelena Isinbayeva, the former gymnast who has redefined the women's pole vault record, breaks the five metres barrier at London's Crystal Palace.

24 July FRANCE
U.S. cyclist Lance Armstrong narrowly avoids a crash just before entering the Champs Élysées in Paris to win his seventh successive Tour de France in his final race before retiring at the age of 33.

21 September MEXICO
Argentine-born Rubén Omar Romano, the coach of one of Mexico's richest soccer clubs, Cruz Azul, is freed after a 65-day kidnap ordeal. Less than three months later he is fired.

25 September BRAZIL
Fernando Alonso takes over from Michael Schumacher as the world Formula One champion, winning the title in São Paulo after the longest season in history, comprising 19 races. He celebrates again in Shanghai by giving Renault their first constructors' title.

17 November GERMANY
Soccer referee Robert Hoyzer is sentenced to two years and five months in jail for his part in Germany's biggest match-fixing scandal.

25 November UNITED KINGDOM
Northern Irishman George Best, possibly the most gifted soccer player the British Isles ever produced, and certainly the most glamorous, dies in a London hospital at the age of 59 after years of alcohol abuse.

March

19–20 March FRANCE
Ethiopian Kenenisa Bekele, still devastated by the death of his 18-year-old fiancée during a training run at the start of the year, completes a fourth successive long and short-distance cross-country double near Saint-Étienne in central France. No other man has won both races since the short race was introduced in 1998.

April

10 April UNITED STATES
Tiger Woods, who has remoulded his swing in the relentless quest for perfection, holes a 15-foot birdie putt to beat Chris DiMarco on the first playoff hole to win the U.S. Masters.

14 June GREECE
Jamaican Asafa Powell, a soft-spoken son of a preacher man, reduces the world 100 metres record by one-hundredth of a second to 9.77 seconds at the Athens grand prix.

July

6 July SINGAPORE
Twice Olympic 1,500 metres champion Sebastian Coe, head of the London 2012 Olympic bid team, reaps the reward for relentless hard work when London is awarded the Games over long-time favourite Paris. The next day suicide bombers strike London's transport system, killing 52 people.

August

6–14 August FINLAND
Torrential storms interrupt the world championships in Helsinki but fail to deter Olympic 100 metres champion Justin Gatlin, who completes a 100–200 metres gold medal double, while Yelena Isinbayeva sets her 18th world record in the women's pole vault after claiming her first world title.

September

12 September UNITED KINGDOM
At the end of a glorious autumn day at the Oval cricket ground in London, England regain the Ashes by winning their first series against their oldest enemy Australia for 18 years.

October

12 October BRAZIL
Brazil successfully complete a two-year, 10-team, 18-match marathon to qualify for the 2006 soccer World Cup. Under new FIFA rules they no longer qualify automatically as the defending champions.

26 October UNITED STATES
The Chicago White Sox win their first baseball World Series since 1917 by defeating the Houston Astros 4–0.

26 November UNITED KINGDOM
The New Zealand All Blacks complete only their second grand slam in history by beating Wales, Ireland, England and Scotland on successive Saturdays. They had already reasserted southern hemisphere rugby union supremacy by defeating the British Lions 3–0.

December

4 December CROATIA
Croatia win the Davis Cup final for the first time with a 3–2 victory over the Slovak Republic. They are the first unseeded team to win the men's tennis team event.

WORLD TIMELINE OF SPORT 2006

February

12–26 February ITALY
Benjamin Raich leads an Austrian clean sweep in the slalom and also wins gold in the giant slalom at the Turin winter Olympic Games. Austrians dominate the Alpine skiing with 14 of the 30 medals.

18 February ITALY
Norway's Kjetil André Aamodt becomes the first Alpine skier to win four winter Olympic gold medals with victory in the Turin Games super-G at the age of 34. Half an hour later Croatia's Janica Kostelić matches the feat with her fourth career gold, in the combined event.

May

4 May ITALY
Newspapers publish transcripts of phone calls intercepted in 2004 in which Juventus general director Luciano Moggi tells the head of the referees' association which officials he wants appointed. The Italian federation and magistrates in four cities open investigations involving Juventus, Lazio, Fiorentina and AC Milan.

June

July

4 July GERMANY
Extra-time strikes from Fabio Grosso and Alessandro Del Piero give Italy a 2–0 win over Germany and a place in the soccer World Cup final. France, who eliminated Brazil in the quarter-finals, defeat Portugal 1–0 in the other semi-final.

9 July GERMANY
France captain Zinedine Zidane is sent off in extra time after headbutting Italy's Marco Materazzi in the Berlin World Cup final with the score tied at 1–1. Materazzi had levelled the score after Zidane scored the opening goal. Italy go on to win the penalty shootout 5–3.

August

7–13 August SWEDEN
Portuguese Francis Obikwelu becomes the first man since 1978 to win the European athletics championships 100–200 metres double. Belgium's Kim Gevaert completes the women's double at the Gothenburg championships.

10 September ITALY
Michael Schumacher says he will retire at the end of the Formula One season after winning the Italian Grand Prix. It is the 90th career victory for the 37-year-old German.

24 September IRELAND
Only six weeks after the death of his wife Heather from cancer, Irishman Darren Clarke helps Europe to an 18½ to 9½ victory over the United States in the Ryder Cup. The win at the K Club is the third in a row for the Europeans.

October

23 February ITALY
Shizuka Arakawa becomes the first Japanese to win an Olympic figure skating title, relegating twice world champion Irina Slutskaya to third place in the women's event.

April

2 April JAPAN
Ethiopian Kenenisa Bekele completes a fifth consecutive long- and short-course cross-country double. The world 5,000 and 10,000 metres record-holder tries to win a sixth long-course title the following year but fails to finish.

9 June GERMANY
Hosts Germany, playing without their injured captain Michael Ballack, open the soccer World Cup with an entertaining 4–2 win over Costa Rica in Munich.

11 June FRANCE
Despite winning only one game in the opening set, Spaniard Rafael Nadal becomes the first man to beat Roger Federer in a grand slam final. Nadal defeats the Swiss 1–6 6–1 6–4 7–6 at the French Open to record his 60th consecutive match victory on clay.

27 June GERMANY
Ronaldo scores a record 15th World Cup goal as Brazil defeat Ghana 3–0 to enter the quarter-finals.

23 July UNITED KINGDOM
Tiger Woods wins the British Open by two shots in his first golf major since the death of his father Earl. The American uses his driver only once on a sun-baked Royal Liverpool course, shaping his victory with immaculate iron play.

27 July FRANCE
The Swiss-based Phonak cycling team announce that Tour de France winner Floyd Landis of the United States tested positive for excessive amounts of the male sex hormone testosterone after finishing first in the 17th stage.

21 August UNITED KINGDOM
Pakistan become the first team to forfeit a cricket test when they refuse to take the field after tea on the fourth day of the fourth test against England at The Oval in London. Their protest follows the umpires' decision to dock them five runs for alleged ball tampering.

September

9 September ITALY
Italy's Serie A soccer season starts two weeks late. Juventus are in Serie B for the first time, on minus 17 points. Fiorentina, Lazio and Reggina stay in the top division with heavy points penalties. AC Milan, docked eight points, are allowed to stay in the Champions League despite being censured by UEFA.

16 October PAKISTAN
Pakistan pace bowlers Shoaib Akhtar and Mohammad Asif are withdrawn from the Champions Trophy squad after becoming the first test cricketers to test positive for steroids. Shoaib is suspended for two years and Asif for one before the bans are overturned by a Pakistan Cricket Board tribunal due to 'exceptional circumstances'.

November

21 November AUSTRALIA
Australia's five-times Olympic swimming champion Ian Thorpe retires at the age of 24. Thorpe won three gold medals at the 2000 Sydney Olympics and two more at the 2004 Athens Games. He also won 11 world titles and set 13 world records, including the 200 and 400 metres freestyle marks.

WORLD TIMELINE OF SPORT 2007

January

5 January AUSTRALIA
Australia take brutal revenge for England's unexpected 2005 Ashes cricket victory with a 5–0 whitewash in the subsequent Ashes series. Shane Warne and Glenn McGrath, their two finest bowlers, retire from test cricket after the final match in Sydney.

February

4 February UNITED STATES
Tony Dungy becomes the first black coach to hold the Vince Lombardi Trophy aloft after the Indianapolis Colts defeat the Chicago Bears 29–17 in Miami to win Super Bowl XLI. Quarterback Peyton Manning completes 25 of 38 passes for 247 yards and one touchdown.

April

28 April BARBADOS
Australia complete a unique hat-trick of cricket World Cup triumphs with victory over Sri Lanka in a rain-shortened final. In a shambolic finish, umpires call the players back for a further three overs in the dark although the match is already concluded under International Cricket Council rain regulations.

June

29 July INDONESIA
Iraq's soccer team bring a rare moment of collective joy to their war-torn homeland by beating Saudi Arabia 1–0 in the Asian Cup final in Jakarta. Captain Younis Mahmoud heads the winning goal in the 71st minute from a corner.

August

2 August POLAND
Online firm Betfair void bets on a match between Russian world number four Nikolay Davydenko and Argentine Martin Vassallo Arguello in Sopot because of unusual betting patterns. An Association of Tennis Professionals investigation clears Davydenko, who retired hurt in the third set, of any wrongdoing.

12 August UNITED STATES
Tiger Woods clinches his 13th major title in the U.S. PGA championship at Southern Hills in Oklahoma. Fellow American Zach Johnson won the 2007 Masters, Argentine Angel Cabrera the U.S. Open, and Irishman Padraig Harrington the British Open.

26 August–2 September JAPAN
American Tyson Gay (left) emulates compatriots Maurice Greene and Justin Gatlin by winning the world championships 100-200 sprint double in Osaka. Kenyan-born Bernard Lagat, now running for the United States, becomes the first man to complete a 1,500–5,000 double.

September

October

5 October UNITED STATES
Triple Olympic champion Marion Jones admits in a U.S. federal court that she used steroids before the 2000 Sydney Olympics and pleads guilty to lying to federal agents about her drug use. All her athletics results dating back to September 2000, including five Sydney Olympics medals, are annulled.

20 October FRANCE
South Africa claim their second rugby World Cup by defeating defending champions England 15–6 at the Stade de France in Paris. A monotonous final decided entirely by penalties followed an entertaining tournament highlighted by the performances of the minor nations in the opening round.

March

17 March–1 April AUSTRALIA
American Michael Phelps wins an unprecedented seven gold medals at the world swimming championships in Melbourne with victories in the 200 metres freestyle, 100 and 200 butterfly, 200 and 400 individual medley and the 4x100 and 4x200 freestyle relay. He also breaks five world records.

18 March JAMAICA
Pakistan cricket coach Bob Woolmer, 58, dies after being found unconscious in his hotel room following his team's shock World Cup defeat to Ireland. Police launch a murder inquiry after a post-mortem report says he was strangled. Pathologists later say he died of natural causes and an inquest records an open verdict.

10 June FRANCE
Spaniard Rafael Nadal ends Swiss Roger Federer's hopes of holding all four grand slam titles in the same calendar year with a four-set win in the French Open final at Roland Garros. He is the first man to win three successive French Open titles since Björn Borg in 1980.

July

3 July SPAIN
Swiss syndicate Alinghi defeat Team New Zealand by one second in a dramatic seventh race to take the 32nd America's Cup 5–2 in the waters off Valencia. Alinghi, skippered by a New Zealander, are the first European team to successfully defend yachting's elite trophy.

5 August SCOTLAND
Mexican Lorena Ochoa leads from start to finish to win her first golf major by clinching the women's British Open at St Andrews. Ochoa took over from Swede Annika Sörenstam as world number one in April.

7 August UNITED STATES
Barry Bonds of the San Francisco Giants cracks the ball deep into the stands in right field before an ecstatic home crowd to break Hank Aaron's career home-run record of 755. Bonds, in his 22nd major league baseball season, is later charged with lying to a federal grand jury in 2003 when he denied steroid use.

13 September FRANCE
Formula One leaders McLaren are stripped of all their 2007 constructors' points and fined $100 million after a dossier of data from rivals Ferrari is found in the possession of their chief designer Mike Coughlan.

20 September UNITED STATES
American 2006 Tour de France champion Floyd Landis is banned for two years after a U.S. arbitration panel finds him guilty of doping violations. After a further spate of doping scandals in the 2007 Tour, Deutsche Telekom withdraw their support from team T-Mobile at the end of the year.

21 October BRAZIL
Finn Kimi Raikkonen, driving for Ferrari, ends Lewis Hamilton's dream of becoming the youngest Formula One champion in his debut season. Raikkonen takes his first title by one point over Hamilton and McLaren team mate Fernando Alonso after victory at the Brazilian Grand Prix.

December

10 December UNITED STATES
Atlanta Falcons quarterback Michael Vick, a three-times Pro Bowl selection with a 10-year, $130-million contract, is jailed for 23 months for his role in a dog-fighting and gambling ring.

January

4 January PORTUGAL
The 6,000-km Dakar Rally, held uninterrupted since 1979, is called off one day ahead of the start in Lisbon after the killings of four French tourists the previous month in Mauritania, which had been due to host four stages.

May

21 May RUSSIA
English champions Manchester United win the Champions League by beating Chelsea 6–5 on penalties after the Premier League rivals were tied 1–1 following extra time.

June

4 June UNITED STATES
Detroit Red Wings captain Nicklas Lidström from Sweden becomes the first European to lead a team to win the Stanley Cup. The Red Wings defeat the Pittsburgh Penguins 3–2 in game six to win the National Hockey League series 4–2.

July

July 6 UNITED KINGDOM
Rafael Nadal defeats Roger Federer in an epic, rain-interrupted, five-set Wimbledon final to become the first man since Björn Borg to win the French Open and Wimbledon titles in the same year. Nadal also thwarted Federer's bid to become only the second man to win six consecutive Wimbledon titles.

August

10 August UNITED STATES
Irish golfer Padraig Harrington follows his repeat victory in the British Open by winning the U.S. PGA Championship at Oakland Hills. He is the first European to win the USPGA since Scottish-born Tommy Armour in 1930.

24 August DUBAI
The International Cricket Council postpone the eight-nation Champions Trophy scheduled for Pakistan in September after South Africa withdraw because of safety and security fears and four other countries say they will follow suit. The one-day tournament is rescheduled for October 2009.

September

21 September UNITED STATES
Paul Azinger's U.S. team win the biennial Ryder Cup golf competition for the first time since 1999 after beating Europe 16½ to 11½ at the Valhalla Club in Kentucky.

October

10 October UNITED STATES
Former world 100 metres record holder Tim Montgomery of the U.S. is sentenced to five years' jail on heroin possession and selling charges.

17 October INDIA
Sachin Tendulkar overtakes West Indian Brian Lara's world-record test runs tally of 11,953 on the opening day of the second test against Australia in Mohali. The 35-year-old Indian already held the world record for the most one-day international runs and the most centuries in both forms of cricket.

29 January AUSTRALIA
India spinner Harbhajan Singh is cleared of racial abuse after an appeal to the International Cricket Council. Harbhajan had been suspended for three tests for allegedly calling Australia all-rounder Andrew Symonds 'a monkey' during the second test.

February

3 February UNITED STATES
New York Giants quarterback Eli Manning fires a 32-yard pass to wide receiver David Tyree for the winning touchdown in Super Bowl XLII against the New England Patriots, sealing a 17–14 win for the underdog Giants and stopping the Patriots becoming the first National Football League side to go 19–0 for the season.

20 February INDIA
The Chennai franchise pay $1.5 million for India one-day captain Mahendra Dhoni in an unprecedented auction to determine who plays where in the inaugural Indian Twenty20 Premier League.

16 June UNITED STATES
Tiger Woods, battling crippling pain in his left knee, defeats fellow American Rocco Mediate in a 19-hole playoff at the U.S. Open in San Diego. He takes the remainder of the year off after undergoing reconstructive surgery.

29 June AUSTRIA
Spain claim their first major soccer title for 44 years with a 1–0 win over Germany in the European Championship final in Vienna. Liverpool striker Fernando Torres scores the only goal of the match in the 33rd minute.

8–24 August CHINA
A spectacular opening ceremony in the futuristic Bird's Nest stadium precedes an immaculately organized Beijing Olympics. By the end, China head the medals table with 51 golds, ahead of the United States.

8–24 August CHINA
Swimmer Michael Phelps wins an unprecedented eight Olympic gold medals, including seven world records, to better the record set by fellow American Mark Spitz 36 years before.

8–24 August CHINA
Jamaican Usain Bolt breaks the world 100 and 200 metres records in the greatest exhibition of sprinting witnessed at an Olympics.

1 September UNITED KINGDOM
An Abu Dhabi-based company agrees a deal to buy English Premier League side Manchester City from former Thai premier Thaksin Shinawatra. A spokesman for the company says it aims to make City the biggest club in the world's richest soccer league.

9 September UNITED STATES
Seven-times Tour de France champion Lance Armstrong announces he is coming out of retirement and plans to race in the 2009 Tour.

14 September ITALY
German Sebastian Vettel becomes the youngest man to win a Formula One race with victory in the Italian Grand Prix at the age of 21 years 74 days.

November

2 November JAPAN
Frenchman Sébastien Loeb survives a late spin in heavy rain to finish third in the Japan Rally and clinch a record fifth consecutive world rally championship. Loeb surpassed Finn Tommi Makinen's previous record of four championships from 1996–99 to become the most successful rally driver ever.

2 November BRAZIL
Lewis Hamilton moves from sixth to fifth on the final lap of the season-ending Brazilian Grand Prix to become the youngest Formula One drivers' champion.

Additional Photo Credits

pages 358–59

Mike Blake, 30 January 2000
Rajesh Jantilal, 9 April 2000
Mohsin Raza, 26 May 2000
Tony O'Brien, 2 July 2000
Ruben Sprich, 6 July 2000
Dylan Martinez, 8 July 2000
Kieran Doherty, 9 July 2000
Kai Pfaffenbach, 21 July 2000
Ferran Paredes, 23 July 2000
Kai Pfaffenbach, 15 September 2000
Ian Waldie, 16 September 2000
Mike Blake, 23 September 2000
Andy Clark, 23 September 2000
Gary Hershorn, 25 September 2000
Susumu Toshiyuki, 8 October 2000
Mike Segar, 26 October 2000
Albert Gea, 10 December 2000

pages 360–61

Mark Baker, 27 January 2001
Duffin McGee, 18 February 2001
Megan Lewis, 27 August 1997
Jayanta Shaw, 15 March 2001
Gary Hershorn, 7 April 2001
Mike Hutchings, 22 April 2001
Stefano Rellandini, 6 June 2001
Kieran Doherty, 9 July 2001
Mark Baker, 14 July 2001
Mark Baker, 29 July 2001
Jason Reed, 6 August 2001
Shaun Best, 9 September 2001
Mike Blake, 5 October 2001
Gary Hershorn, 6 October 2001
Haruyoshi Yamaguchi, 14 October 2001
David Leeds, 30 October 2001
Mike Blake, 4 November 2001
Eriko Sugita, 27 November 2001

pages 362–63

Mark Baker, 26 January 2002
Colin Braley, 3 February 2002
Jerry Lampen, 8 February 2002
Mike Blake, 17 February 2002
Andy Clark, 24 February 2002
Paul Hanna, 17 February 2002
Andrew Winning, 23 February 2002

Stephen Hird, 14 April 2002
Desmond Boylan, 31 May 2002
Mike Hutchings, 11 April 2000
Gary Hershorn, 8 June 2002
Desmond Boylan, 29 June 2002
Oleg Popov, 30 June 2002
Robert Pratta, 21 July 2002
Jeff J Mitchell, 3 August 2002
Eric Gaillard, 23 July 2002
Kevin Lamarque, 7 September 2002
Xavier Lhospice, 14 September 2002
Darren Staples, 29 September 2002
Sue Ogrocki, 13 October 2002

pages 364–65

David Gray, 25 January 2003
Mark Baker, 2 March 2003
Mike Hutchings, 23 March 2003
Toby Melville, 13 April 2003
Kevin Lamarque, 22 May 2003
Robert Pratta, 26 June 2003
Tony O'Brien, 24 September 2005
Paul Hanna, 16 July 2003
Jim Tanner, 20 July 2003
Andrea Comas, 25 July 2003
Eric Gaillard, 26 July 2003
Charles Platiau, 24 August 2003
Carlos Barria, 25 August 2003
Jim Ruymen, 14 September 2003
Fabrizio Bensch, 28 September 2003
Bill Hatto, 10 October 2003
Wolfgang Rattay, 12 October 2003
Mike Hutchings, 22 November 2003

pages 366–67

David Gray, 6 January 2004
Kevin Lamarque, 11 April 2004
Jason O'Brien, 14 April 2004
Lucy Nicholson, 24 April 2004
Mike Finn-Kelsey, 25 April 2004
David Gray, 30 August 2003
Alex Morton, 26 May 2004
Lucy Nicholson, 15 June 2004
Kevin Lamarque, 3 July 2004
Kai Pfaffenbach, 4 July 2004
Stefano Rellandini, 25 July 2004

Jerry Lampen, 23 August 2004
David Gray, 17 August 2004
Mike Blake, 28 August 2004
John Kolesidis, 18 August 2004
Pascal Rossignol, 29 August 2004
John Gress, 12 September 2004
Susan Ragan, 17 September 2004
Peter Jones, 27 October 2004
Jessica Rinaldi, 4 September 2004

pages 368–69

David Gray, 30 January 2005
Pierre Ducharme, 6 February 2005
Kevin Lamarque, 10 April 2005
Dylan Martinez, 25 May 2005
John Kolesidis, 14 June 2005
Russell Boyce, 19 February 2005
Sergio Moraes, 14 July 2005
Steven Paston, 27 July 2005
Alessandro Bianchi, 11 August 2005
Kieran Doherty, 12 September 2005
Henry Romero, 22 September 2005
Paulo Whitaker, 25 September 2005
Sergio Moraes, 12 October 2005
John Gress, 26 October 2005
Arnd Wiegmann, 17 November 2005
Darren Staples, 3 December 2005
Jeff J Mitchell, 26 November 2005
Nikola Solic, 4 December 2005

pages 370–71

Leonhard Foeger, 18 February 2006
Wolfgang Rattay, 20 February 2006
David Gray, 24 February 2006
Kimimasa Mayama, 2 April 2006
Daniele La Monaca, 29 June 2006
Kai Pfaffenbach, 9 June 2006
Pascal Rossignol, 11 June 2006
Paulo Whitaker, 27 June 2006
Kieran Doherty, 4 July 2006
Peter Schols, 9 July 2006
Robert Galbraith, 23 July 2006
Stefano Rellandini, 20 July 2006
Yves Herman, 8 August 2006
Luke MacGregor, 20 August 2006
Daniele La Monaca, 9 September 2006

Nikola Solic, 10 September 2006
Darren Staples, 24 September 2006
Mohsin Raza, 28 October 2006
Will Burgess, 21 November 2006

pages 372–73

Tim Wimborne, 5 January 2007
Mike Blake, 4 February 2007
Tim Chong, 1 April 2007
Siphiwe Sibeko, 4 April 2007
Mike Hutchings, 28 April 2007
Francois Lenoir, 10 June 2007
Heino Kalis, 3 July 2007
Russell Boyce, 29 July 2007
Eddie Keogh, 4 August 2007
Richard Clement, 6 August 2007
Robert Galbraith, 12 August 2007
Brian Snyder, 30 August 2007
Gonzalo Fuentes, 13 September 2007
Max Morse, 22 May 2007
Shannon Stapleton, 5 October 2007
Regis Duvignau, 20 October 2007
Sergio Moraes, 21 October 2007
Kevin Lamarque, 10 December 2007

pages 374–75

Hugo Correia, 4 January 2008
Will Burgess, 29 January 2008
Jeff Topping, 3 February 2008
John Sibley, 21 May 2008
Shaun Best, 4 June 2008
Mike Blake, 16 June 2008
Kai Pfaffenbach, 29 June 2008
Ian Walton, 6 July 2008
Reinhard Krause, 8 August 2008
Wolfgang Rattay, 11 August 2008
Gary Hershorn, 16 August 2008
Mike Cassese, 10 August 2008
Nigel Roddis, 21 September 2008
Max Rossi, 14 September 2008
Eddie Keogh, 21 September 2008
Adnan Abidi, 17 October 2008
Nigel Marple, 29 August 2008
Toby Melville, 5 November 2008

Acknowledgments

Project Director

Jassim Ahmad joined Reuters in 2000 and works in the Media division as Head of Visual Projects, with responsibility for producing photographic books, exhibitions and other visual communications. He also worked on *Reuters – The State of the World*, which has been published as a book in 10 languages and staged as an exhibition in 30 cities internationally. Recent projects include the bestselling collector's series *Reuters – Our World Now* and award-winning multimedia essay *Bearing Witness*.

Picture Editor

Hamish Crooks spent 11 years working at Magnum Photos in a variety of roles including Online and Deputy Director. He co-edited the bestselling book *Magnum Football*. Hamish joined Reuters in 2005 to manage analysis and development of Reuters Pictures data, workflow and content. He has written sports features for national online newspapers and guest lectured on photography at universities in the United Kingdom.

Contributing Writers

John Mehaffey joined the Reuters Sports Desk in 1981 after working as a general news and political reporter in New Zealand, Australia and England. Since then he has reported on a variety of sports from more than 30 countries, including track and field at six summer Olympic Games. He has attended 10 world athletics championships, the soccer, rugby and cricket World Cups plus the winter Olympics, world championships in amateur boxing, gymnastics and cross-country running, professional boxing, squash, the Wimbledon tennis championships and the U.S. Masters golf. He has also covered the International Olympic Committee and written extensively on sports politics and the problem of drugs in sport.

Clare Fallon has been a Reuters journalist since 1982, first in news and economics in London and Rome and, since 1987, on the international Sports Desk in London. She has reported on three summer and three winter Olympic Games, as well as the Auckland and Victoria Commonwealth Games, the 1990 soccer World Cup in Italy and the inaugural Goodwill Games in Moscow in 1985. She has covered world and regional championships in athletics, gymnastics, swimming, Alpine skiing, table tennis and show-jumping as well as numerous editions of the Wimbledon and French Open tennis championships, Davis Cup tennis finals and world and European boxing title fights.

Special thanks to Paul Barker, Catherine Benson, Valerie Bezzina, Jonathan Bramley, Lynne Bundy, Jane Chiapoco, Timothy Collings, Ayperi Karabuda Ecer, Dominic Favre, Shannon Ghannam, Emma Goh, Philip Kelly, Jeremy Lee, Simon Newman, Paul Radford, Jonne Roriz, Peter Schols, Alexia Singh, Victoria Stenson, Akio Suga, Thomas Szlukovenyi, Sara Veness and Monique Villa.

Contributing Photographers

This book features images by 259 Reuters and Action Images photographers of 56 different nationalities on rotating locations around the world. The country that follows each name represents the photographer's nationality.

Adnan Abidi, India
Ahmad Masood, Afghanistan
Albert Gea, Spain
Alejandro Ruesga, Spain
Alessandro Bianchi, Italy
Alessandro Garofalo, Italy
Alessia Pierdomenico, Italy
Alex Grimm, Germany
Alex Morton, United Kingdom
Alexandra Beckstein, Germany
Alexandra Beier, Germany
Ali Jarekji, Syria
Allen Fredrickson, United States
Alvin Chan, China
Aly Song, China
Andrea Comas, Spain
Andreas Meier, Switzerland
Andrew Budd, United Kingdom
Andrew Winning, United Kingdom
Andrew Wong, United Kingdom
Andy Clark, Canada
Anthony Phelps, New Zealand
Anwar Mirza, Pakistan
Arko Datta, India
Arnd Wiegmann, Germany
Babu, India
Bazuki Muhammad, Malaysia
Beawiharta, Indonesia
Bill Hatto, Australia
Bob Martin, United Kingdom
Bobby Yip, Japan
Bogdan Cristel, Romania
Brendan Mcdermid, United States
Brian Snyder, United States
Bruno Domingos, Brazil
Caren Firouz, Iran
Carl Recine, United Kingdom
Carlos Barria, Argentina
Charles Platiau, France
Chris Helgren, Canada
Christian Charisius, Argentina

Christinne Muschi, Canada
Christopher Herwig, Canada
Claro Cortes IV, Philippines
Claudia Daut, Cuba
Claudio Papi, Italy
Colin Braley, United States
Crispin Thruston, United Kingdom
Damir Sagolj, Bosnia
Dan Chung, United Kingdom
Dan Riedlhuber, Canada
Dani Cardona, Spain
Daniel Munoz, Colombia
Daniele La Monaca, Italy
Danilo Krstanovic, Bosnia
Darren Staples, United Kingdom
David Gray, Australia
David Leeds, United States
David Mercado, Bolivia
David Moir, United Kingdom
David W Cerny, Czech Republic
Desmond Boylan, Ireland
Dimitar Dilkoff, Bulgaria
Duffin McGee, United States
Dylan Martinez, United Kingdom
Eddie Keogh, United Kingdom
Eduardo Munoz, Colombia
Enrique Marcarian, Argentina
Eric Gaillard, France
Eric Miller, United States
Eriko Sugita, Canada
Euan Denholm, United Kingdom
Fabrizio Bensch, Germany
Fadi Al-Assaad, Lebanon
Fatih Saribas, Turkey
Felix Ordonez Ausin, Spain
Ferran Paredes, Spain
Fran Veale, Ireland
Francois Lenoir, Belgium
Fred Greaves, United States
Gary Cameron, United States
Gary Hershorn, Canada

Giampiero Sposito, Italy
Gonzalo Fuentes, Mexico
Gopal Chitrakar, Nepal
Grace Liang, China
Grigoris Siamidis, Greece
Haruyoshi Yamaguchi, Japan
Hazir Reka, Kosovo
Heino Kalis, Germany
Henry Romero , Colombia
Howard Burditt, Zimbabwe
Hugh Gentry, United States
Hugo Correia, Portugal
Ian Hodgson, United Kingdom
Ian Waldie, Australia
Issei Kato, Japan
Jacky Naegelen, France
Jason Lee, China
Jason O'Brien, Australia
Jason Reed, Australia
Jayanta Shaw, India
Jean-Paul Pelissier, France
Jeff Haynes, United States
Jeff J Mitchell, United Kingdom
Jeff Mitchell, United States
Jeff Topping, United States
Jeff Zelevansky, United States
Jerry Lampen, Netherlands
Jessica Rinaldi, United States
Jim Ruymen, United States
Jim Tanner, United Kingdom
Joe Chan, China
John Gress, United States
John Kolesidis, Greece
John Sibley, United Kingdom
Jorge Silva, Mexico
Jose Miguel Gomez, Colombia
Joshua Lott, United States
Juan Medina, Argentina
Kacper Pempel, Poland
Kai Pfaffenbach, Germany
Kevin Lamarque, United States
Kieran Doherty, United Kingdom
Kim Kyung Hoon, Korea
Kimimasa Mayama, Japan
Kin Cheung, China
Koen van Weel, Netherlands
Laszlo Balogh, Hungary

Lee Mills, United Kingdom
Leon Neal, United Kingdom
Leonhard Foeger, Austria
Louafi Larbi, Algeria
Lucas Jackson, United States
Lucy Nicholson, United Kingdom
Lucy Pemoni, United States
Luis Cortes, Mexico
Luke Macgregor, United Kingdom
Marc Koeppelmann, Germany
Marc Serota, United States
Marcelo del Pozo, Spain
Marcos Brindicci, Argentina
Mark Baker, New Zealand
Mark Blinch, Canada
Mark Horsburgh, Australia
Mark Wallheiser, United States
Marsh Starks, United States
Matt Sullivan, United States
Max Morse, United States
Max Rossi, Italy
Megan Lewis, Australia
Michael Dalder, Germany
Michael Regan, United Kingdom
Michaela Rehle, Germany
Miguel Vidal, Spain
Mihai Barbu, Romania
Mike Blake, Canada
Mike Cassese, Canada
Mike Finn-Kelsey, United Kingdom
Mike Hutchings, United Kingdom
Mike Segar, United States
Milan Rasic, Serbia
Miro Kuzmanovic, Austria
Mohsin Raza, Pakistan
Nacho Doce, Spain
Nigel Marple, New Zealand
Nigel Roddis, United Kingdom
Nikola Solic, Croatia
Nir Elias, Israel
Noh Soon-taek, Korea
Ognen Teofilovski, Macedonia
Oleg Popov, Bulgaria
Parth Sanyal, India
Pascal Deschamps, France
Pascal Lauener, Switzerland
Pascal Rossignol, France

Paul Hanna, United States
Paul Vreeker, Netherlands
Paulo Whitaker, Brazil
Pawel Kopczynski, Poland
Petar Kujundzic, Serbia
Peter Andrews, Poland
Peter Jones, Canada
Peter MacDiarmid, United Kingdom
Peter Muhly, United States
Petr Josek, Czech Republic
Phil Noble, United Kingdom
Philippe Wojazer, France
Pierre Ducharme, United States
Punit Paranjpe, India
R. Marsh Starks, United States
Radu Sigheti, Romania
Rajesh Jantilal , South Africa
Ray Stubblebine, United States
Rebecca Cook, United States
Regis Duvignau, France
Reinhard Krause, Germany
Richard Chung, Taiwan
Richard Clement, United States
Richard Heathcote, United Kingdom
Rick Wilking, United States
Robert Galbraith, United States
Robert Pratta, France
Ronen Zvulun, Israel
Ruben Sprich, Switzerland
Russell Boyce, United Kingdom
Sean Gardner, United States
Sebastian Derungs, Switzerland
Sergei Karpukhin, Russia
Sergio Moraes, Brazil
Sergio Perez, Spain
Seth Wenig, United States
Shamil Zhumatov, Kazakhstan
Shannon Stapleton, United States
Shaun Best, Canada
Siggi Bucher, Switzerland
Simon Baker, New Zealand
Siphiwe Sibeko, South Africa
Stefano Rellandini, Italy
Stephen Hird, United Kingdom
Steve Dipaola, United States
Steve Marcus, United States
Steve Schaefer, United States

Steven Paston, United Kingdom
Stuart Milligan, Australia
Sue Ogrocki, United States
Sukree Sukplang, Thailand
Susan Ragan, United States
Susana Vera, Spain
Susumu Toshiyuki, Japan
Tami Chappell, United States
Thierry Gouegnon, Ivory Coast
Thierry Roge, Belgium
Tiffany Brown, United States
Tim Chong, Malaysia
Tim Shaffer, United States
Tim Wimborne, Australia
Toby Melville, United Kingdom
Todd Korol, Canada
Tomas Bravo, Mexico
Tony Gentile, Italy
Tony O'Brien, United Kingdom
Toru Hanai, Japan
Umit Bektas, Turkey
Victor Fraile, Spain
Victor Tonelli, France
Vincenzo Pinto, Italy
Vivek Prakash, Australia
Will Burgess, Australia
Win McNamee, United States
Wolfgang Rattay, Germany
Xavier Lhospice, France
Yannis Behrakis, Greece
Yaw Bibini, Ghana
Yiorgos Karahalis, Greece
Yuriko Nakao, Japan
Yves Herman, Belgium
Zainal Abd Halim, Malaysia
Zeev Rozen, Israel

Index

Aamodt, Kjetil André 370
Aaron, Hank 16, 177, 366
Abellán, Miguel 243
Abramovich, Roman 9, 18, 227, 345, 365
Adams, Andre 46
Addo, Eric 25
Adlington, Rebecca 91
Afghanistan
    body building 265
    buzkashi 266–67
    soccer 235
    golf 290–91
    wrestling 251
Africa, athletes from 12
African Nations Cup 31
African Stars Soccer Academy 234
Agassi, Andre 19, 37, 188–89, 190, 364
Agostini, Giacomo 170
Akhtar, Shoaib 46, 371
Akram, Wasim 359
Alekna, Virgilijus 70
Ali, Muhammad 9, 11, 19, 200
Allen, Ray 145
Alonso, Fernando 118, 121, 166, 168, 368
Alonso, Xabi 142
America see United States of America
America's Cup (2003) 12, 112, 113, 373
anabolic steroids 16
Anderson, John 129
Angelopoulos, Gianna 63
Anquetil, Jacques 365, 367
Apel, Katrin 98
Aragonés, Luis 61, 136
Arakawa, Shizuka 371
Arguello, Martin Vassallo 372
Armstrong, Lance 18, 192–95, 197, 358, 363, 365, 367, 368, 375
Aro, Samuli 114
Artemev, Sasha 76
Arthur Ashe Stadium, New York 336
Asian Games 68, 96, 135, 256, 333
Asif, Mohammad 371
AT&T National Pro-Am championships (2004) 44
Aussie Stadium, Sydney 29
Australia
    Australian Open (tennis) 39, 41, 360, 362, 363, 364, 368
    dragon boat racing 308
    surfing in 302
    Sydney-to-Hobart race (2004) 115
    Sydney Olympics (2000) 9, 12, 14, 15, 18, 19, 75, 81, 84, 172, 184, 199, 200, 202, 203, 215, 331, 333, 359, 371, 372
Azharuddin, Mohammad 198, 359
Azinger, Paul 144, 374
Azteca stadium, Mexico City 26
Azul, Cruz 368

badminton 87
    see also individual players
Badminton horse trials, Gloucestershire 131
Baillet-Latour, Henri de 15
Balaa, Basseem 48

BALCO laboratory 16, 18, 177, 203, 361
Baldini, Stefano 319
Ballack, Michael 139, 371
Banville, Melanie 77
Barajas, Carla 281
bare-knuckle fighting 251
Barmao, Samson 57
Barretos Rodeo, Brazil 249
Barrichello, Rubens 364
Barros, Alex 325
baseball 34–35, 58, 176–77, 312–13, 345, 349, 358, 361, 367, 369
    club owners 347
    in Cuba 236
    Hall of Fame 177
    managers 228
    mascots 338
    on TV 8
    World Series 144, 228
    see also individual players
basketball 48–49, 145, 172–75, 315, 329, 360, 366
    in China 172, 237
    hooliganism 352, 353
    in Kosovo 239
    managers 228
    NBA 172, 173, 174, 175, 228
    see also individual players
Bass, Brandon 48
Basso, Ivan 197
Bateer, Menk 172, 345
Batistuta, Gabriel 25
Bautista, Alvaro 124
Becker, Benjamin 37, 189
Beckham, David 25, 150–51, 226, 340, 343
Beijing Olympics (2008) 9, 10, 12, 14, 18, 19, 48, 64, 65, 67, 72, 73, 78, 91, 94, 107, 133, 145, 172, 183, 199, 203, 205, 206, 207, 212, 323, 329, 331, 333, 355, 371
Bekele, Kenenisa 12, 206, 364, 369, 371
the Belfry, Warwickshire 45
Belgium, Spa-Francorchamps 367
Bell, Ian 47
Benoit, Chris 51
Berdych, Tomas 189, 193
Berezhnaya, Yelena 102, 363
Bergqvist, Kajsa 73
Best, George 148–49, 368
Bikila, Abebe 68
billiards, in Tibet 256–57
Bing Crosby Pro-Am 44
Bjørndalen, Ole Einar 105, 362
Blackwood, Wayne 100
Blair, Tony 348
Blanco, Raúl González 139
Blatter, Joseph 'Sepp' 346
Blom, Alice 89
bobsleigh 100
bodybuilding 260–61
    in Afghanistan 261
bog snorkelling 297
Bollettieri, Nick 188
Bolt, Usain 205, 375
Bommel, Mark van 325

Bonds, Barry 16, 176–77, 361, 365, 366 , 373
Böschenstein, Niki 81
Bosnia, soccer in 294–95
Botha, Francois 219
Bowe, Riddick 220
boxing 9, 52–53, 55, 218–21, 361, 363, 366
    in Cuba 10, 238
    promoters 346
    in South Africa 262–63
    in Uganda 236
    see also individual boxers
Bradley Center, Milwaukee 48
Bradman, Don 161, 361
Braemar Highland Games 252
Brazil
    Indigenous Nations' Games 254–55
    rodeo festivals 245
Britain
    Badminton horse trials 131
    British Grand Prix (Formula One) 321
    British Open (golf) 371
    Cheltenham Festival 133
    Henley Regatta 321
    London marathon 207, 365
    London Olympics (2012) 365
    the Oval, London 47, 142, 365, 367
    Royal Ascot 214, 321
    social season in 320–21
    Wimbledon 39, 41, 179, 181, 183, 184, 187, 188, 190, 358, 359, 360, 367, 374
Bruno, Frank 220
Brunsbüttell, Mud Olympics 300
Bruschelli, Luigi 268
Bryan, Bob 190
Bryant, Kobe 173, 175, 228, 342, 345
Buchanan, John 229
Budd, Zola 68
Buesa Arena, Vitoria 128
Buffon, Gianluigi 11, 138
bullfighting 240–43
    see also individual bullfighters
bull-taming, in India 245
Burgess, Jerry 170
Burnett, Simon 212
Busch, Kurt 122
Bush, George W. 349, 351, 363
Bush, Reggie 33
buzkashi 266–67

Cafu 146
Calzaghe, Joe 52
Campbell, Darren 58
Canadian Grand Prix (Formula One) 122
Canary Islands, windsurfing in 304
Candida, Stefano 127
Cannavaro, Fabio 25, 146
canoeing 117
Cantona, Eric 226
Capriati, Jennifer 360, 362
Cao Zhongrong 323
car racing 9, 281–85, 374
    solar car racing 282
    women racers 281

see also Formula One racing; NASCAR; rally car racing; stock car racing
Carlos, Roberto 146
Carrière, Eric 325
Carvalho, Jacqueline 89
Cepeda, Fernando 243
Cervantes, Ivan 114
Chamberlain, Wilt 173
cheerleaders 336, 339
Cheese Rolling Championships, New Zealand 297
Chela, Juan Ignacio 191
Cheltenham race course, Gloucestershire 133
Chen Yibing 79
Cherono, Stephen see Shaheen, Saif Saaeed
Chess 308–09, 333
Cheste track, Valencia 147
China
    basketball 237
    Beijing Olympics (2008) 9, 10, 12, 14, 18, 19, 48, 64, 65, 67, 72, 73, 78, 91, 94, 107, 133, 145, 172, 183, 199, 203, 205, 206, 207, 212, 323, 329, 331, 333, 355, 371
    golf 240
    gymnastics 234–35
    sports education 232–33
    swimming 232
Ching Li 86
Chirac, Jacques 155
Cho, Kwan-hoon 93
Churchill, Winston 12
Clarke, Darren 42, 370
Clijsters, Kim 41
Coe, Sebastian 54, 369
Cole, Andy 128
Collazo, Luis 53
Collina, Pierluigi 225
computer games 352
Connors, Jimmy 190
Conte, Victor 16, 18, 177
Cooper, Charlotte 14
Cortés, Salvador 243
Cotto, Miguel 55
Couples, Fred 42
Coutts, Russell 364
Cracknell, James 215
cricket 46–47, 222–23, 338, 344, 358, 361, 365, 366
    the Ashes 61, 142, 145, 223, 229, 348, 369, 372
    and drugs scandals 371
    in India 8, 234
    managers 229
    match fixing 198, 359, 359, 362, 371
    the Oval, London 47, 142, 223, 365, 367
    World Cup 46, 198, 223, 229, 359, 361, 368, 369
    world records 364, 367, 374
    see also individual players
Cronje, Hansie 198, 358, 362
Crosby, Sidney 108
Cuapio, Julio Perez 134
Cuba
    baseball 236

boxing 10, 234
Cumani, Luca 216
cycling
    and drugs scandals 18, 371
    extreme cycling in Mexico 279
    fans and supporters 328, 329
    Giro d'Italia 134, 197, 361
    Tour de France 18, 134, 193, 194, 197, 327, 358, 363, 365, 367, 368, 373, 375
    Tour of Qatar 135
    Tour of Spain 56, 58, 134, 135, 326
    track cycling 133
    see also individual cyclists

Davenport, Lindsay 41, 184, 187, 191, 359
Davydenko, Nikolay 39, 372
de la Hoya, Oscar 53
De Rossi, Daniele 25
decathlon 70
Dechy, Nathalie 353
Del Piero, Alessandro 26
Delgado, Miguel Angel 240
Demeester, Arnaud 127
Dementieva, Elena 187
Dempsey, Charlie 359
Dempsey, Jack 9
Desgrange, Henri 18
Despatie, Alexandre 92
Dettori, Frankie 214
Devers, Gail 209
Dhoni, Mahendra 375
Diaz, Douglas 301
Dickens, Scott 61
DiMarco, Chris 369
Dionne, Deidra 102
discus 61, 70
Dityatin, Alexander 214
diving 4, 94–95
Djoković, Novak 39
Domenech, Raymond 140
Donington Park, Derby 126, 174
Dragila, Stacy 75, 361
dragonboat racing 304–05
Drechsler, Heike 15
dressage 129
Dreyer, Jenna 92
Drogba, Didier 140
Drummond, Jon 56
Drury, Sarah 61
Dudek, Jerzy 142
Duff, Damien 22
Dungy, Tony 372
Duran, Roberto 346

eagle hunting, in Kazakhstan 272–73
Earnhardt, Dale 360
Ecclestone, Bernie 346
Écija bullfighting school, Spain 240
Eden Park, Auckland 29
El Guerrouj, Hicham 367
Elena, Daniel 145
elephant polo, in Nepal 270–71
Elizondo, Horacio 155
Elliott, Stewart 131

Els, Ernie 45
endorsements, celebrity 342–45, 354
enduro motorcycle racing 116
Engadin ski marathon 85, 98
Escobar, Julián López (El Juli) 246, 247
Essien, Michael 25
Eto'o, Samuel 139
Evans, Cadel 134
Eyethu Boxing Club, Mdantsane 267

Fàbregas, Cesc 136, 138
Fabris, Enrico 111
Falla, Alejandro 181
Fangio, Juan Manuel 362, 365
fans 326–29
Federer, Roger 19, 39, 178–81, 183, 366, 368, 371, 373, 375
fencing 82, 147
Feofanova, Svetlana 361
Ferguson, Alex 226
Ferreira, Vitor Borba (Rivaldo) 148, 165, 229
Ferrer, Fernando 107
Ferrero, Juan Carlos 359
field hockey 323
figure skating 9, 61, 102, 211, 363, 371
finger-wrestling, in Bavaria 264–65
Fischer, Birgit 115
Fisher, Derek 56
fist-fighting, in South Africa 255
flags 324–25
Flanagan, Nicholas 355
Flushing Meadow, New York 37, 39
Foe, Marc-Vivien 365
football *see* soccer; American football
football, American 31–33, 146, 236, 358, 362, 368
    injuries 325
    Super Bowl 33, 318, 344, 358, 362, 368, 372, 375
    see also individual players
Foreman, George 364
Formula One racing 9–10, 118–21, 164–69, 319, 346, 358, 360, 364, 365, 373, 375
    Bahrain Grand Prix 120, 346
    Brazilian Grand Prix 164
    British Grand Prix 168
    Canadian Grand Prix 122, 319
    DIY Formula One car 282
    Formula One World Championship, 120, 368
    French Grand Prix 121, 362
    Indianapolis Motor Speedway 335
    Italian Grand Prix 166, 370, 375
    Malaysian Grand Prix 166
    Monaco Grand Prix 164–65
    Singapore Grand Prix 120
    Spa-Francorchamps 367
    Spanish Grand Prix 118, 120
    U.S. Grand Prix 120, 123, 168, 346
    see also individual drivers
Foster, Norman 358
Foster, Tim 215
France
    French Grand Prix 121, 362

French Open (tennis) 179, 183, 184, 188, 371
    Nice triathlon (2004) 84
    Tour de France 18, 134, 193, 194, 197, 327, 358, 363, 365, 367, 368, 373, 375
    world athletics championships, Paris (2003) 56, 364
Francis, Charlie 16, 203
Frans, Tonky 301
Frazier, Joe 19
Freeman, Cathy 14, 200, 331, 359
Friesacher, Patrick 118

Gaines, Jashaad 33
Ganguly, Saurav 341
Garcia, Sergio 45
Garnett, Kevin 145
Gatlin, Justin 16, 201, 372
Gatting, Mike 223
Gay Games, Chicago 258–59
Gay, Tyson 372
Gayle, Chris 46
Gebrselassie, Haile 206, 359, 365
Gehrig, Lou 361
Geinub, Manfred 288
Gelder, Yuri van 79
Germany
    Bavarian finger-wrestling 264–65
    mud flat racing in 276
    Soccer World Cup (2006) 22, 25, 26, 148, 155, 158, 159, 161, 163, 164, 225, 231, 239, 310–11, 317, 325, 326, 337, 341, 351, 359, 366–71
    Tour Players' Championship, Gut Kaden 45
Gerrard, Steve 142, 368
Gevaert, Kim 370
Al-Ghasara, Ruqaya 68
Gilardino, Alberto 25
Gilchrist, Adam 46
Gimelstob, Justin 39
Giro d'Italia 136, 147, 361
Glazer, Malcolm 344
golf 11–12, 160–63, 216, 367
    in Afghanistan 290–91
    AT&T National Pro-Am 44
    British Open 45, 163, 358, 371, 372, 374
    in China 236
    LG Skins Game, La Quinta 42
    Masters 163, 360, 369
    in the media 8, 357
    in Namibian desert 288
    PGA Tour 45, 216, 359, 364
    Ryder Cup 9, 42, 45, 144, 360, 358, 363, 366, 370
    Singapore Open 45
    Tour Players' Championship, Gut Kaden 45
    U.S. Open 358
    see also individual players
Gonzales, Pancho 8
González, Aitor 134
Graf, Steffi 19, 188, 192
Graham, Trevor 16

Greece
    Athens Olympics (2004) 12, 16, 21, 50, 54, 61, 63, 65, 67, 70, 71, 74, 76, 77, 81, 82, 86, 88, 90, 92, 93, 96, 97, 106, 107, 144, 172, 199, 201, 207, 212, 319, 331, 362, 363, 367
Greene, Maurice 201, 372
Gregory, Dick 12
Gretna Football Club, Scotland 293
Gretzky, Wayne 108
Grimes, David 33
Grosjean, Sébastien 189
Grosso, Fabio 26, 325, 370
Guerrero, Chavo 51
Guinness World Records 303, 308
Guo Jinjing 93
Guo Shiqiang 345
Guttmann, Sir Ludwig 106
Guus Hiddink stadium, Gwangji 228
gymnastics 74, 76–81
    in China 232–33

Habana, Bryan 29
Hackett, D.J. 33
Hackett, Grant 90
Hair, Darrell 222
Hall, Dougie 61
Hall, Gary 214
Hamilton, Lewis 168–69, 319, 373, 375
Hamm, Paul 76
hammer throwing 73
Harkleroad, Ashley 187
Harrington, Padraig 45, 372, 374
Harvick, Kevin 122
Hasselbeck, Matt 33
Hatton, Ricky 53
Haubrich, Randy 284
Hayden, Matthew 364
Hayden, Nicky 124, 170
Hayman, Carl 29
Heiden, Eric 211
Hellebaut, Tia 73
Helliniko Olympic complex, Athens 117
Henin, Justine 41, 341
Henley Regatta 321
Henninger, Rod 284
Henry, Thierry 341
Heras, Roberto 135
Hernandez, Edgar 26
Hernandez, Jesus 56
Hewitt, Lleyton 39, 181, 359, 360, 368
Hiddink, Guus 227
high jump 73
Highland Games, Scotland 256
Hill, Damon 9, 164, 168
Hinault, Bernard 365, 367
Hingis, Martina 360, 362
Hoffa, Reese 70
Hogan, Ben 367
Hoiles, Stephen 29
Holmes, Andy 215
Holmes, Kelly 54, 366
Holyfield, Evander 219, 220
Hoogenband, Pieter van den 358

hooliganism 320, 350–51
Hopkins, Bernard 52
Horan, Cornelius 319
horse racing 129, 130–31, 214, 292, 323, 325
    on ice 276
    International Endurance Race 288
    on mud flats 276
    the Palio, Siena 268–69
Horton-Perinchief, Katura 92
Hoyzer, Robert 225, 368
Hungary, European Aquatic Championships
    (2006) 91
Hunter, C.J. 15, 16, 203, 358
Hunter, Steven 48
hurdles 65

Iaquinta, Vincenzo 25
Ibrahim, Karam 50
ice hockey 108–9, 322, 358, 370
    pond hockey 287
ice skating 9, 61, 82, 102, 111, 210–11, 363, 371
India
    bull-taming 245
    cricket 10
    pole mallakhamb 253
    wrestling 251
Indigenous Nations' Games, Brazil 254–55
Indurain, Miguel 358, 365, 367
injuries 56–57, 324–25
International Association of Athletics
    Foundation (IAAF) 199
International Olympic Committee (IOC) 14,
    15, 347
Inzaghi, Filippo 139, 318
Ipatov, Dmitry 111
Ironman Triathlon, Hawaii (2003) 94
Isinbayeva, Yelena 72, 368, 369
Italy
    Giro d'Italia 136, 147, 361
    Italian Grand Prix (Formula One) 370
    the Palio, Siena 268–69
    Turin Olympics (2006) 101, 102, 105, 111,
    134, 211, 213, 371
Ivanišević, Goran 360
Iwata, Satoru 354

Jackson, Colin 65
Jackson, Phil 173, 175, 228, 366
Jallikattu bull-taming festival 249
James, LeBron 48
javelin 70
Jeter, Derek 35
Johnson, Ben 15, 16, 203
Johnson, Jimmie 122
Johnson, Michael 202, 205, 236
Johnson, Zack 372
Jones, Bobby 9
Jones, Cullen 91
Jones, Geraint 47
Jones, Marion 14, 15, 16, 18, 199, 203, 347, 358,
    362, 365, 372
Jordan, Michael 12, 19, 174, 184, 228, 360
El Juli (Julián López Escobar) 242, 243

K Club, Ireland 42, 146
Kabul Golf Club, Afghanistan 294
Kahn, Oliver 341
Kaká 139
Kaniskina, Olga 67
Kanouté, Frédéric 327
Kasamatsu, Shigeru 74
kayaking 117
Kazakhstan, eagle hunting in 272–73
Keller, Klete 90
Kemboi, Ezekiel 67
Kenteris, Costas 199, 367
Kenya
    Nairobi marathon (2005) 57
    ostrich racing 275
Khandker, Tushar 325
Khannouchi, Khalid 363
Kidd, Jason 48
Kildow, Lindsey 355
Kim Dong-sung 82
Kingston, Richard 25
Kirilenko, Maria 187
Kipchoge, Eliud 206
Klassen, Cindy 211
Klim, Michael 90
Klitschko, Vitali 220, 221, 366
Klose, Miroslav 22
Klüft, Carolina 73
Knabe, Morgan 61
Ko, Lai Chak 86
Kosaxi, Soultana 76
Kosovo, basketball in 235
Kostelić, Janica 15, 209, 363, 370
Kotomitsuki 248
Kournikova, Anna 12
Krasnianska, Irina 77
Kuffour, Samuel Osei 25
Kuznetsova, Svetlana 187
Kwon, Kyung-min 93

La Russa, Tony 228
Lahm, Philipp 136
Lampard, Frank 22
Landis, Floyd 16, 196–97, 342, 371, 373
Lara, Brian 367, 374
Larrionda, Jorge 140
Laver, Rod 179
Le Gougne, Marie-Reine 102
Lebedeva, Tatyana 73
Lee, Ho-Suk 82
Lehmann, Jens 26, 136
LeMond, Greg 197, 363
Leonard, 'Sugar' Ray 346
Lewis, Carl 14, 15, 207
Lewis, Lennox 9, 218–21, 361, 362
Lezak, Jason 214
Li Ning 331
Lidstrom, Nicklas 374
Lima, Vanderlei de 319
Lin Ma 86
Liu Peng 237
Liu Xiang 65
Lochte, Ryan 90
Loeb, Sébastien 116, 145, 375

Lombardi, Vince 368
Lomu, Jonah 29
long jump 70, 71, 73
Lonnis, Erick 157
Lorifice, Rob 305
Lough, Gary 207
Louis, Joe 9
Louisiana Superdome, New Orleans 31, 33
luge 101
Lysenko, Tatyana 73

MacArthur, Ellen 216
Maccabiah games 333
Madden, John 352
Mahmoud, Younis 372
Maier, Hermann 208
Malik, Salim 198, 359
mallakhamb, in India 257
Malone, Karl 174
Manaudou, Laure 91
Mancebo, Francisco 58
Manning, Eli 375
Manning, Peyton 33, 372
Mansell, Nigel 358
Maradona, Diego 152–53
marathons 306–07
    Athens Olympics (2004) 63, 208, 321
    Chicago (2002) 208, 363
    filming 357
    London 207, 365
    Nairobi 57
    New York 207, 306
    world records 207, 363, 364, 365
    see also individual athletes
Marciano, Rocky 9, 220
Marco, Francisco 243
Marks, Dominik 225
Marsh, Geoff 229
Martin, Mark 122
Martinez, Robinson 107
Masaryk circuit, Brno 174
mascots 340
Massa, Felipe 118, 120
Materazzi, Marco 11, 154, 370
Matsuda, Takeshi 212
Matsuzaka, Daisuke 312, 340
Matthews, Derry 53
Mauresmo, Amélie 41, 187
May, Bob 359
Mays, Willie 177
Mayweather, Floyd Snr 53
McBride, Kevin 219
McCall, Olivier 222
McCline, Jameel 346
McFadden, Bryant 33
McGinley, Paul 362
McGrath, Glenn 372
McGwire, Mark 177, 361
Mealamu, Keven 29
media and sport 354–55
Mediate, Rocco 375
Melandri, Marco 124
Menchov, Denis 135

Merckx, Eddy 365, 367
Messi, Lionel 138, 341
Mexico
    chess 308
    extreme cycling 279
Michalczewksi, Dariusz 'Tiger' 53
Mickelson, Phil 167, 367
Mileson, Brooks 293
Miller, David 14
Mishin, Alexei 211
Mitrev, Bozhidar 140
Mizutori, Hisashi 74
Modi, Lalit 344
Moen, Travis 109
Moggi, Luciano 370
Mongolia, Nadaam festival 246–47
Monroe, Craig 35
Montano, Aldo 144
Monterola, Keisa 74
Montgomery, Tim 16, 18, 203, 362, 365, 374
Montoya, Juan Pablo 122
Morris, Tom 358
Morrison, Roland 284
Moskalenko, Alexandre 81
Mosley, Shane 53
motocross 114, 126–27
motor racing 9
    see also Formula One racing; motocross;
    NASCAR, rally car racing; solar car
    racing; stock car racing
motorcycling 116, 126–27, 128–29, 170–71,
    281, 284, 325
    women racers 281
Mourinho, José 227, 345
Mud Olympics, Brunsbüttel 296
mud racing, Netherlands 298
Mühlegg, Johan 362
Müller, Gerd 157
Muralitharan, Muttiah 222
Murray, Andy 39, 179
Mutola, Maria 54
Mutombo, Dikembe 175

Naadam festival, Mongolia 246–47
Nadal, Rafael 10, 179, 181, 182–83, 371, 373,
    374
Namibian desert, golf in 292–93
NASCAR 9, 122
Nash, Steve 48, 343
Navratilova, Martina 190–91
Nelson, Bryon 367
Nemov, Alexei 81
Nepal, elephant polo in 270–71
Nesterenko, Yuliya 21
Newlands Cricket Ground, Cape Town 202
Ngong racecourse, Nairobi 278
Nicklaus, Jack 161
Nikitin, Yuri 81
Nikkhah, Mohammad 48
Nintendo 354
Nowitzki, Dirk 315
Nozadze, Ramaz 50
Nozdran, Elena 87

Obikwelu, Francis 370
Ochoa, Lorena 373
Ogilvie, Lauryn 97
Ohno, Apolo Anton 82
Okocha, Jay Jay 25
Oliver, David 64
Olonga, Henry 358
Olympic Games 9, 10, 12–16
    Athens (2004) 12, 16, 21, 50, 54, 61, 63,
      65, 67, 70, 71, 74, 76, 77, 81, 82, 86, 88,
      90, 92, 93, 96, 97, 106, 107, 144, 172,
      199, 201, 207, 212, 319, 331, 362, 363, 367
    Atlanta (1996) 175, 200, 202, 205, 215,
      225
    Beijing (2008) 9, 10, 12, 14, 18, 19, 48,
      64, 65, 67, 72, 73, 78, 91, 94, 107, 133,
      145, 172, 183, 199, 203, 205, 206, 207,
      212, 323, 329, 331, 333, 355, 371
    Berlin (1936) 10, 11
    London (2012) 207, 212, 369
    Nagano (1998) 105, 208, 211
    Olympic flame 14, 63, 172, 199, 200, 331,
      359
    opening ceremonies 15, 63, 172, 200, 329,
      331, 333, 371
    Salt Lake City (2002) 14, 15, 82, 102, 105,
      209, 211, 213
    Seoul (1988) 16, 203, 220
    Sydney (2000) 9, 12, 14, 15, 18, 19, 75, 81,
      84, 172, 184, 199, 200, 202, 203, 215, 331,
      333, 359, 371, 372
    Turin (2006) 15, 100, 101, 102, 105, 111,
      132, 209, 211, 318, 333, 370
    see also Paralympic Games
O'Neal, Shaquille 173, 175, 181, 228, 366
O'Neil, John 293
opening ceremonies 332–35
orang-utan kickboxing 274
Ortega, Ariel 25
ostrich racing, in Kenya 275
Otto, Sylke 101
Oval Lingotto, Turin 111
Owens, Jesse 10, 11, 14, 15

Paes, Leander 190
Pakhalina, Yulia 93
Palestine, soccer in 239
Palio, Siena 272–73
Panathinaiko stadium, Athens 63
Pang Panpan 78
Pang Qing 102
Pantani, Marco 16
Paralympic Games 105, 106–7
Parker, Willie 33
Pasarell, Charlie 8
Pauleta, Pedro 327
Payne, David 64
Pedersen, Maya 101
Pelé 10, 157, 161, 362
Pelletier, David 102, 363
Perec, Marie-José 200
Peterhansel, Stéphane 116
Phakula, Dina 68
Phau, Björn 183

Phelps, Michael 19, 90, 212–13, 355, 364, 366,
    373, 375
Phillips, Dwight 71
Pi, Hongyan 87
Pierce, Paul 145
Ping, Whitney 86
Pinsent, Matthew 215
Pistorius, Oscar 107
Pirlo, Andrea 25, 142
Plushenko, Yevgeny 211
pole mallakhamb, in India 253
pole vaulting 15, 72, 75, 361, 368
Poliandri, Maria Sol 77
politicians, interest in sport 350–51
pond hockey 291
Ponting, Ricky 47, 145
Popescu, Daniel 76
Popov, Alexander 365
Postiga, Hélder 56
Pound, Dick 16, 347
Powell, Asafa 9, 369
powerboat racing 112
preparations for sporting events 338–39
Price, Yetunde 188, 365
product endorsement 19, 180, 342–45, 354
Prost, Alain 360
Puyol, Carles 136

Qatar, Tour of Qatar 137
Qi Chen 86

racism and sport 11, 204
Radcliffe, Paula 207, 363, 365
Rafter, Patrick 358, 360
Rahman, Hasim 361
Raich, Benjamin 370
rally car racing 116–17, 170, 285, 360, 374, 375
Ramos, Sergio 136, 145
Rathore, Rajyavardhan Singh 96
Red Bull Down Taxco, Mexico 279
Redgrave, Steve 215, 359
Reed, Jasna 86
referees 227
Retrosi, Samantha 101
Reyes, Anthony 58
Ribéry, Franck 139
Ricceri, Alberto 268
Richardson, Quentin 48
Riis, Bjarne 144
Ripken, Cal 361
Rivaldo 146, 159, 226
Robben, Arjen 140
Roberts, Kenny 170
Robertson, Grant 127
Robinho 138
Robinson, Jackie 11
Robles, Dayron 64
Roddick, Andy 39, 181, 364
rodeo festivals, in Brazil 245
Rogge, Jacques 211, 347
Romano, Rubén Omar 368
Ronaldinho 146, 159, 226, 340–41, 352
Ronaldo 146, 156–57, 159, 363, 371
Ronaldo, Cristiano 140, 226

Rossi, Graziano 170
Rossi, Valentino 124, 170–71
rowing 215, 323, 359
Royal Ascot, Berkshire 214, 323
Rudman, Shelley 101
rugby 58, 61, 360, 369
    fans 329
    Hong Kong Sevens 327
    managers 229
    streakers 318
    wheelchair rugby 107
    World Cups 11, 28–29, 229, 361, 368
    see also individual players
running 9, 12, 14–15, 54, 56, 58, 64, 65, 68, 73,
    199–207, 359, 362, 369–75
    cross-country 369, 371
    and drugs scandals 16, 199, 201, 203,
      358, 366, 367
    filming 357
    steeplechase 67
    see also individual athletes; marathons
Russia, tennis players in 12
Ruth, Babe 16, 161, 366, 367

Safin, Marat 39, 368
sailing 12, 112–13, 216, 364, 373
Salé, Jamie 102, 363
Salt Lake City, Olympics (2002) 14, 15, 82, 102,
    105, 210, 211, 213
Samaranch, Juan Antonio 14
Sampras, Pete 19, 190, 358, 360, 365
Sánchez, Laura 4
Sanders, Corrie 366
Sant Jordi stadium, Barcelona 116
Sapina, Ante 225
Sartor, Diana 101
Sastre, Carlos 144
Schalken, Sjeng 39
Scheckter, Jody 164
Schilling, Curt 34
Schumacher, Michael, 118, 121, 123, 164–67,
    168, 326, 358, 360, 362, 365, 367, 370
Schwarzenegger, Arnold 260
Scolari, Luiz Felipe 226
Scotland, Highland Games 252
Scott, Adam 45
Seaman, David 159
Šebrle, Roman 70
Seddigh, Laleh 281
Selariu, Dorin Razvan 81
Senft, Didi 327
Senna, Ayrton 9, 168
Shaheen, Saif Saaeed 12, 67
al Shanfari, Ali 127
Sharapova, Maria 41, 184, 334, 342, 343, 367
Sheffield, Gary 34
Shevchenko, Andriy 140, 142, 345
Shishahai Sports School, Beijing 232
shooting 96–97, 105
shot put 8, 70, 358
showjumping 130
Shropshire, Darrell 33
Siena, Palio 272–73
Sikharulidze, Anton 102, 363

Silverstone, Northamptonshire 321, 357
Silvestre, Mikael 7
Simeone, Diego 25
Simpson, Bob 229
Simpson, John 53
Singapore Open (golf) 45
Singh, Harbhajan 375
Singh, Vijay 44, 163, 367
Sisler, George 35
skateboarding, in Los Angeles 305
skating
    figure skating 9, 61, 102, 213, 363, 371
    speed skating 82, 111, 213
skeleton racing, women's 101
skiing 15, 98–99, 105, 357, 362, 370
    cross-country 85, 98
    downhill 8, 208
    ski jumping 102, 111
    super-G 15, 105, 208, 209, 255, 370
    see also individual skiers
skikjöring, St Moritz 276
Skvortsov, Nikolay 212
Slutskaya, Irina 371
Šmicer, Vladimír 142
Smith, Joe 48
Smyth, Ryan 109
Snead, Sam 367
snowboarding 132
soccer 61, 136–43, 144, 145, 146–47,
    150–51, 224–27, 293, 318, 365, 368,
    374, 375
    in Abidjan 239
    in Afghanistan 239
    African Nations Cup 31
    in Bosnia 294–95
    club owners 344–45
    Euro 2000 225
    Euro 2004 151, 154, 226, 227
    Euro 2008 136, 138, 145, 227, 327, 355, 375
    UEFA Champions League 138, 139, 140,
      142, 144, 225, 227, 293, 359, 367, 368, 371
    fans 326–27, 328
    FIFA 9, 239, 243, 348, 314, 317, 346, 352
    Gretna FC 296–97
    hooliganism 350–51
    injuries from 325
    managers 226–27
    in New York 240
    in Palestine 239
    referees 225
    in South Africa 238
    on TV 8, 316–17, 355
    transfers 12
    women's in Thailand 314
    World Cups 9, 11, 15, 22, 25, 26, 56,
      136–37, 140, 146, 151, 152, 154, 155,
      157–59, 225, 226, 227, 231, 234, 239,
      310–11, 317, 325, 326, 337, 341, 346, 351,
      359, 365, 366, 367
    see also individual players
Soderling, Robin 39
Soi, Edwin Cheruiyot 206
Solberg, Petter 116
Sörenstam, Annika 42, 216, 364, 373

South Africa
  boxing 262–63
  fist-fighting 255
  soccer 9, 238
Spain
  bullfighting 240–43
  Spanish Grand Prix 120
  Tour of Spain 56, 58, 136, 137
speed skating 61, 82, 111, 213
Spitz, Mark 212, 364, 375
sponsorship 18–19, 342–45
sporting novelties 278–79
Sports Illustrated 174
Springer, Nicholas 90
squash 8
Srebrenica 298
Stanley Cup 108
steeplechase (athletics) 67
Stehlik, Henrik 81
Steiner, Matthias 145
Steinbrenner, George 345
steroids 16
  see also drug scandals
Stewart, Tony 122
stock car racing 9, 124
Stoner, Casey 124, 170
streakers 318, 364
Sukur, Hakan 363
sumo wrestling 248–49
supercross 128
supporters 326–29
surfing 61, 302–03
Surtees, John 174
swimming 12, 19, 61, 84, 90–91, 94–95,
  212–13, 298, 361, 364, 373
  in China 232
  diving 92–93
  synchronized 94
  world records 358, 361, 364, 371, 373, 375
  see also individual swimmers
Superdome, New Orleans 31, 33
Sydney
  dragon boat racing 308
  Olympic Games (2000) 9, 12, 14, 15, 18,
  19, 75, 81, 84, 172, 184, 199, 200, 202,
  203, 215, 331, 333, 359, 371, 372
  surf 298
Sydney-to-Hobart race (2004) 115

table tennis 86
Tan, Paey Fern 86
Tashnick, Anthony 303
Tendulkar, Sachin 374
tennis 11, 19, 36–41, 178–191, 336, 372
  Australian Open 39, 41, 179, 181, 183,
  184, 187, 189, 191, 350, 355, 360, 362, 363,
  364, 368
  Davis Cup 39, 336, 359
  French Open 179, 183, 184, 188, 371
  hooliganism 352
  Rogers Cup 39
  Russian tennis players 12
  tennis court preparations 338
  on television 8

U.S. Open 37, 39, 179, 181, 183, 184, 189,
  190, 191, 336, 360, 363, 366
Wimbledon championships 39, 41, 179,
  181, 183, 184, 187, 188, 190, 358, 359, 360,
  367, 374
WTA tennis championships 41, 336, 338
  see also individual players
Tergat, Paul 359
Thailand, women's soccer in 314
Thanou, Katerina 199, 366
Thorpe, Ian 12, 90, 358, 361, 362, 371
Tibet, billiards in 256–57
Tiozzo, Fabrice 53
Tochinonada 248
Tolo Harbour, Hong Kong 308
Tomita, Hiroyuki 74
Tomescu, Constantina 207
Tong Jian 102
Toni, Luca 136
Torres, Ricardo 55
Totti, Francesco 26, 138, 326
Tough Guy Event, Preston 287
Tour de France 18, 134, 358, 363, 365, 367,
  368
Tour of Qatar 135
Tour of Spain 56, 58, 134, 135
Trent Bridge, Nottingham 47
Trézéguet, David 359
triathlons 84, 94
Tunney, Gene 9, 220
Turkey, oil wrestling in 250
Tyree, David 33, 375
Tyson, Mike 9, 218–19, 220, 363

UEFA Champions League (soccer) 138, 139,
  140, 142, 144, 225, 227, 293, 359, 367,
  368, 371
Uganda, boxing in 236
Ullrich, Jan 197
United States of America
  AT&T National Pro-Am 44
  Chicago marathon (2002) 208, 363
  Indianapolis Motor Speedway 337
  New York marathon (2004) 207
  Salt Lake City Olympics (2002) 14, 15, 82,
  102, 105, 209, 211, 213
  U.S. Grand Prix (Formula One) 123
  U.S. Masters 360, 369
  U.S. Open (golf) 358
  U.S. Open (tennis) 37, 39, 179, 181, 183,
  184, 189, 190, 191, 336, 360, 363, 366
  U.S. PGA championship (2000) 359
  U.S. swimming championships (2006)
  92–93
Urzica, Marius 76

Valuev, Nikolai 346
Vanderkaay, Peter 90
Vaughan, Michael 142
Ventoso, Francisco 135
Verón, Juan 25
Vettel, Sebastian 375
Vick, Michael 373
video games 354

Villeneuve, Jacques 9, 164
Vincente Calderón soccer stadium 325
Vlašić, Blanka 73
Volandri, Filippo 39
volleyball 61, 88–89

WADA (World Anti-Doping Agency) 16, 347
Waddell, Tom 258
Wadi Rum, International Endurance Race 288
Wales, bog snorkelling in 301
Walker, Tyler 105
Wallace, Ben 48
Walsh, Courtney 358
Wang Zhizhi 172
Ward, Cam 109
Warne, Shane 145, 222, 223, 229, 365, 372
Warner, Kurt 358
Watt, Winston 100
Wattolümpiade (Mud Olympics) 300
Waugh, Steve 229, 366
Wawrinka, Stanislas 39
Weah, George 12
Webber, Chris 48
Welch, Noah 109
Wensink, Caroline 89
Wess, Timo 323
Westwood, Lee 45
White, Kelli 16, 364, 365, 367
White, Shaun 132
Whitehill, Jake 258
Whitfield, Simon 84
Wie, Michelle 216, 342
Wiegersma, Lucy 129
Wiggins, Bradley 133
Wilander, Mats 19, 366
Wildhaber, René 283
Wilkinson, Jonny 28, 229, 365
Williams, Danny 218–19
Williams, Esther 94
Williams, Richard 11, 184
Williams, Serena 11, 41, 184–87, 359, 364,
  365
Williams, Shane 318
Williams, Steve 163
Williams, Venus 11, 184–87, 359, 363, 364, 365
Wimbledon tennis championships 39, 41, 179,
  181, 183, 184, 187, 188, 190, 358, 359, 360,
  367, 374
windsurfing, in the Canary Islands 301
Wołowiec, Monika 101
Woodman, Trevor 29
Woods, Tiger 10–11, 160–63, 340, 352, 358,
  359, 360, 367, 369, 371, 372, 375
Woodward, Annette 97
Woodward, Clive 229
Woolmer, Bob 373
Woosnam, Ian 42
World Anti-Doping Agency (WADA) 16, 349
World Cups (soccer) 9, 11, 15, 22, 25, 26,
  56, 136–37, 140, 146, 151, 152, 154, 155,
  157–59, 225, 226, 227, 231, 234, 239,
  310–11, 317, 325, 326, 337, 341, 346, 351,
  359, 365, 366, 367
World of Speed, Utah 281, 284–85

wrestling 50–51, 247–51
  in Afghanistan 251
  by Bolivian women 251
  oil wrestling 250
Wu Minxia 93

X Games 301
yacht racing 12, 114–15, 218, 364
Yagudin, Alexei 211
Yao Ming 12, 172–73, 340, 345

Zablocki, Courtney 101
Zanetti, Javier 25
Zelezny, Jan 70
Zhang Nan 77
Zidane, Zinedine 10–11, 140, 146, 154–55,
  359, 370
Zvonareva, Vera 187